The Names
of Things

A Memoir

David Helwig

The Porcupine's Quill

Library and Archives Canada Cataloguing in Publication

Helwig, David, 1938–
    The names of things / by David Helwig.

ISBN-13: 978-0-88984-286-1
ISBN-10: 0-88984-286-8

1. Helwig, David, 1938–.   2. Authors, Canadian (English) – 20th century –
Biography.   I. Title.

PS8515.E4Z465 2006   C818'.5409   C2006-900211-8

1   2   3   4   •   08   07   06

Published by The Porcupine's Quill, 68 Main St, Erin, Ontario NOB 1TO.
http://www.sentex.net/~pql

Readied for the press by John Metcalf.
Copy edited by Doris Cowan.

Represented in Canada by the Literary Press Group.
Trade orders are available from University of Toronto Press.

We acknowledge the support of the Ontario Arts Council and the Canada
Council for the Arts for our publishing program. The financial support of the
Government of Canada through the Book Publishing Industry Development
Program is also gratefully acknowledged. Thanks, also, to the Government
of Ontario through the Ontario Media Development Corporation's
Ontario Book Initiative.

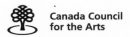 Canada Council
for the Arts   Conseil des Arts
du Canada

 Canada

 ONTARIO ARTS COUNCIL
CONSEIL DES ARTS DE L'ONTARIO

This memoir is dedicated, with love,
to my grandchildren, Simone Maria Helwig,
Émile David Royer and Pascal Nicholas Royer.

their 'soup and fish'. My mother explained the metaphoric expression to me, and my interest in the odd turn of phrase is the reason the jigsaw stayed in my mind. I also remember a sense of physical distress from that illness, a feeling of oppression, as if one were struggling to rise but too much weighted down to do it.

Palpitations: that Victorian-sounding word is used by one of the medical people to describe what I'm going through. It was just after going to bed that I noticed the oddity in my pulse. The evening had been spent at the Saturday night dinner of the Writers' Union annual gathering. I skipped most of the business sessions: meetings drive me mad. I was at the founding session in Ottawa thirty years ago, in 1973, at the peak of the excitement about new possibilities in Canadian writing and publishing, and I have felt some kind of loyalty to the organization, but many of those who were on hand in the early days have left the union or seldom attend meetings. Some – Margaret Laurence, Marian Engel, Matt Cohen, Tiff Findley – have died. Still, especially since I moved to Prince Edward Island, far from my old haunts, I sometimes turn up in the hope of running into friends and acquaintances. Tonight I was surrounded by familiar faces, old cronies.

'I'll see you in another ten years,' one of them said to me as I was leaving that dining room at the National Arts Centre. Yes, it was probably that long since Catherine and I had met, sometime when I was living in Montreal. Catherine was once, in another time and place, my lover. Her glittering and marmoreal beauty prompted poems thirty and more years ago, back before the first of her three marriages. I can reread the poems and recall the past. She has a son starting university.

Marian Hebb, the Union's lawyer, sat at the same table. Though she began to work for the Union only after it was up and going, we have known each other longer than most people in the room, and she is a reminder of the high spirits and idealism of the early days when every year a journalist from one of the Toronto papers would come to the meeting and report that the Union was about to fall apart over some contentious issue, but somehow it never did. I don't think the meetings get in the papers any more.

And Maggie was there, my first-born child, eleven years old at the time of that first meeting, and now the mother of my granddaughter Simone. One of the earliest of the poems I've kept in print is about Maggie, not yet three as the poem says, on an autumn day in a deserted lakeside park in Kingston, everything being taken by the wind. Her second novel was recently bought by Chatto and Windus in England and Knopf in Canada, and I know she came to the meeting, in part, because she felt she ought to do the things that writers do, and in part to visit with me, since I wasn't getting to Toronto on this trip.

On my right at dinner was Isabel Huggan, in Canada from her home in France for the launch of *Belonging,* her collection of memoirs. I published Isabel's fine story, 'Sorrows of the Flesh' in the Oberon Best Stories collection in 1983, and excited by it and the previous stories of hers that I'd seen, I suggested to Oberon that she probably had a collection ready, and that led to the publication of *The Elizabeth Stories,* which, in its various editions, created for her a substantial reputation.

The last time we spoke was 1984, the year of the publication of that book. On that occasion too I was in Ottawa for a Writers' Union meeting. Ken Adachi, who was covering the meeting in his capacity as book columnist for the *Toronto Star* and had recently written a highly favourable review of *The Elizabeth Stories,* was looking bored, and I proposed to him that we skip out for long enough to have lunch with Isabel if she was free. So I phoned her and we did that. Five years later, Ken Adachi, to my mind the most intelligent and literate book reviewer in the country, was accused of plagiarizing part of a column, was fired by the *Toronto Star* and committed suicide. How could that happen? I have only the tiniest, most meagre, unconvincing clues. The other world – chaos, hopelessness – is nearby, close as the other side of the coin. I might have died tonight.

Also at that big table was Hugh MacDonald, who drove up from PEI with me and is to drive back with me the next day. I have a firm arrangement to pick him up at eleven in the morning, and he is staying in one of the residences at Carleton University where he is inaccessible by telephone. As Maggie and I sit through the night, first waiting to see if the heart will convert to a regular rhythm, then waiting for an anaesthesiologist to be found so they can convert it by electroshock, we invent various complex and intricate plans for notifying him or getting the car to him, since Maggie doesn't drive.

Finally, as the morning shift comes on, someone is found to administer the anaesthetic. I am shocked, converted, quickly come back to consciousness. My ECG is, they tell me, 100 percent, and so we walk out into daylight and take a cab back to Hull, where we're both staying in my daughter Kate's house while she and her family are away at a conference of art conservators on the west coast. Cleaned up, packed, the cat safely locked in the house, I drive to Carleton where Hugh is waiting for us, and after dropping Maggie at the train and picking up Joe Sherman, who's been attending a meeting of the League of Canadian Poets, we set off east through Quebec, spending the night in a motel on the south shore of the St Lawrence.

At breakfast I'm delighted to learn a new French idiom, *miroir* for 'sunny side up'. We roll past the odd rock formations near Kamouraska, bits of the Appalachian chain rearing up out of the alluvial flatlands, and on through the hills and forests of New Brunswick and across the long Confederation Bridge to the Island, and when I get back home in the evening, Judy throws her arms around me and says, 'Did you do anything I wouldn't do?'

'Well,' I say, 'there was the night in hospital.'

The little island of red earth has become my home. Odd how these things come about, life we call it, decisions, accidents, you're one place then another, you're a sick child then a grandfather whose heart is acting up. Is it possible to say how it all happened?

In our Sunday best.
Hamilton, Ontario, May 1942.

Two

Everyone is the child of someone.
That is the heart of our pain
and our tenderness.

Families are the first language we have for destiny. As an only child brought up in a close family, I was enriched and overwhelmed by the daily presence of it all. My parents lived on into their eighties. I was there with them until the last, though in both cases I was absent at the moment of death. There was no great drama about either death. What was coming was obvious, and it came. It was death, and final, and they were gone from my life.

They met at twenty or twenty-one, waited to marry for financial reasons, but they were together for much of their lives. They developed a common world, and their assumptions about the world and its values were similar enough that their differences of character seemed to exist within the marriage, not against it. If my mother was difficult, unbending, fierce and proud, she also had real moral intelligence and clear principles. If my father was high-strung, moody, perhaps more often depressed than he ever admitted, he was also kind and gentle and generous. Each one had some difficult family history to accommodate.

* * *

When I drove to the cemetery in November, the funeral flowers had been piled over the grave and were slowly rotting. It was grey and wet, and I thought of my father's body there below, embalmed, encased in wood, beginning to deteriorate, buried far down in the earth. They would not let me plant anything on the grave, not even daffodils.

He wanted to be cremated, but my mother was unable to accept that, in part because she couldn't think what to do with the ashes, could not face the sullen comedy of having the remains around the house.

So there he was, in the earth, and I parked the car nearby on a wet afternoon and looked at the pile of ruined flowers on the ground where a small horizontal stone would be placed – the only kind allowed in this cemetery with many rules – and I thought that what I would wish to see carved on the stone was a quotation from *Great Expectations:* 'God bless that gentle Christian man.'

Oh, he had his faults, and especially in the last five years of his life had grown querulous, irritable with the world, something in him thwarted, disappointed. Going to a restaurant with him was a terrible experience. Nothing pleased him or lived up to his expectations. By now, his vision had deteriorated, and sight had always been the way he took hold of things. His visual memory was very accurate. After his retirement I'm not sure he missed his trade – after years of hard work as a cabinetmaker he was prepared to let that go – but he loved taking pictures. He liked attractive things, good clothes, for himself and even more for my mother. The world was, most acutely, what he saw. Even in the last weeks of his life, when he was very weak, dying of cancer, it was the blindness that he complained about. When he could hardly walk, he was bitter because he couldn't see.

He was proud, quick to see slights, nervous. His principles were not clearly thought out or especially coherent. His courage and goodness were the products of a kind heart and a sensitive nature, not the result of thought. His thinking was concrete, not abstract, and religion, which he took seriously, was a trouble to him.

Part of it went back to his mother's suicide. She had some kind of unchurched, hugger-mugger burial, and in his last months he was still bitter about a clergyman who, when my father asked why that should have been so, evaded the issue. All his life he had dreamed about that suicide. He was sixteen, the youngest of four sons, the last left at home. He did some hunting and trapping, kept a rifle in the house, and his father had told him never to keep bullets there. She was known to be suicidal. Her eldest son was an air force navigator shot down during the First War, and the fear may have begun to unbalance her. My father told me how he'd come home from school and found his parents in the kitchen, his mother on her husband's knee, her feet in the warm oven: they had just received the news.

It was several years later, her son safely back from a German prison camp, when she got some insecticide – Paris Green – and ate it. Her death was slow and my father was allowed to go into her room and see her. All she said to him was that she would be much happier dead. No gesture of affection. No goodbye. At eighty-four, dying of cancer, he was bitter about that too.

He was losing himself in those last years. I suspect that he had fought against depression all his life and that as he got older he was unable to fight so hard. Maybe some of it was just the failure of an aging brain. When someone he liked – his granddaughter, a pleasant nurse – was with him, he could focus his energy. He was still very alert to human facts. He asked me if Nancy and I might separate. (It was in the cards and happened not long after his death.)

In the last months of his life, it seemed to me that people were put off by him as he was then, nervous, impatient, uneasy, apparently inattentive, and I became irritably protective of him. He was not dying with exemplary stoic calm, nor had he lived with it, not that but something perhaps better, a kindness and gentleness and generous strength that overrode worry and sadness, with a sense of humour that was sweet and sudden and never cruel.

The stories I remember. During the second war, my mother's sister, married very young, was alone with her children. Her husband was overseas. She was a feckless soul, and at least once, in winter, ran out of coal for the furnace, with no money to buy more. We had no car, so my father took a sack of coal from our basement, put it on the back of my wagon, with its noisy steel wheels – no rubber in wartime – and pulled the wagon loaded with coal through the streets of Toronto to my aunt's house to keep her furnace going.

Christmas, when I was very young. They were poor and couldn't afford a tree. On Christmas Eve my father went to all the lots where trees had been sold and gathered up loose branches, brought them home, drilled holes in a broomstick and fastened them on to make a tree.

We had bad luck with dogs. One, bought as a puppy, quickly came down with distemper, with seizures, uncontrollable diarrhea. My father built it a large box so it couldn't run wild and hurt itself and then he stayed up all night with the dog, fed it brandy, drop by drop, bits of cheese. The dog survived.

In his old age, he dreamt about his mother's death, and he dreamt about me, his son, calling out for help. When he mentioned it, I'd almost forgotten the incident. We were trout fishing in a creek that ran down the Niagara escarpment. It was a new and promising place, in a large woods. We were there with another man, a friend. I went off into the woods on my own, to find a way down, lost my footing and fell several feet. The wind was knocked out of me and I lay there paralyzed and frightened until my breath came back. I couldn't see how to climb back out, and I shouted for help. They came, and I was got out, and the moment when he heard me, my child's voice calling for help through the trees, came back forever in his dreams.

When I was very young my father went off to work in various factories, carrying a lunch bucket, but when I was seven or eight, he started in business for himself, first making small pieces of office furniture in the basement of our house, then in a workshop built behind the house. In 1948, he bought a furniture repair and refinishing business in Niagara-on-the-Lake.

We lived an old-fashioned, almost pre-modern life. The barn where my father worked was only thirty feet or so from the back door of the house. It is a commonplace these days for men to talk about distant mysterious fathers, fathers who commute to work in unknown offices and only appear on weekends. I knew where my father worked and what he did. It is still close and vivid.

The barn had wide solid doors that could open for a car or truck to drive in. Once, apparently, the building had been a livery stable. In the middle of one of the doors, there was a small entrance. To avoid interfering with the door frame, it ended several inches above the ground. You had to step up and over to get inside. Once inside, the place was large and dim. A wide wooden staircase led to the upper floor which was full of old furniture, chairs hanging from the rafters, ancient dry lumber. There was a huge old loom, built of black walnut, and on it, a half-finished piece of fabric. The four-sided roof rose to a peak in the darkness above. Wooden doors, at floor level in the low walls, looked out front and back. There was dust and sunlight and the shimmer and ache of the past.

Downstairs the car was parked, and then there were two doors, their glass panes half opaque with sawdust, which led to the workshop. A bandsaw, planer, joiner, a circular saw, a worktable and workbench, and in a corner, beside the drill press, a hot-plate where glue was kept warm in a pot of simmering water.

Most of the machines were run from a single electric motor, and above the room were huge wooden pulleys that drove the wide leather belts. With the motor on you couldn't hear much of anything else, but

her temper. She threw knives and mixing bowls. Once when I was very young, her brother was staying with us, and he told her about his astonishment when he heard his fierce and dangerous sister sitting on the back steps patiently explaining to her tiny son why he shouldn't behave in a certain way.

Her way of expressing affection for someone was to worry. Anyone who stepped through the door was offered something to eat. For a while she kept a diary, a bare factual document, but she recorded what she wore to work every day she went. She never forgot or forgave a slight. In the room which for a while was called the office, she had a newspaper clipping with the headline, PEACE OF MIND, A RARE QUALITY, COMES FROM WITHIN. When she had to leave home at seventeen to take a job outside Toronto, she was shattered by loneliness and fear. She said, not without a certain satisfaction, that she had once punched my father and knocked him out.

* * *

A hot Sunday in late April, and I got down from the train at an empty platform. The small station was boarded up, under repair. The ticket office was closed. One taxi had come to meet the train, but I ignored it, and it soon drove off. Across the bridge over the tracks was a pub, and I crossed over to see if they might rent rooms. Then I could drop my bags. But no. So I set off down the street, two bags on my shoulder, one in my hand. I was soon sweating as I went along a street of row houses, shops, an old warehouse; everything in English cities is so small and close. This was a factory town by the looks of it. It was not for the beauties of the place that I was here, but to find one particular house: 147 Taunton Road, Bridgwater, Somerset.

July, the year before. I'm standing beside a bed in a hospital in Niagara-on-the-Lake. It is five in the morning of an early summer day, and the thin morning sunlight shows my mother's fine features. The night before she struggled for breath, her face distorted by convulsions, her tongue bleeding, torn by a sharp tooth. Now the face is at rest, but the colour is wrong. Yet more human, it seems, than it was the previous day, when it was possessed by the symptoms of some neurological damage after a stroke. There are roses beside the bed – what is that colour, coral? – deep pink with a hint of orange – roses that I'd brought from her garden and put there in a green bottle. I stand by the bed, her only child, much loved (too much for my own good I sometimes think) and I have come all the way to the end with her, though I missed her death, minutes, an hour, earlier, through a stupid misunderstanding with the nurse who phoned me to tell me that she was dying, but whose words, describing symptoms that sounded unchanged, didn't get through to my sleeping brain.

It was a long haul through the streets of Bridgwater, with stops at one pub that didn't rent rooms and another that did but was full up. Most places were full up, the publican said, as the other men in the pub stared. There was some kind of building project on. He gave me some advice about finding a bed and breakfast, on Taunton Road, down to the corner, right to the roundabout, then left.

Taunton Road.

In an hour, I was standing by a row of small brick houses. Some of them had been turned into shops, but 147 was still a house, one of those late Victorian workingmen's houses, two up and two down with some kind of scullery on the back. As far as I know, my mother was born here. Certainly this is her parents' address on her birth certificate. That birth certificate is one of the clues in a lost story, and while it was partly my mother's death that brought me here, it was not her story – at least to begin with – but my grandmother's. Though the story of my mother's birth may explain a part of what she was.

My grandmother had been gone for more than twenty years. I was in a hotel in Neepawa, Manitoba, when I heard of her death. That was a Sunday too. I was driving to the west coast with friends, and we had stopped for gas. There was that small town silence. The hotel lobby, it seems to me, was deserted, except for a desk clerk. Signs announced local events.

I remembered the last time I'd seen her, a few months before, when I'd gone to visit the church residence for the old where she was living. She was alone, although there was a second bed in the room, where some other woman slept. My mother had warned me that my grandmother might not recognize me, that her mind was not always reliable, and she lapsed into long silences, but I never for a moment believed that she wouldn't know me and speak. So I'd stopped, with Maggie and Kate, my two young daughters, at the pleasant, comfortable, well-run United Church home in the middle of orchards, near Beamsville. She was asleep when we came in, and I sat by the side of the bed, spoke, and touched her. Waking, she was shocked to find me there, as if I had interfered in her dreams or blurred the line between sleep and waking, but in the first moment, she called me by name, in her familiar voice with its trace of Yorkshire.

It was a painful visit. 'I don't like it here, David. I'm not happy here,' she would say, over and over again. Her eyes had the white circles of cataracts around the iris. She was tiny and frail and paid little attention to the children who stood in awkward polite silence.

I remembered another visit, a few years earlier, somewhere else. 'Oh David, I'm about ready for the garbage can,' she'd said, but smiling, laughter in her voice, her attention going immediately to the children who had come to visit her. Memory is deceptive, of course, but while I can remember her angry or impatient with her husband and other adults, I can never remember her angry with a child. 'Naughty Peter,' she'd say to any mischievous child, with laughter in her voice; she seemed always able to laugh at children's mischief. When we lived in Toronto, I enjoyed stopping at her house for lunch on school days when my mother was away at work. My grandmother would send me up the street to buy the rare treat of a newspaper full of fish and chips.

Sometimes I stayed overnight at her house, on a folding bed near the laundry tubs in the basement. There was always a package of Rickett's Blue, that cobalt powder that was used to keep the whites from yellowing. We didn't have that at home; I think my mother used Javex.

Rickett's Blue, and fish and chips, and a plate rail in the dining room with china on it, including a Wedgwood teapot my grandmother had been given when she was in service in England. On Saturday nights my grandparents attended the Yorkshire Club, which for some reason was pronounced with the accent on the second word.

My impression of my grandmother is still the one I developed in early childhood, a sense of kindliness, of acceptance, of easy laughter. She was always a small woman, and as she got older, an inherited disease bent and bowed her legs and made her smaller, though she never had to struggle with the grotesque barrel staves on which some of her older brothers and sisters hobbled around. (It startles me now, in this world of modern nutrition and medicine that I took for granted that my mother's aunts and uncles should be half-crippled, distorted, dwarfish figures.)

I thought of my grandmother as a small, kind, warm, rather plain woman. Yet in her wedding photograph, she looks very pretty. No doubt some of that is youth and happiness. That photograph is in an album of ancient pictures of members of her family, an album full of the flavour of

Victorian England, where she was born and raised. There are photos entwined in a lithograph of English roses and decorated with a little scene of boats near the shore that might be an illustration to David Copperfield. Built into the back cover of the album is a music box that plays two little marches with a metallic carnival gaiety. Many of the figures are anonymous: an old woman in her bonnet and a long dress of a spotted material, sitting straight in the photographer's upholstered chair, her arm across a carved table; a young man in his best suit standing in front of a blank background, one hand on his hip, the other leaning on a small table where his bowler hat waits complacently. A few are labelled: *Mr and Mrs Pickles, Mrs Maud Morris and Edgar, Vinnie, Uncle Will's first wife, died in childbirth.* A pop-eyed little boy sits on a wooden horse. A blurred photograph of a young woman in mid-Victorian dress. On the back is the photographer's label, Smith, 33 Park Lane, Leeds.

I have only once been in Leeds, in 1961. My parents, my wife Nancy and I drove there, in a rented car, to visit my grandparents' only living relative, my grandmother's sister-in-law. She and her husband lived on a narrow little street on a hill, one of those smoky terraces of darkened brick built in the nineteenth century to house men and women who worked in the factories that were making England prosperous. Nothing built by man can quite equal the ugliness of those industrial towns in the north of England. On the street we were visiting, the rows of small identical brick houses were set back to back; laundry was hung on lines stretched across the narrow street. The houses had been darkened by a century of smoke.

Inside, the house was clean, crowded with furniture and bric-a-brac, not unlike the houses of my great-aunts and uncles in Toronto. As we sat and talked, a gob of soot fell from the chimney into the fireplace and out onto the floor, to the grievous embarrassment of our hostess.

I remember only one moment of the conversation. The woman, the sister of my grandfather, David Abbott, was talking about my grandmother.

'We always tried to love her,' she said, 'for David's sake.'

It was one of those remarks in which a certain meanness of spirit has garbed itself in the robes of charity, and behind it lay a story my mother told me when I was seventeen or eighteen, one dark winter afternoon. What she told me was the story of her own illegitimate birth. The man I had always known as my grandfather wasn't my mother's father. My grandmother, in her teens, had fallen in love with a married man who wrote poetry and played the double bass and sometimes preached in the spiritualist chapel she attended. When she found herself pregnant, they went away together to Somerset, where my mother was born, in that house on Taunton Road I must assume. On the birth certificate, the man is described as a printer, the two of them as husband and wife. Later he went back to his wife and two sons, and my grandmother emigrated to Canada. My mother was five years old when my grandmother married David Abbott, who was younger than she was and had been her father's apprentice.

I have the wedding picture in front of me. The young woman who was my grandmother is striking for the warmth and vivacity in her face, and her five-year-old bastard daughter is in the picture with her and her new husband. This child of love was not to be concealed or ignored. There was nothing weak or shame-faced about the woman.

In 1906, when her daughter was born, out of wedlock, infant mortality rates were high. Germaine Greer, in her book on birth control, has suggested that there was a good deal of only-half-accidental infanticide. It would have been easy for a young girl in circumstances that can only have been thought shameful (sixty years later her sister-in-law was still proud of forgiving her) to wish the child gone, but when my grandmother spoke, once, of my mother's birth, the story went all the other way. The child was weak and couldn't hold down food; it seemed possible that she might die. My grandmother told me how she walked up and down the garden, up and down, holding the baby in her arms and swearing that it would not die, she would not let it die.

When I found the house in Bridgwater where those events happened, I remembered what she'd said. Had there been a body of water at the end of the garden, or had I made that up? I went down side streets and paths, and I found a canal flowing between mud banks, but it was further away, well past the garden's end. But they must surely have walked there sometimes, on a Sunday, that summer of the child's birth.

There is no explanation of why they came to this town in Somerset, or when, or how long they stayed. The small row house wouldn't have been very old then, perhaps even a desirable sort of place for a working man and his family. Of all these things, I can only say, I don't know.

When my grandmother married David Abbott, the child was in the wedding picture, and he, such is the force of human decency and love, treated my mother not only as well as his own children, but sometimes, she thought, better. My mother was expressing her gratitude I suspect, when she named her only son after him. He had loved my grandmother since the days when he was a boy apprentice and she was older and unattainable, and he failed her only by dying young and leaving her too long alone.

Who was that other man, my other grandfather? I know his name, and I can't help seeking myself in him or him in me. He wrote poetry, he was musical, he had the temerity to stand up before an audience and speak. I recognize myself in all that. When I asked my grandmother about him, she told me only a little. She believed that she had known the time of his death; the connection had endured that long. She was in her house, one day, working, and suddenly she felt that he had just died.

When she came to Canada, she tried to leave him behind. Sometime during the trip, she went on deck and threw into the Atlantic all her keepsakes, his poems and letters. She remembered only a few lines of one of his poems, which she told to his daughter many years later.

Be careful, my darling,
our secret defend
but best of all
be true to the end.

He wasn't, of course. He went back to his wife, and there were rumours that Rosina Brett wasn't the first of his young conquests, though perhaps the first to bear a child.

Where, in that dim city, did they see each other? Where did they go together? My grandmother worked as a housemaid. Perhaps he came round to the house where she was in service and waited for her there. He must have seemed, I suppose, heroic and exceptional, a musician and poet, lay preacher, something shining in the dark streets of working-class Leeds.

On the testimony of those four remembered lines, he wasn't a very good poet, but to declare yourself a poet at all, in those circumstances, was remarkable enough. Whatever he was, he is unreachable now and his importance is in the passion and heroism that his actions summoned from the young woman whose eyes shine so brightly, who sits so straight, so proudly, in that wedding photograph. I have no doubt that she loved him; there was no hint of the thoughtless, the merely carefree about her. She could love and recognize love.

It is a small story, which took place among ordinary people, with consequences in only a few anonymous lives, and not everything in it reflects well on the people among whom the events occurred. My mother remembered sly remarks in her childhood, and when she was sixteen, one of her aunts felt it her business to tell the girl's first boyfriend the tale. Perhaps it was my mother who paid the price for her own mother's passion and courage, her father's heedlessness.

I stood there by the bed in the hospital, where my mother lay, her fine face calm, beside the roses from her garden. She had lived eighty-seven years since the day of her birth in Somerset. At her funeral, a stranger came up to me and said, 'She was always a lady.' Well, that left out a good deal, but it wasn't altogether wrong-headed, and much as I loved my grandmother, I didn't think that was a phrase anyone would have used of her. Was it in her own defence that my mother had invented that role for herself, a life with dignity and propriety? Along with it, of course, the ferocity and determination. After her death it was impossible not to wonder how much of her complicated and difficult character might have been formed by her strange position in her family.

They are gone now, my mother, and Rosina Brett and David Abbott, and that other man, whose name is of no importance to mention. Pictures come to me: a girl meeting a man in the dark streets of Leeds near the spiritualist chapel, a young woman standing at the rail of the steamship *Corsican* as it crosses the Atlantic, and there, out of sight of land, throwing her keepsakes and love letters into the sea, a woman growing older, at work in her kitchen and suddenly getting, from somewhere, the news that the man she had once loved was dead.

Three

Lanes of Toronto, inner ways
of the old city, mud and cinder
playground of my childhood,
summer journeys
less than a block long.

Now I come hand in hand with Simone
to splash cold puddles.
Under a sky of bare trees
and February sunlight
our shadows follow us.

When I started school in 1943 we were living in small yellow brick house
at 274 Nairn Avenue, four tiny rooms strung out one behind another, my
bedroom at the front, a little room with built-in shelves and drawers my
father had constructed, my parents' room next along the narrow hall,
behind that the living room and then the kitchen. The bathroom was in
the basement where there was a coal furnace and something called a
'jacket heater' (for hot water, I think), which took a different and smaller
kind of coal. Everyone burnt coal, which was varied and specialized in
kind, delivered by men with blackened faces who slung on a shawl of
heavy leather to protect their shoulders and backs as they hefted the hun-
dred-pound sacks along the alley and dumped them into a coal chute
through a basement window. Coal came in trucks, but the breadman, the
milkman and the junkman moved along the streets in horse-drawn wagons, their nags dropping balls of manure along their way. In the summer
the iceman came by, a pearl-white, translucent block of ice carried in his
tongs, dropped in the well of the icebox in the kitchen, melting there,
keeping food edible in the boiling August days, when, as they said, you
could fry an egg on the sidewalk. Behind the houses were the back lanes,
those moody secret places of weed and mud and English sparrows.

Mortality was there. Dead birds were buried with due ceremony in an empty box which had contained wooden matches. A rumour spread among the neighbourhood children of an evil girl who had killed a baby by sticking it with pins. My cousin Judy, one of my aunt Jean's twins, was found dead in her crib, and my aunt ran screaming down the street to her mother's house. During the funeral I stayed with our neighbour, Mrs Hamp, who taught me to tell time. Where we lived, the nearest green space was Prospect Cemetery, and on Sunday we sometimes went there for a walk up the quiet road among the trees and graves.

An Easter Pageant: Pilate is about to wash his hands, declare himself innocent of the blood that will soon be shed. The scene is acted out at the front of Earlscourt United Church in Toronto, a performance for the church congregation. A small ash-blond boy, clean, polite, and biddable, I present a bowl of water to the man impersonating Pilate so he can perform the symbolic cleansing.

Each day I set off to Rawlinson Public School, down Nairn Avenue to Rogers Road with its metal tracks and streetcars warmed in winter by a coal stove tended by the conductor. (On weekends or holidays we might ride the streetcar to its terminus at Oakwood and St Clair and transfer to another that travelled east along St Clair and then down Bay Street to Eaton's and Simpson's department stores, the big movie theatres – Shea's and Loew's.) On the way to school I wandered along Rogers Road past the oil grass – whipped on bare skin it would leave a dark streak – to the busy corner at Dufferin Street, the tall house where my grandparents lived (part of the upstairs rented out to a woman named Bessie Bourne) and where I stayed for lunch when my mother was working at her part-time job as a stenographer. She had spent her high school years doing a commercial course, and I grew accustomed to seeing her notes to herself written in the strange little lines and hooks of shorthand, her private language.

The war, the illuminated backdrop of my imagination, went on until I was seven. One day I would learn these events as history but now they were embodied in the leering cartoon faces of Japs and Krauts, events bright and iconic as a distant banner, the clear outlines of a comic strip, the Bayeux tapestry. One of my uncles was overseas, my father rejected by the army because he had pernicious anaemia. I read about the battles in the pages of the *Toronto Star*. The CBC produced a series called *L for Lanky* about the crew of a Lancaster Bomber serving in Europe. I listened avidly, and I remember the haunting tune of the Air Force March, its theme music. Tanks and destroyers and bombers, ours and theirs, battle and victory, Hitler, Churchill, it was all lurid and magnificent and left its stain on my memory. We had ration books, my father worked at DeHavilland Aircraft in Test Flight, adapting and repairing the famous wooden aircraft, the Mosquito. My mother's friend Madge married a young man who went off to war with the RCAF and never came back. Cards from cereal boxes instructed me in the various planes and guns that were in use by the troops, but the painful reality of the war existed a long way off.

In the summer and after school I played in the streets, Red Rover, May I, Kick the Can. I shared the febrile excitement when a group of neighbourhood boys set out to catch the huge rat nesting under the house where one of my friends lived. On school days, while I was at home for lunch my mother and I would listen to Bert Pearl and the Happy Gang (*Knock knock knock. Who's there? It's the Happy Gang. Well, come on in!*) and a soap opera called Big Sister, 'Big Blister' my mother sometimes called it. (My mother knew someone who knew someone who worked for Bert Pearl and reported that he had 'bad nerves'. For some reason, I took that phrase as code for something secret, unspeakable.) We listened to the radio news, and to some of the popular American crime series, *The Whistler, The Green Hornet,* or *The Shadow,* with its portentous opening words each week: *Who knows what evil lurks in the hearts of men? The Shadow knows.*

Our next-door neighbours lived in a low-built, shabby house, the door down a narrow alley. Large man, tiny woman with bad teeth and a loud voice like a street-vendor when she was heard calling out as one long word, 'Freddyandjohnny, Freddyandjohnny,' to bring her two sons home from wherever they were playing in the streets and lanes. One day as I passed by on the sidewalk I saw a boy named Warner, older than I was and who seemed to me very confident and sure of himself, being beaten with a newspaper by his mother on the front porch of their house, in full view of the street. And crying.

The workaday world ambled along like the junkman's skinny horse, but there were breaks in its regularity, as startling to a child as a divine intervention. My father went to a Toronto Maple Leafs hockey game and came back with a hockey stick for me, signed by the gentlemanly Syl Apps, the team captain. My mother and father bought a jar of burnt cork, dressed up in fancy clothes, and put on blackface like Al Jolson to go to a costume party. Once when my parents were away I was in charge of making lunch-time tea for Ronnie, who was working for my father in the little workshop out back. I think I boiled the tea after setting it to steep, but Ronnie was from Newfoundland and perhaps he liked it strong.

Once every summer, to escape the busy streets and burning side-walks, we would go to a cottage, first my grandparents' at Wasaga Beach, and later to a rented cabin on Lake Simcoe, or at Bowmanville, where the water was so cold my father and I could only dive once and run back to shore and where I caught perch with a home-made fishing rod. One of those summers I fell in love. I think I was eight years old, and I saw a lovely girl child and was stirred, felt that I knew her and she knew me. My uncle Bob and aunt Muriel bought a little resort in Haliburton, and one summer we spent our holidays there, and I learned to dive from the rocks into the clear water of Hall's Lake. It was there my father met someone who knew someone who was selling a business, and within a few months we had left Toronto.

Friends: Kennie Sandford, Jim Petropolos, Bob Yerex, the Gooch twins, George Dunkley, all lost to sight when we moved. Girls: some were pretty and some were cruel, and I picked out one, blue-eyed and golden-haired, to yearn for, but then we moved away, so I never grew up to walk with her through those dim back lanes.

> The wind chills me as we stand
> on the hidden side of the world
> my grandchild unafraid
> of all this winter. She reaches the corner
> brave and running.

Four

I was ten years old when we arrived in Niagara-on-the-Lake. My father had bought an antique and furniture repair business in the somnolent historic town with its Georgian houses and exotic stories. The house next to us on the main street had uncut grass, tall burdock, unpainted clapboard walls. The old man who lived in there was never seen. Much of the town was decayed, especially the older houses and older families. The local livery stable – horses for rent less than a block from the Town Hall – was owned by Jack Greene. He lived in an ancient house with a sister who never appeared in public. Around town he had other properties, but he didn't use them or rent them out. He paid just enough taxes to keep them from being seized, and he let the houses stand empty until they fell down. The town was ghostly, full of secrets. When I came to read William Faulkner's story, 'A Rose for Emily', I felt that I had lived at the fringes of the world he portrayed.

Not long after we arrived my father was brought for repair a delicate desk with a curved marquetry front. Kids had broken into the owner's house and hacked at the delicate inlay with a hatchet, hoping to find valuables inside. They hadn't succeeded in opening it, but they had violated the finely patterned surface. Houses falling down, the eccentric spinster descendants of the old families, beautifully made things smashed by violence, to be restored by my father's strong clever hands: all this was a rich brew of daily experience, and of course the great disturbance of puberty began not long after.

Sex, like everything else, was closer and more intense in this small community. The first or second day I appeared in school it was whispered that the fire chief's daughter was in love with me. I listened to the tale of a girl driven from school by harsh teasing.

'Why are you so mean to her?' the teacher said to the boys who had driven her out.

'Well, sir,' a grinning little monkey replied, 'she fucked.' With all of Toughy Russell's gang, it appeared. (Small towns are enduringly mysterious. I never again heard mention of Toughy Russell or learned just who made up his gang.)

The bank manager's son, who'd previously lived in the city of Windsor, had a story about a girl found dead on a beach near there. He was a toothy, snuffly boy who claimed that she'd been fucked to death, and his grotesque account of the anatomical state in which she was found was unconvincing to me, even at eleven or twelve years old. (Much of my own sex education came from secretly searching through magazines like *Ladies' Home Journal.* Expert in things like tubal pregnancy, I was selective in what gossip I believed.)

At the public beach, floating in the water like pale dead fish, the white condoms, dropped in here or upriver to come down with the current, French safes they were called then, shaping themselves to the movement of the ripples, washing softly along just off the shore.

Out on the lake, the low black shapes of the freighters moving on the flat plane of the water. The steamer from Toronto arrived twice a day, gradually appearing over the horizon and landing at the dock where the boys swam and bobbed for coins, and where there was deep water and a diving tower. Sometimes late in the morning of our swimming lessons we would go there, a short walk along the river past the fishermen's shacks and the reels of drying nets. A boy named Tommy Houlihan set out one morning from the steamer dock, accompanied by a rowboat, and swam across the wide powerful river and back.

A swimming lesson: it was the second year. The lifeguard and teacher the previous year had been a husky pleasant no-nonsense blonde, whose name I can still remember. But the second year, the teacher was smaller, dark, and her name will not come back, though it is just at the edge of recall. I was eleven or twelve that year, and one of the regulars at the morning sessions sponsored by a local service club. We were studying the breast stroke that day, and the teacher sat on the sand in front of us to illustrate the frog kick, and leaning back on her arms, she spread her legs to their fullest extent, and just before she brought them down and together for a powerful thrust through the imaginary water, I saw the little bouquet of black hair at the edge of her bathing suit.

How old was she? Seventeen, eighteen? Perhaps she was perfectly innocent and had no idea what the white rubber things were that floated past the beach. Or perhaps she thought that these children just on the point of puberty were as inert as stones. Or perhaps showing herself gave her the same half-embarrassed moment of exquisite pleasure that it gave me to see that secret hair.

It was not long after our move to Niagara that I heard, on CBC's *Stage 49*, a radio adaptation of Conrad Aiken's story 'Mr Arcularis'. I think I had come on the program by accident. It was produced by Andrew Allen with original music by Lucio Agostini. Mr Arcularis was played by that wonderful actor John Drainie. Fifty-five years later I can remember the intensity of my reaction to the ghostly story of a man approaching death and haunted by the mysteries of the universe, the spectral emptiness that surrounded the voices on radio. I was scared, fascinated, possessed by it even. It was perhaps my first experience of something like art, of my response to art. Would it be an exaggeration to say I owe my soul to CBC radio?

My parents took me off to church with some regularity after we moved to Niagara, where the church was close by, and traditional hymns were probably the first kind of poetry I knew. Some, of course – the kind set to be sung by children – were dreadful trash:

Climb, climb up Sunshine Mountain.
Heavenly breezes blow.
Climb, climb up Sunshine Mountain
Faces all aglow.
Etc.

But a certain number of traditional hymns were impressive for their poetic power. Their embodiment of old ways of speech, their habit of metaphor taught me something. I'm not sure we ever sang the settings of George Herbert in those days, but many of Charles Wesley's verses have real poetry in them.

Christ whose glory fills the skies,
Christ the true, the only light,
sun of righteousness, arise,
triumph o'er the shades of night.
Day-spring from on high, be near;
day-star in my heart appear.

I soon reached the age when the children's books I'd been reading – I was a fan of Doctor Doolittle – began to pall, and of course there was no such thing as young adult novels. I was not one of those prodigies who immediately devoured all the great books. I went to the movies a lot, seeing westerns, musicals, the Bowery Boys, the Three Stooges. Over the next years I read an odd assortment of things, magazines like *Outdoor Life* and *Field and Stream,* a huge book about travels north of Lake Superior, and the novels of wilderness life by James Fenimore Cooper, *Deerslayer, Pathfinder, The Last of the Mohicans.* I took my dog into the fields outside the town to chase rabbits and pheasants, and I spent hours on the riverbank above the wide Niagara River, which here lost itself in the flat distances of Lake Ontario. On the other side of the river, the American Coast Guard station below Fort Niagara at Youngstown, N.Y., flew weather flags, and I learned which flags were set for various weather conditions. Liked best the windy days when the flags warned boats to keep off the water. I was pleased to be able to decode the pennants that waved over the river in that other country a mile away. I grew expert at spotting the various breeds of ducks that stayed all winter. I had some fantasy of a wilderness life – Dave the cunning wilderness guide – a fantasy of the kind of existence that my contemporary Margaret Atwood actually lived in her early days. I had no particular talent for hardy survival in the wild. It was all poetry, I think, and the first poem that I read and loved expressed it.

Cedar and jagged fir
uplift sharp barbs
against the grey
and cloud-piled sky;
and in the bay
blown spume and windrift
and thin, bitter spray
snap
at the whirling sky;
and the pine trees
lean one way.

Those are the opening lines of 'The Lonely Land', a poem first published by A.J.M. Smith in 1936. I found it in a high school anthology and wrote it out in a small red covered notebook, so that it became my own.

By now I had begun the five years of daily bus rides to a high school on the outskirts of Niagara Falls. Much of my life was spent on those buses, the delinquents or would-be delinquents at the back leading the singing of 'Roll Me Over in the Clover' and other richly salacious ditties. If he got on first, my friend Arno saved me a seat. The transmission on some of the buses was near death and the driver would have to wrestle with the stick shift to change gears. Sometimes one of buses broke down, and we sat there on some empty country road till we were rescued and delivered to school late. The route varied, but most commonly we went west on the Stone Road as far as Virgil, then turned south on the Creek (pronounced 'crick') Road to St David's, then up the steep hill of the escarpment and through Stamford to the school. There were separate boys' buses and girls' buses, though given the complication of finding every kid on every country road, sometimes the genders got mixed, for at least part of the ride, and the driver expected better behaviour, or at least cleaner language, if there were girls on the bus. The distance from school meant that your participation in extracurricular activities was limited, but there was a period between the end of the last class and the arrival of the school bus that allowed you to join one or another club. By my first year of high school I must have been somewhat bookish, since one of the clubs I joined that year was the library club. The other was the technical club, which, among other things, learned about theatrical lighting.

Among the others at the top of the arena, he chaffs, chatters,
the lighting crew in wait,
the follow-spot
switched off until the next of the young skaters,
her routine of figures prepared, perfected, glides out.

He is adolescent, gauche, half grown,
staring with captive gaze
as he sees
her taking her place out on the white ice, the one
girl, the darkly beautiful, the elegant thighs.

He will only later come into the best of himself – male,
bearded, say thirty-three,

but she,
slender strider on those bright edges of steel,
at her mere fifteen is faultless to his hungry eye,

and though wordless of praise, he will perfectly give it
in the sweep of the spot
left and right,
his long-barrelled instrument on its double pivot
holding her in its moving circle of light.

But that was later. Perhaps it was the librarian herself who drew me to the library club in that first year. Hélène de Mouilpied came from the Channel Islands and so had been raised bilingual. My high-school teachers were generally competent, one or two a bit more than that, but Miss de Mouilpied had about her something exceptional. She had the force of character that makes for impressive teachers, a tiny woman that six-foot country boys treated with respect. In my final year I observed her give an impromptu monologue in front of a French class, setting off into a diatribe prompted by quite authentic annoyance, her recital growing more and more theatrical until by the end she was weeping crocodile tears and trying unsuccessfully to repress her laughter. One wanted to shout 'Bravo!' but wouldn't quite have dared. Miss de Mouilpied kept the library, taught the senior French courses and ran the drama club, and in my first year she directed a production of *Twelfth Night* that intoxicated me. Live performance on stage and Shakespeare to boot. I'm not sure it was an especially good production, but I saw it at least twice. The same thing with next year's *HMS Pinafore*. The theatre, the theatre: something there I couldn't help but love.

In the course of exploring the library in those short hours after school I came on Somerset Maugham's selection of the world's ten great-est novels, which he presented mildly abridged. An obscure but dominat-ing appetite was dragging me forward, toward knowledge, cultivation, a quality of being for which I had no words. I decided that if these were the ten greatest I must read them. So there I was on a school bus full of rowdies leading us in obscene songs (I liked the songs), reading my way through *War and Peace*.

I wanted to know the best of what there was, but even so, I was of two minds, uncertain. Latin and Greek: I ended up studying both, but I remember how, near the end of grade nine, the school Latin teacher, Magister Liddy as he called himself, appeared in a history class, a very short, very broad man wearing spectacles with immensely thick lenses, a man about whom school rumour swirled *(he used to be six feet tall but had undergone the removal of a large piece of his spine; he was heavily addicted to tobacco for certain and probably booze; he was too blind to know what the smart-alecs were doing in his class* – and this last may have been true, for I more than once saw him hold a sheet of paper directly against the end of his nose to read it). He was in that history class to recruit for his Latin course which began the next year in grade ten. Who was planning to take Latin? A few put up their hands. I didn't. Who had high marks in English? A few put up their hands. I did too. If I had such good marks in English, he said, I must certainly take Latin. No, I said, I didn't want to. I was determined that I would not do it. Was it pure cussedness? The belief that a wilderness guide had no need of a dead language? The determination to do everything the hard way?

By the beginning of the next school year, I had changed my mind. I did study Latin – though Magister Liddy vanished in mid-year – booze? blindness? – and was replaced by a plain, nervous, well-meaning young woman. I won the Latin prize in my final year, and I feel immense grati- tude for those four years of study, since it was through the analytic work on the old language, learning the precise and regular way an inflected lan- guage proceeded, that I came to understand the nature of syntax. Like so many, I learned English grammar by studying Latin.

And Greek? A similar roundabout approach when a year later a geography teacher of unusual accomplishment offered to teach a Greek class at noon hour or after school. A couple of people I knew enrolled. Once again I turned it down, stubborn, stubborn, but two months later all of the others had fled and I had become the sole Greek student and went on to get a grade twelve credit in the language two years later. I learned verb tenses and vocabulary and parsed sentences and struggled through some pages of Xenophon.

Then, whether or not I was ready for it, we moved on to Homer, and the episode of the *Odyssey* which is usually named after its heroine, Nausicaa. I sat in a front desk on the left-hand side of the room. My teacher, a man of middle height, with straight hair and a pale blue suit and a characteristic, almost elegant way of moving, stood in front of me as I translated. How long did we spend over that passage? One class?

Several? Those lines, the
embody the essence of p
that.

A high-born girl se
to the shore where they
wait for the fabric to dr
voices rouse Odysseus
and naked and ruined
himself.

That summary c
in the original was so
shore, the washing, t
recognized for the fir
common things of
vision of the high-born Nausicaa
pings of heroism, who is only a naked man lying on the shore. And
white cloth drying in the bright sun.

Sea and shore, traveller and household, the stranger who comes from
the dangerous waters and she who welcomes him, in sunlight: I trans-
posed it into a lyric poem I wrote in university.

White, salt white as Aphrodite's heels
 dancing on the cobbles, on the sand, the sails
 flame fine as the glad sound of long waiting
 as oaken keels salute the bright foam, riding
 homeward.

And she out of the ground too, the dark,
 will dance across the silver spears, will break
 the brown hemp binding helion who shall seize
 the salt-washed breadth of burning sky and raise
 a standard.

The poem appeared in a student publication, but I never reprinted it
in a book. Does that third line, which sounds so pleasing, actually mean
anything? But the rhythmic energy, the half-rhymes, the delightedness of
it are all things I can still respect, a footnote to my joy in that only known
passage of Homer's Greek.

At the time I entered Stamford Collegiate, the school presented, what must sound very old-fashioned now, a yearly verse-speaking contest. Harked back, perhaps, to the days of elocution. Eager to shine, I entered the contest, reciting a high-blooded piece of melodrama about the death of Bonnie Dundee, which galloped along to a wonderfully noble and rampageous ending.

> Strike! and when the fight is over,
> If ye look in vain for me,
> Where the dead are lying thickest
> Search for him that was Dundee!

I believe I placed second or third. In later years – verse-speaking having been abandoned – I entered the public speaking contest, for which you had to deliver a prepared and memorized speech and then an impromptu one based on your choice from a number of set topics. There is a picture of me in a school yearbook tied for second place with a dark and smiling young woman, Barbara Rosberg, her name was, daughter of the owners of a large store in downtown Niagara Falls, and to be better known in later years under her married name – Barbara Frum.

Barbara Frum and I were of the generation that came to maturity as everything in Canada was changing. CBC radio had made itself an important historical and cultural voice by the 1950s and CBC television began its first experimental years. In that decade Irving Layton published *A Red Carpet for the Sun*, Hugh MacLennan had an international success with *The Watch that Ends the Night*, and Mordecai Richler discovered his own voice in *The Apprenticeship of Duddy Kravitz*. There was a new Canadian nationalism, both implicit and gradually more explicit, and a talented young woman could move from a high school speaking contest to public notice on radio and later to celebrity on TV. A decade earlier, I think, Barbara might well have spent her life as a dentist's wife, clever but finding an outlet in volunteer work.

What I heard, read, studied, recited – all that led me toward the decision that I would be a writer – was a small part of the life I lived. I fished, swam, played badminton, later a lot of golf. I sang in choirs, played piano badly, worked hundreds of hours weekends and summers in a butcher shop.

We heard him arrive in the August heat,
  and he stank like hell,
the man who came for the bones and fat,
  so you'd catch the smell

as grinning and sweating, he climbed from a truck
  already half full
parked on the mud of the yard out back,
  and we would pull

bushel baskets of ribs and shanks
  and ivory fat
out of the sawdust cooler's ranks
  of beef and get

a dollar or two for what was waste
  when the meat was sold,
the fat rendered to lard, the rest
  to be ground or boiled

and fed to the soil or to beast or to man
  in some disguise,
all piled on that travelling garbage can
  in a haze of flies,

as he climbed into the cab and was gone
  in the hot August sun,
and his rattling truck went rattling on,
  goes rattling on.

I endured the horny sweat of adolescent lust. I had a short awkward involvement with a precociously sexy girl younger than I was, but I turned away from it. If I look back to that now – how I saw her kneeling by the manger as the Virgin in the United Church Christmas tableau, in a dark blue garment, one end drawn over her head as a scarf, with all the classical beauty of a Raphael Madonna, or remember that she once baked me a cake – I'm aware that I really knew nothing of the girl. I was perhaps sixteen, and like any boy of sixteen, I was wired for sex, and I knew little enough of men and women and the world. The only way I could have known what she was like – Jeannie was her name – was to have had an easy, fulfilled sexual connection, and even assuming she had the same desire, there was no way for that to happen. Is it easier for young people now? Maybe. I think I didn't want the conventional imitation of marriage – going out, going steady, being a couple. I didn't want to be part of a couple. My guess is that we would never have been suited, but I really have no idea. Not too much later she married a public school friend of mine. It was still the day of the shotgun wedding, and I was grateful for whatever instinct had saved me.

A story told by a friend of mine during our university years: he was working in Montreal, and after meeting an acquaintance from Oshawa – in the big city on a visit and eager for action – he agreed to accompany him and two Montreal prostitutes to their place of business, where there was an awkward scene because the lad from Oshawa expected more than any self-respecting prostitute had on offer. As this got sorted out, the manager of the establishment remarked to my friend, 'Your friend doesn't want to fuck. He wants love.' I suspect many young men, at least at that era, had some difficulty with the distinction. Young women too, no doubt.

Another memory: the high school choir put together a production of *Brigadoon*, and I played the hero, Tommy. I got the part because I had a strong baritone voice. Imagine me spreading my arms and opening my throat for the high notes at the end of 'There But for You Go I.' I was largely unmoved by the pretty young woman I was singing to, my romantic interest in the sentimental Broadway tale, but I was half secretly half in love with a tall girl of finely sculpted features, crippled by polio, who looked up and smiled as she accompanied me on the piano.

I survived adolescence – we do somehow – though I had begun to experience the pattern of moods that would be all too familiar in the coming years. A good deal of the time I was confident to the point of arrogance. A well-loved child, a clever student, I thought highly of myself and won all the prizes. Yet I could become prey to powerful hypochondriac fears, anxiety and cold panic occurring suddenly and continuing for weeks, to be kept hidden as much as possible.

I was scared. I would be shamed. There were great holes in the universe – death, failure, humiliation – and nothing could be counted on. I could fall, keep falling, nothing to save me.

44

There was the period when I was afraid that I would vomit in a public place. Never stray too far from a washroom, a place to escape. I'm not sure whether this began on the occasion when I did in fact throw up in public, in the Parliament Buildings, just outside the parliamentary restaurant. I had been taken there for dinner by my member of parliament while on a tour sponsored by a service club. It's even possible that the embarrassing moment cured me of the hypochondriac fear.

Steinbeck and Hemingway were my favourite writers in those days, and I had done a couple of imitative little pieces in Hemingway's manner, just as I had written poems in imitation of 'The Lonely Land'. In my final year of high school, we were assigned *King Lear*, and I can see myself still, the night I read it, sitting in a high-backed antique wing chair that later found its way to a museum. (Furniture came and went like that. We couldn't afford to keep the best pieces if my father got a good offer.) I was alone in the house, and I knew gloriously that I was engaged in reading a masterpiece, a vision of great bleak spaces unlike anything else that the genius of humankind had produced.

I was seventeen years old, and I had invented a man that I would set out to be, a man who was adequate to the appreciation of greatness, a man who had the right to explore his own ability to capture things in words, to experience and record. That was what I wanted, needed. One night I was sitting with my friend Arno Letkemann. He was Mennonite in background like a number of my school friends, and he had some skill in drawing. It was a summer evening, about to grow dark, and thrilling with some inner hunger, I asked him if he didn't feel an urgent desire to capture the moment, to draw something, to record it. No, he said, he didn't. Simple as that. So why did I? No knowing, but I did. I had given myself the gift of a new ideal of life, one still not very common in Canada, the life of a writer. Wanted to be a journalist, I said, pretending to be realistic, but that wasn't what I planned. I wanted to create the world. No doubt there had been, from my earliest childhood, some unspoken message from my mother that I was to be special, but a writer wasn't what she had in mind. Poking around in the treasure trove of the old barn behind the house, I would come on things like an ancient schoolbook, find Keats's 'Ode to a Nightingale', and read the line, 'She stood in tears amid the alien corn,' and something in me shivered and caught its breath.

All the same, at the time of the Christmas exams, I half thought I might change my mind about my aim in life and become a doctor specializing in biochemistry. I'd read a book about it. I had most of the required math and science courses. All I lacked was grade thirteen algebra. I was a good mathematics student, and since I had to spend the afternoon of the algebra exam at school waiting for the bus, a couple of friends decided they would teach me the course over lunch and I would write the exam.

We didn't quite manage it, so I had to become a writer after all.

Five

It's a sunny Saturday morning in October. Judy is outside planting tulip bulbs. It's been a warm fall, and a few red hollyhock flowers blossom at the edges of the yard. Ragged chrysanthemums survive, and an occasional snapdragon among all the dried stalks, the dead goldenrod in the field behind us a rich burnt brown. Something, perhaps picking apples last weekend, has brought Robert Frost to my mind, and ever since I woke, I've been singing to myself one of Randall Thompson's settings of a Frost poem, and as I'm doing it I realize that what I'm singing is not the melody, but the bass line – what I rehearsed and learned. I can't exactly remember the melody. A lesson of sorts: what we remember is our own part of the harmony; we depend on others to know the rest.

Judy has an up-to-date computer and some experience and expertise in family history, and with her help I've recently tried to find my lost biological grandfather in the English census records from a hundred years ago. I know his name – it is inscribed on my mother's birth certificate – but no amount of searching in the census records will turn up a character who seems possible. They are too old, too young, in the wrong part of the country, one way or another not the right man. It doesn't matter, of course, but I'm puzzled to find that this man who was my origin has vanished from the public record. One of the lost.

I think of the boy I'm writing about, observe the somebody/nobody who exists in my memories, somehow the same person I am now, the man who has cut a few chrysanthemums, yellow, gold, dark red, and set them on his work table in a blue-and-white china vase, who writes these words on a laptop, but so young then, and callow and full of urgent needs, improvising. Time is the most obvious and still the most mysterious thing we know. Judy's youngest daughter, who lived with us on and off from the age of eleven, is now at the same point in her life I had reached then, at school in Halifax, scarcely beyond the rawness of childhood, yet autonomous, a young soul creating itself minute by minute, as others have done, as others will.

Six

The smartest thing I ever did was to get myself born in 1938. What that meant was that I was just a few years ahead of the baby boom that came along after the war, my own more thinly populated generation catching most trends on the way up. I left high school in 1956 and only six years later I had a full-time teaching job at Queen's University. I had never intended to be an academic, or wished to, but I was married at twenty-one and a father at twenty-three, so when the job offers began to arrive – I was in England, with a wife and a child and no money – it was impossible to turn them down.

When I graduated from high school, I had high marks and some money in the bank from my job in the butcher store. I went back for the summer, putting up the orders that would be sent out later in the day. Or I served at the counter where local residents and the rich Americans with estates on the edge of town came to buy their meat. Or I lifted and carried crates of vegetables, bags of potatoes. Replaced the delivery man and drove the truck when he was on holidays.

My parents would certainly do their best to try to help me get a university education, but they had very little in the way of spare cash. So I had applied for scholarships, and I received a generous one from General Motors. (*What's good for General Motors is good for the country.*) One of the pieces of information required for that scholarship was my parents' income, and the guidance counsellor thought I'd made a mistake, unable to believe how little money my father took out of the business as a salary to cover their weekly expenses. So I was poor but clever and GM put me through four years of English Language and Literature. I have, I suppose, lived by my wits ever since.

When I arrived at the University of Toronto, a sunny morning in September, my parents' car parked in a laneway so I could carry the boxes of my possessions into the residence where I had a room, I was excited, but also nervous and unsettled. I wanted to leave the little world of my family, but this new universe was enormous and very accomplished. I was moving into Taylor House in the Sir Daniel Wilson Residence at

University College, a new yellow brick building constructed around an inner quadrangle at 73 St George Street, the large building divided into six 'houses', each with a graduate student or lecturer as Don. Just across the lawn of the quadrangle was the west wing of the old college building, nineteenth-century Romanesque, and the little attached house where the principal lived. As I settled in, the more senior students would appear at my door, shake hands, all of them friendly and welcoming, but for all that, I found my situation solitary, chilling.

Still, I was intrigued by the possibilities of the place and leapt in with both feet. In the first couple of weeks I auditioned for the Hart House Glee Club (Michael Rasminsky, who lived in my house, was the assistant director), turned up to work at the *Varsity* (where Peter Gzowski was the editor – back at the university to do the job after a year or so as a newspaper reporter), and auditioned for a play at Hart House Theatre, where Robert Gill, the flushed, quick-speaking professional director listened to my reading and said, 'You're a singer.' It was not a question. I was accepted for the Glee Club, given a part of the Hart House production of *The School for Wives*, and deemed a possible candidate at the *Varsity*.

In a sudden panic I quit them all. I started over, going to class, gradually getting to know a few people, working hard. My history class contained perhaps three hundred people, and there was no single textbook. Well, there was this one and there was that one; each had its virtues. High school history was a subject where I could know *everything* – what had been printed in the text and what had been presented in organized form by the teacher. The first thing the University of Toronto taught me was that there was more out there than I or any of us would ever know.

My indispensable scholarship depended on my marks, and I was surrounded by men and women immensely more sophisticated than I was. I could fail and go under. This was a not uncommon fear among scholarship students, those who were starting on their way up by the use of their brains – the new meritocracy. One of my friends from residence, a year or two ahead of me, turned up at the health service every year before examination time and got his prescription for tranquilizers. He survived, with excellent marks, and went on to be a science professor and a successful university administrator.

So I worked, gradually got to know the other English students and spent my spare time with a few friends from the residence. The most senior students were on the top floor. I had known James Woodruff from

Niagara-on-the-Lake. He was enough older that we overlapped in high school by only one year, and he was now doing his first year of graduate studies in English literature. He was one of the first people to whom I showed poems I'd written. Across the hall lived his high-spirited friend William Whitla, who had turned a bare residence room into a tiny high church sanctuary. Bill was a devout Anglican who went to mass – daily I believe – at St Thomas's (called, for its fog of incense, Smoky Tom's), situated just up Huron Street. In England some years afterward I received a card asking me to pray for William Whitla on the occasion of his ordination as a deacon. Though he was later ordained as a priest, Bill's career was mostly spent as a professor of English at York University – a couple of years ago I met him and his wife at Toronto's Holy Trinity where he has been serving since his retirement from the university. The effect of his room: the crucifix, the leather-bound books bought by mail from catalogues sent from England, the page of Gregorian chant on the wall, the order and harmony of it; it might have been nineteenth-century Oxford, Hopkins just down the hall writing strange poems and considering whether to go over to Rome. In my picture of the time Bill is always writing a long paper on T.S. Eliot's *Four Quartets*. And laughing. He had a delightful and ebullient sense of humour, scholarly, astute and innocent.

This was one new vision of how one might live. Of course the other rooms of the house were less elegant. Mike Rasminsky – a gifted scientist and musician with whom I later wrote a musical – lived in the middle of complete disorder, the rubbish pushed away in February when he finally began serious academic work. I can still in imagination walk myself down the halls of the house and name and describe almost every young man who lived there.

I was returning to Toronto, where I'd been born, after eight years away, but to a different part of the city, a different kind of life. One evening I took public transit out to Weston to visit my Aunt Glad and Uncle Bill. Their older children, Carol and Allen, were close to my age, and when we lived in Toronto, we saw quite a lot of each other. Bill had cancer and I knew that he was going to die, and I felt some kind of duty to take a break from my narrow life within the university world and make the visit. My aunt warned me before I walked into the bedroom to see him, but I didn't really take it in, and I stood speechless facing the flesh-less, yellowed skull that stared at me and tried to smile. He was propped up in bed, his voice when he spoke almost inaudible. He lay there waiting to die. I found a few words to say and left, returned to the university where we were all young and hopeful and where I was beginning to feel at home.

Apart from James Woodruff my only high school friend at the university that year was George Loewen. (Harvey Shepherd, whom I'd known since public school, turned up a year later.) George had come to Niagara not long after I had. His family was Mennonite, and he was born in Russia in one of the settlements of German Mennonites who had lived there since their ancestors were invited to move to Russia by Catherine the Great. When George was a child, his father was seized by the Russian authorities, never to be seen again. During the Second War, the German army, as it retreated, dragged along all those who appeared to be of German nationality and marched them back to the fatherland they'd never known – George, his brother Bernie, his mother and maternal grandparents among them. Later they came to Canada among the many displaced persons who arrived in the years after the war. George had a notable artistic talent. We were friends in public school, but then he went away to a church school, reappearing for grade thirteen at Stamford Collegiate. Though by now he was a year ahead of me, he took a year off to earn enough money for university, and we entered first year at the same time.

George, who had an intense and enduring fascination with cosmology and the farther philosophical reaches of science, was enrolled in Math, Physics and Chemistry and had rented a tiny attic room near the university. No one in the dim silent house spoke anything but Chinese, or so it appeared the first time I tried to visit him. I had some difficulty getting in and finding my way up to his room. (I used that dark mysterious maze of a house in a story I wrote later and sold to *The Montrealer*.) George, in those days, drew as naturally as he breathed, and he gave me some of the things he'd done. Every day now as I climb the stairs of our Island house, I see a pencil drawing he made that winter looking out the window of his room, roofs covered with snow, trees, a glimpse of the back lane. The cheap drawing paper has darkened over the years and is covered with tiny brown spots of foxing, and the effect is of a rich golden surface, lightly touched with grey lines.

Here is a landscape of emptiness,
roofs, back stairs, alleyways,

garden tools in snow, and a silence
that cannot be spoken, some pain

no doubt, but the bare trees
do not tell it, nor does the snow.
We cannot speak of the loneliness
of such backyards with broken fences,

things undone that hardly matter.
Icicles melt, vanish in water
as the morning star disappears in day.
We turn from it. Let all things be.

George was an intent, inward young man, heavily built, with thick glasses, unassuming, though he seemed to make friends easily. Everyone in first year had to participate in some form of athletics. He choose the most exotic of sports, fencing, and pursued it with some success. Absent-minded, he would sometimes forget to go to the bank on Friday, and in his diffident way would wait until he was desperate before coming to the residence to borrow enough cash to get something to eat.

Preoccupied with the meaning of science, not the mechanics, George failed his year, and back in Niagara it was a few months before he found work. Living in one tiny room in the minuscule house he shared with his mother and brother – his grandparents lived in one almost equally small just across the yard – he had nothing to do but paint and read and think, and when I visited him on my trips home, he would talk for hours about the multitude of things that preoccupied him. His passion for understanding was volcanic. We would go for long walks, up the little road where he lived to the golf course, round the lakeshore that edged the course, down the streets of the town, George talking and talking – not mere garrulity, but the overflow of passionate thinking. I would intervene now and then with an idea, and then we'd go on, perhaps drop in to see my parents, who liked him and saw more of him for many years than I did, since they lived there in Niagara while I was always far away. I think it was in this period that George began to work in black and white in a new technique he'd invented. He would take a good-sized brush and beat it against a hard surface until the hairs were wildly disordered, and then he would begin to draw in black ink, the mashed-up brush inevitably splashing the ink so that he was forced to adjust to these accidental events. It was his own kind of Zen calligraphy, the images often slightly abstract landscape forms, though he gave me two very different pieces, a splendid surreal bird with upraised wings, and an Ecce Homo, the image of the man in the crown of thorns partly derived from Hieronymus Bosch but reimagined in this black-and-white technique.

After a few months of isolation George got work as a land surveyor and over the years passed his Ontario Land Surveyor's exams and became the city surveyor for St Catharines, Ontario. We've never, since those years, lived in the same place or even close by, but we've never lost touch. As is the way of things, marriage, children and work got in the way of his painting, though I have a fine collection of his lovely Christmas cards.

It was in my first weeks at university that I was taken out to dinner by Bob Vandersluys. I'd met him while I was working at the store in Niagara. I was outside on the main street cleaning the big plate glass windows with a brush and a rubber squeegee when he stopped and spoke to me. Both a musician and an artist, Bob worked for CBC as a graphic designer. Most weekends, at least during the summer, he came back to Niagara-on-the-Lake, where his parents had recently built a house, and where he played trombone with a concert band that gave concerts in the Niagara area. I became a regular visitor at his parents' house on those weekends. Bob had one of the new high-fidelity sound systems and he would play records for me. Only the best, and the best was Toscanini, or perhaps Bruno Walter. Or the Chicago Symphony playing 'Pictures at an Exhibition' under Fritz Reiner. A brass player, he loved the Gabrieli Canzons for Brass and the jazz trombone duo of J. J. Johnson and Kai Winding.

Bob had graduated from the Albright Art School in Buffalo. He'd attended with Tony Urquhart. He worked at the CBC with notable painters like Graham Coughtry. One of his close friends, Joey Umbrico, was appointed first trumpet of the Toronto Symphony. He knew the worlds of art and music from the inside. At some point, I introduced him to George, who was becoming as obsessed with music as with art, and sometimes the three of us would get together. It was the period of Abstract Expressionism, and sometimes I messed around with paint, and maybe got a glimpse of what those people were up to.

There was the day Bob decided to teach me to play trombone so I could play simple duets with him. The unforeseen problem in this was that I had a false tooth in front – the original lost in a floor-hockey game –

and when I tried to play the trombone I blew out my partial plate. On a later occasion the three of us were sitting around in Bob's Toronto studio trying to sing a passage of Beethoven's Sixth symphony which contains the Great Bassoon Joke. (It's possible that all music for that instrument contains the Great Bassoon Joke.)

My dinner with Bob was at the Swiss Chalet, which was brand new then and almost classy. Then we went further along Bloor Street to a café, German or Hungarian. This was 1956, and such places were a novelty. European immigration was changing Toronto the Good. While we were eating a pastry and drinking coffee, a pretty, slender young woman in a yellow dress came striding in, greeted by all the regulars. One of them took her hand to kiss and as he did she bent and kissed the back of her own hand.

I've never known what the gesture meant, whether the act was spontaneous, unique to her, but I was captured by it.

It's hard for me to give an accurate account of the scene I've described because it became a longer, more detailed, dramatically significant passage in my novella 'The Streets of Summer'. That young woman I saw for a few minutes at most was the first image of one of the book's central characters, and I can't separate what I saw from what I later invented, adapted, shaped. It's like the uncertainty now and then about whether an intensely remembered moment was experienced or dreamed. Once written, events take on a new reality, more vivid and complete than the original moment. The scene written is permanently possessed. I can look it up.

I know she kissed the back of her own hand, and I know that in the next days or weeks I put together a little vignette about that girl. That's what I wrote then, prose vignettes, mood pieces, because that was how the world came to me, in fragments, in moods. Only later did I start to construct stories. I wasn't a precocious writer. It took me a long time to get where it was possible to go, and even then it was a chancy business. There were others around the university who were more developed. David Lewis Stein, who won writing awards early on for some very polished stories, once pointed out to me that in a story something had to happen. In my vignettes nothing did. Another friend, Christopher (later Leonard) Priestley, son of a University College English professor, had a remarkably polished poetic technique, a mastery of rhyme and metre. I had verbal skill and a hungry eye, but I had much less sense of who I was or might be. I had to try everything. I'm not sure that hasn't remained true throughout my life. I've written a great deal and in a wide variety of forms, and the best of it couldn't have been achieved any other way.

There were a lot of aspiring writers around the university in those days. Among those at University College who later wrote and published extensively were John Robert Colombo, Henry Beissel, Edward Lacey, as well as David Stein and I. (And Erna Paris, though her books began to appear many years later.) Barry Callaghan was at St Michael's College, Adrienne Poy (later Clarkson) was at Trinity College, Dennis Lee at Victoria College, as was a young woman who published as M. E. Atwood. I didn't meet her in those years, though I did know, through Chris Priestley, a young man named Jay Ford, to whom, they say, she was later engaged.

Robert Weaver was the editor of the CBC literary program *Anthology*, and the little group of us at UC reminded him of his own time there with various young writers including James Reaney and Henry Kreisel, so he took an interest and accepted an invitation to speak to something called – just imagine – the Modern Letters Club, and he began to buy poems or stories from some of us. I distinguished myself, the first time I was invited to have lunch with him, by – ever absentminded – forgetting all about it and having to call apologetically an hour late. He seems to have forgiven this.

Both Matt Cohen and Douglas (later George) Fetherling have given accounts of the archetypal Toronto literary experience, coffee with Bob Weaver, Matt's account a little embittered, Fetherling's offhand and closer, for me, to the actual experience of those meetings at the Four Seasons where Bob messed with his pipe and told stories and at the end of the session, if you were lucky, told you what he was going to buy.

It was during the period when he was showing an interest in our little group of university wits that Weaver said to me something that stuck, for better or worse. He often discovered work, he said, by talented university students, but most of them soon stopped writing. I took that to heart and remembered it, and it's possible that it helped to drive me to be as prolific as I've been.

At the end of my first year of university, I finished up my essays, wrote the exams and went back to Niagara to work as a tourist guide at the modern restoration of the nineteenth-century Fort George. I had, really, no idea of just how well I'd done. Any mark would have seemed equally possible. I would get the scholarship back or not. On chilly mornings when no one came to the Fort, I huddled in a corner of the little wooden ticket booth and read Sherwood Anderson's book of stories *Winesburg, Ohio*. In those days the University of Toronto results were first given out by publication in the Toronto newspapers. Came a Saturday and I'd been playing golf, and as I was walking up the street the two blocks toward our house, I saw our car, with both my parents in it, hurtling toward me. They pulled over and handed me the newspaper with the endless list of names. They weren't sure they'd been able to interpret correctly the arcane system of listings.

The university was openly and proudly competitive then, elitist to use a word that would be used pejoratively later on. Marks in the honours courses were listed by grade, first, second or third class, and within those, by place, at least down to third class, where everyone was equal. The figures II:3 meant you ranked third among those with second class honours. There I was, at the top of the heap, I:1. I got to keep receiving the money that General Motors offered, and from then on, I was aware that I was not in over my head with all those smart men and women. It was a great relief.

Seven

Would it have been better for me as a writer if I had struggled, failed, become one of the unemployed? It's a conventional pattern. 'He joined a fraternity and had a good time but failed in all his subjects'. (Nathanael West that is.) Years later Edward Lacey, half ruined after a chaotic and peregrine life, his travels ended with a nearly fatal traffic accident in Bangkok, told me that he had always regarded me as a very intelligent conformist. Well, Edward – who was in a hospital bed when he said that, undergoing or refusing to undergo some kind of rehabilitation – also habitually stood I:1, in Modern Languages, though he was already setting out on his career of self destruction.

By my last year of university I had written a one-act play and had it produced, done the book and lyrics for a folk opera, seen poems come out in campus magazines, published a story in *Canadian Forum,* had it read on CBC *Anthology,* and had another one accepted for publication, for real money, in *The Montrealer,* where I'd once read Hugh MacLennan and Mordecai Richler.

And I was married.

It was at the beginning of my second year that I went to a residence dance in a large dim basement room and noticed for the first time a small, very attractive girl with strikingly dark hair and eyes and wearing a bright red velvet dress, one of those wide skirts with a crinoline beneath. Nancy Keeling her name was. The romantic story goes a little awry at this point – not exactly the flowering of love at first sight – since I was also smitten by a cute girl from Smith College in Massachusetts who was at UC on a year's exchange program. Nancy and I were both in the college show that fall, and we went to the cast party together, but I continued to pursue that girl from Smith – who had (I was very impressed by this) actually spent her summer in New York, working for Doubleday – but she was to return to the U.S. at the end of the year, and besides she came to prefer a handsome scoundrel from Trinity. It was a year later, after a fortuitous meeting in the Honey Dew on Bloor Street at the beginning of term that Nancy and I got seriously involved with each other.

Though she was slender, pretty in the *gamine* style of Leslie Caron, there was a strong jaw that suggested defiance and determination, a notable streak of tomboy independence. She spent her summers pumping gas in a service station in an age when girls didn't do such things. She had been a figure skater and played on the college girls' touch football team, a speedy backfielder who, though she wasn't much at handling the ball, could outrun everyone on the field once she had it in her grip. Once, in public school, her oldest brother had discovered her in the middle of a fight in which she was thrashing one of the boys in her class. She was horrified that her brother separated them and then bought candy for the defeated boy. Surely, she'd believed, it was the winner who should be rewarded.

Raised as the middle child in a family of five in Owen Sound, her doughty independence had been encouraged by her father, owner of a local car dealership, who was intense, hard-bitten, ambitious and, though uneducated, very smart. He had made his stake, the money which allowed him to buy the Mercury dealership, by running a lumber camp near Mac Tier. Nancy, along with her brothers and sister, spent at least a couple of summers there. The logging crew included German prisoners of war, who sometimes gave her candy they'd been sent. Once while hauling a bucket of water back to the house she found herself at close quarters with a rattlesnake; when she shouted for help her oldest brother arrived to kill the menacing creature. They had a tin full of rattles from snakes they had killed. It made for a raw kind of childhood. When the prisoners went on strike, their food was cut off until they went back to work. The nearest neighbours of the camp were two families who were slack and inbred and inclined to burn down each other's houses.

Her father was not the stereotype of the small-town businessman. He would have considered Babbitt a fool. His manners were rougher than those of the small-town middle class. A few years before, he had been the sponsor and manager of a hockey team, the Owen Sound Mercurys, when they won the Allen Cup. That was in the days of the six team NHL, so Senior A hockey was of very high quality. A number of players from that team worked in Jim Keeling's business, and Harry Lumley, one of the best goalies in the NHL, was a partner. Nancy had grown up surrounded by the game of hockey. Her father was a hard man, but he had a goodly number of eccentricities as well as a raffish and inventive sense of humour. He went to bed early, no matter who was in the house; if there was company, he went anyway. He rose early, napped in the afternoon. Nothing interfered with his habits. He had a nervous stomach, was a fussy eater, and there were few subjects that could be safely raised at the dinner table. It was safer to eat in silence. Or he might look at his dinner and say, 'Crack me an egg.' One day, his wife said, she'd crack it over his head. As a way to keep himself occupied while he was thinking things out, he did jigsaw puzzles. Once a drinker, he was fiercely on the wagon – no brandy in the Christmas cake at his house. In business his word was his bond and he was bluntly honest, but about unimportant matters the truth bored him and he preferred what he could invent. His fabulations were legion. Still alive and in business at ninety, he claimed to a reporter that he'd once had his family tree checked out but had given it up because it was full of horse thieves. As a child Nancy was expected to be tough as nails until puberty when she was to metamorphose into a lady like her mother. When she worked one summer in the office of the car dealership, she actually had the nerve to start organizing a union of the employees and to approach her father with their demands. Not much he could do; he'd trained her to be fierce and had always admired her determination. He called her Nugget. Jim Keeling and I never liked each other much – at least once I walked out of his house in a rage when he criticized my daughter Maggie – but over the years we developed a certain wary mutual respect.

The arts faculty of the University of Toronto in those days was divided into four colleges, three of them, St Mike's, Victoria and Trinity, religious foundations, the fourth, University College, which I attended, secular. If you were Jewish, inevitably, you went to UC, so many of my close friends were Jewish. Nancy's father, anti-Semitic at least in principle, had been warned about this before our wedding, which was held just before the beginning of term in my (and her) final year. At some point in the proceedings, held in the large front parlour of their house in Owen Sound, he turned to one of my friends, all strangers to him, and said, 'Which ones are the Jews?'

It was an occasion for that kind of behaviour. I'm told that just as Nancy and I and the minister and our two witnesses appeared at one end of the large living room to begin the ceremony, my friend Henry Shapiro, not unlike Jim Keeling in taking a certain defiant delight in saying the wrong thing, turned to his neighbour and muttered in a stage whisper, 'My God, they're actually going through with it.'

Nancy, who had grown up with her ferocious father, the prisoners of war, and the rattlesnakes, was habitually brave and defiant, and I was unswayed by mere common sense, and we did go through with it. We were both, I suppose, driven people, always needing to feel we were accomplishing something, and we understood that in each other. Nancy was more sociable, almost without intention. People would pour out their problems to her at bus stops. Though I had friends, strangers were shy of me. Men and women told Nancy that they were sure I disliked them when I had no such feeling. I suppose we were complementary in that way. Nancy drove herself, did everything – work, mothering, house-cleaning – with a concentrated intensity, worked hard even when her body told her to stop. The depression that had haunted her mother hovered somewhere, and she had to move at high speed to avoid it. Of course we were too young when we married, and of course we paid for that, though we stayed together, though with spells of separation and periods of pain and chaos, for just over thirty years and have remained on good terms since we've been apart, happy to confer about children and grandchildren and gossip about the friends we shared. Say this for us: we never once in all those years argued about money.

The summer before the wedding, the last hot months of our courtship went on in the crazed conditions of a season of summer stock with Straw Hat Players, Nancy acting with one of the two companies that moved back and forth between Peterborough and Port Carling, while I was permanently in Peterborough being what Fred Euringer, in his splendid theatrical memoir, *A Fly on the Curtain,* describes pretty accurately as 'business manager/cum company manager/cum jack of all trades.' Nancy had acted in high school and during the academic year she had played the fierce and evil little girl in Bill Davis's production of Lillian Hellman's *The Bad Seed.* (She always looked younger than her years. When she was thirty, bartenders would still refuse to serve her.) Bill, working with Karl Jaffary, who was later to be a Toronto alderman, was producing the season of summer stock, and he hired Nancy for it during a boozy party at a Toronto hotel. (I don't know why we were at a boozy party at a Toronto hotel.) I had played the romantic lead in the UC Follies in my second year (being able to sing can get you a long way), and had appeared in a small part in Robert Gill's production of *Death of a Salesman.* I got to fire Willy Loman, who was wonderfully performed by a young actor named Ray Stancer. When I stood on the stage with Ray I learned from close up what real actors can do. (Small-world footnote: the young woman who played my secretary was to be Dennis Lee's first wife.) With this much experience I was deemed reliable enough to appear on stage as a journalist or a butler when I wasn't doing my many other jobs.

Which were: overseeing ticket sales at the Gell travel bureau; picking up the tickets at the end of the day and opening and running the box office; depositing money and handling the pay cheques (to be delivered to the actors never later than Friday noon so they had time to get to the bank); distributing posters in Peterborough stores and in resorts within half a day's drive; writing press releases, both a weekly one about the play and an interview with one of the actors for the local daily (the Peterborough *Examiner*, then still edited by Robertson Davies, who invited the company round one evening and stood in his library in front of the tall shelves of books, pontificating); arranging interviews with the other weekly newspaper and with the local radio station; preparing program copy and dealing with the printers; helping to strike the set and pack it on the truck on Saturday night after the end of the show; and on at least one occasion, driving all night to Port Carling to pick up a costume that had been left behind, leaving after I'd closed the box office and getting back in time to handle what needed to be handled the next day. That particular outing got complicated when the old car's generator began to fail somewhere near Washago. I got as far as an all-night restaurant, telephoned the theatre at Port Carling, where the stage crew was still at work, and waited till they could bring me the costume and then follow my car to the all-night garage at Gravenhurst (daylight by now) where I hung around until a second-hand generator was installed. Then I drove back, did a day's work, fell fast asleep and was roused by a telegram from the National Film Board. I'd been given the exceptional opportunity of writing a script for their *Comparisons* series, and I was supposed to be doing it in my spare time. What spare time? It was late.

Later in the season I did the same long haul to pick up some needed item, though on this occasion I was able to stay overnight, spending a couple of hours asleep on somebody's couch and, the next day being roared around Lake Muskoka by the ebullient John Douglas (later, before his early death, my producer at CBC radio), who was being a convincing Mr Toad at the controls of a rented motorboat.

Another of my jobs, early in the season, was to find rooms for the actors to stay in, preferably convenient to the public school where the plays were rehearsed and presented. My system was simple and effective. I walked up and down the streets near the theatre, knocked on the doors of complete strangers and asked if they would like to rent a room to an actor. Since there were two companies, moving back and forth between Port Carling and Peterborough, two actors would use each room, moving in and out on alternate weeks. On the whole it worked out well, but I confess that I never looked at the rooms. A room was a room so far as I was concerned.

Company A opened the season playing some piece of British froth, then carried it off to Port Carling while Company B came and opened *Gigi*. That week, Fred Euringer, who was directing the show, took possession of a room about a half block down the street from the school. At the beginning of the next week, Timothy Findley was arriving from Toronto to join Company A, who were coming back from Port Carling. I had been told a little about Tiff, that he'd acted at Stratford, where he'd met Alec Guinness, who encouraged him to move to England. He'd appeared in theatre there, travelled to Russia with a production of Hamlet. I also heard the gossip about his recent and short-lived marriage, doomed, they said, because he was a homosexual and she a nymphomaniac. (Oh, the grim sexual attitudes of the time.) Bill Davis called Tiff the best young actor in Canada, and I recalled that I had seen him the previous winter at the Crest Theatre playing Archie Rice's son in *The Entertainer*. When he arrived, I drove him to the house where Fred Euringer had been staying and dropped him off.

Tiff was, then and always, a delicate, sensitive man, and I gather that the room was not especially pleasant. Years later I might have had the sense to look at it, try to make it welcoming, flowers, something. Tiff was one of those artists who need protection and should have it, but I was twenty-one and careless, so I took him to the door and left. He wasn't happy there. I don't know how much of it was the room and how much distress about various other things in his life, but Tiff dealt with it, as he did in those days, by drinking quite a lot of gin. Then he turned up at the theatre. He was wearing a rather sexy outfit – very brief powder blue shorts – but was perfectly coherent, and I chatted with him at the box office until he wandered into the downstairs dressing rooms where he passed out.

All that sounds undramatic enough now, but this was small town Ontario in 1959. Bill Lord, the production manager, was convinced that the school caretaker would catch on and we'd be thrown out of the school, the whole season wrecked. So after the show came down, Tiff was surreptitiously carried out to one of the company cars. Heartless to the end, I was all for dumping him in a hotel room, but instead I drove him to the house that Karl Jaffary and his wife had rented for the summer, and which was a kind of headquarters for the company. It had an extra room – where Nancy was staying every second week – and once he woke up in the back seat of the car, I persuaded him, after a certain amount of drunken melodrama, to go in there for the night. He stayed for the rest of the season, so that from then on, he had at least some company around him when he came back from work. As he didn't drive I delivered him to his publicity interviews – where I discovered that he was a writer, or beginning to be one – and he bore no grudge about the unseemly room.

Then there was the shaggy dog.

Audiences for this first year of revived summer stock in Peterborough weren't terribly good, but there wasn't a lot of money for more advertising. Bill Lord came to me one day and said maybe I could think of some interesting ways of getting us free advertising. There was, for example, the shaggy dog in *King of Hearts*. Though I was doing a walk-on in the play, this was the first I'd heard of the shaggy dog, but it became my job to find one for the production and get us some free publicity.

The first thing I did was place a want-ad in the Peterborough *Examiner*. WANTED: SHAGGY DOG TO APPEAR WITH STRAW HAT PLAYERS. And I got a reply.

'I called about the dog.'

'The ad in the paper?'

'That's right'

'So you've got a dog you think we could use?'

'Yeah. You can have him.'

'Is he shaggy?'

'You could say that.'

'Can I come and have a look it him sometime.'

'You just come when you like.'

I got an address and phone number. Then I got in touch with Arthur Mandel. I'd met him at University College, and I knew he was spending his summer as a photographer with the *Examiner*. He agreed to come out to Douro Township, where the animal was currently in residence, and photograph for the newspaper the dog's audition.

King of Hearts features not only a dog but children. In fact Ron

Hartman, the show's director, had been heard to mutter, 'Only I would be hired to direct a show with two kids, a dog, and Tiff Findley.' Tiff's drinking had begun to get him a reputation.

I organized the two children – one was a professional named Guy Bannerman, the other had been picked up in Muskoka to play his buddy – and a young actor named Matt Corrigan (who suffered from car sickness), and the four of us, along with Art Mandel, jammed ourselves into a little red car borrowed from Jackie Burroughs and followed the directions I'd been given along a maze of back country roads till we found the farm where the shaggy dog was living. House, barn, chickens, muddy yard, the usual, and the farmer came out and shook hands and the dog appeared for his audition.

The dog was about the colour of an Irish setter, and he was certainly shaggy. Big too, one of those smiling, affable dogs, and he and the kids hit it off, and Arthur took pictures while Matt tried to walk off his car-sickness. The farmer and I got down to business.

'We need the dog for two weeks,' I said.

'You can have him.'

'We could pay you a few dollars. Two weeks' use of your dog.'

He just looked at me.

'I'll bring him back to you, of course, when the show's over.'

'I said you can have him.'

'You don't want him back?'

He indicated that was the case. I looked at the dog, who was wagging his tail, posing for pictures, charming everyone. Was there a hint of chicken feathers around his mouth? Was I going to be stuck with this shaggy dog forever?

'I'll come and pick him up on Sunday,' I said.

That was the day of the dress rehearsal, and late in the morning I drove out to the farm again, a little nervous that by now the dog might have been shot by an irritable neighbour, but there he was, and once again I offered to pay a little something, and once again the farmer said just take him away, so I did. I drove the cheerful, charming creature back to Peterborough and up to the theatre. He allowed himself to be led across the school lawn, perfectly happy about the whole arrangement until we got to the door of the kindergarten/rehearsal room, where he planted his feet. He was a country dog, and an outdoor dog, and he was frightened of doorways. It came to me that this could pose a problem. Somehow (brute force I think) I got him into the rehearsal room and assigned one of the company apprentices – ill-paid young people from Peterborough who had theatrical inclinations – to clean up the dog, getting rid of burrs, mud, chicken feathers and whatever else had come along with him.

Since I had just hired a dog who wouldn't go through doors, I decided that I'd better have some treats with which the actors could bribe him. However this was small-town Ontario (as I may have mentioned) in 1959. Nothing was open on Sundays. Nothing. Well, there was one exception, the restaurant at the local hotel, legally open, I suppose, so that travellers didn't actually starve during the Sabbath. So I drove down there.

Could I buy some wieners from their kitchen?

No.

Price was no object.

Still no.

I picked up a copy of the menu where I found something they called a Swanky-Franky – a hot dog with cheese and bacon.

'I'd like to order,' I said firmly, 'six Swanky-Frankies. But leave out the cheese, the bacon and the bun.'

The waitress stared at me and disappeared into the kitchen.

I got my six wieners, at a wildly exorbitant price, and drove back to the school where we were performing. I equipped the stage manager and the two actors who had to deal with the dog, Matt Corrigan and Tiff, with wieners meant to ease the problem of getting the dog in and out. I'm not sure I explained that the dog had never before passed through a doorway.

Then I settled down to watch the dress rehearsal, entering for my one line when required. Came the dog scene. There was a certain amount of pushing and shoving from offstage and the dog popped through the appropriate opening in the flats. He looked wonderful, shaggy, appealing, still smiling. He didn't piss on the furniture or leap off the stage. The child actors loved him. The audience would love him. Really the scene went swimmingly until it was time for his exit. Tiff was to lead him offstage. Through a doorway.

Tiff led. Dog said No.

This was a dress rehearsal. Any professional knows that you treat it like a performance. Keep going, no matter what. If a bomb goes off you ad lib a remark about the noisy neighbourhood. Tiff was a professional, and I had equipped him for emergencies. He reached in his pocket. He waved his wiener.

The dog ignored it. A wiener was as nothing compared to the terrible possibilities created by a doorway.

Tiff, as I've said, was a professional. Tiff had performed for Tyrone Guthrie at Stratford. Tiff had been to Russia. He did what had to be done when his wiener failed. He picked up the dog. Now Tiff was not a small man, but our hero was not a small dog. Nevertheless Tiff had him off the ground and aimed at the exit.

One of the features of the set of *King of Hearts* was a totem pole, though I can't remember why. As Tiff got hold of the dog, the dog got hold of the totem pole and hung on tight so that one more step would have brought it down.

The audience watching this was three people: Ron Hartman, the director; me, the dog wrangler; and Brenda Davies, wife of Robertson Davies and director of the next show. By this point the three of us were paralyzed by laughter, but somehow, as we unhelpfully fell about, Tiff, still perfectly professional in the face of immense provocation, managed to pry the dog off the totem pole with one arm while holding it in the air with the other, and they got off the stage.

It's possible that I kept my distance after the rehearsal – though I had to pick up the dog and take him to the Humane Society, where I'd arranged his accommodation, but the shaggy dog was a sensible creature, and he gradually learned that entrances and exits wouldn't hurt him. By the second week of the show, the Port Carling week, he had become quite an accomplished performer. I wasn't certain what would happen after the run was over, whether I would dare return the dog to the farm – perhaps I would have to pay them to take him back – but one of the actors had a woman friend visiting from Philadelphia, and she fell for the dog and adopted it.

While I was racing about Peterborough that summer, attending to everything from pay cheques to shaggy dogs, Nancy was performing with one of the travelling companies, beginning the summer as Gigi, a French ingenue who has to mature from childhood to elegance in the course of the play, and following this by playing the mannish middle-aged Miss Casewell in Agatha Christie's *The Mousetrap,* something of a stretch that was, so she padded herself and invented a deep foghorn voice. Then she returned to playing a teenager in *The Late Christopher Bean,* in which her most memorable line was 'Shoot 'im, Pa!'. She ended the summer among the mock Australian accents of *The Summer of the Seventeenth Doll.*

There wasn't much spare time, but on the weeks she was in town we spent what there was together, often getting less sleep than we should. But we were young. As we were tumbling toward the marriage bed, Bill Davis's early marriage – the wedding had been held just after his university graduation that spring – was falling apart. He'd spoken about his uncertainties even before the wedding took place, but the train was on the rails and there was no stopping it. It was clear to anyone observing that summer that he and Cathy had serious problems; he was surly and she was suffering.

As an economy measure, my contract ended before the final show of the Peterborough season, *Visit to a Small Planet*, with Tiff playing the space man. Nancy was finishing up her season in Port Carling and returning from there to Owen Sound. The day I was to leave on a train to Toronto, I was spending my last hour or so in the shared house which had been headquarters for the season. There was a muted but climactic scene between Bill and Cathy, and as he left the house, she went upstairs in tears and began to pack. When she reappeared with a suitcase, I offered to share a taxi to the train station, and we sat together on the train to Toronto, pointedly not discussing her marriage. It was years later that Bill discovered I had run off with his first wife. It had never occurred to me to tell him the story.

(An aside on memory and words: a few pages back I described the shaggy dog as smiling and affable. While this memoir was lying around in manuscript I began rereading James Thurber's lovely book *The Years with Ross*. There I found an account of an editorial wrangle when a writer working for *The New Yorker* said of a dog, 'He stared at us and smiled affably.' Did I really have that phrase tucked away in a corner of my brain for forty years? Perhaps. Now and then I have written a phrase that appears to me a little too familiar. Usually I go around and show it to everyone in sight to see if anyone can place it. They never can. Anyway, as Northrop Frye observed somewhere, books are made out of other books.)

We spent a lot of time with Bill Davis over the next winter. He directed a production of *The Crucible* in which Nancy played Mary Warren, one of the coven of hysterical girls who propel into existence the Salem witch trials, and he also directed *Katy Cruel*, the folk musical that Michael Rasminsky and I had written over the previous months. That production was, if nothing else, a triumph of *chutzpah*. University College had a history of annual shows that went back at least to Wayne and Shuster in their undergraduate days. The shows had died out for a while, but in 1957, Marv Catzman and Phil Cowan revived the tradition with a light-hearted musical about college life, with a certain amount of local satire, of, for example, Toronto's laws on Sunday closing.

On a Saturday night in Toronto,
There's music and dancing and gin,
But the things that are right on a Saturday night
After midnight all turn into sin.

I was in that edition of *UC Follies* and was represented in the 1958 version (by different writers) as an underground character named Earwig.

West Side Story was setting the world on fire in those days, and at some point Michael Rasminsky and I hatched the idea that we would take over *UC Follies* for the next year and write, not a college show, but a serious musical. I knew that Kurt Weill had written a musical based on a folk song and called *Down in the Valley*, though I had never heard a note of it. (Still haven't.) But the notion planted a seed. Early in the summer of 1959 I spent a few days in New York visiting my witty friend Henry Shapiro who was estivating in his parents' house out in Brooklyn, and while I was there I saw and loved productions of *The Threepenny Opera* and *The Fantasticks*, both playing in small theatres in Greenwich Village. Somewhere, probably in a paperback anthology, I had found a folk song with a single haunting verse.

When first I came to town
They called me the roving jewel.
Now they've changed their tune,
They call me Katy Cruel.

There was a story buried in that, and a character in the song's refrain.

Oh, that I was where I would be.
Then would I be where I am not.
Here I am where I must be.
Where I would be I cannot.

So Michael and I went to the student executive of University College and proposed that we would write and produce this show, and they bravely said Yes.

Now all this depended on the assumption that musically Mike Rasminsky could do just about anything, and that was fortunately true. He was a very fine pianist, assistant director of the Hart House Glee Club, and he played good jazz, school of Art Tatum. Though not too tall, he was good-looking, immensely personable when he cared to be, and at parties he would sit down at the piano and every young woman in the place would immediately join him there wanting to ruffle his hair or rub his back. Infuriating man. He was at this point finishing up his last year in Physics and Chemistry and trying, after a belated application, to get into the Harvard medical school. They said he was too late. Not used to being rejected, Michael applied for and won an important scholarship. They said he was still too late – very stubborn, those Harvard people. So he was to spend the next year as a researcher at a cancer clinic while he waited for a place at Harvard.

I sketched out a story – what seemed to me implicit in the folk song that would begin and end the show – and began writing lyrics, now and then tossing in an idea of a tune. Michael set the words I wrote, handed me a couple of existing pieces of his, one a little piano piece written as an exercise in the manner of Bartók, one a three-part fugue in a minor key and I found places for them and gave them words. In a short period we had a draft, and with a small production staff, Bill Davis set about putting it on the stage.

The opening in January of 1960 created some stir, a front-page rave review in *The Varsity,* modest but pleasant notices in the *Star* and the *Globe.* I got a nice letter from the principal of the college. There was talk of reviving the show professionally, talk a little disturbing to Michael's parents. His father was deputy governor (later governor) of the Bank of Canada, and they weren't keen on the idea that their brilliant son might become a theatrical gypsy, but the plans to do something more with the show came to nothing, and Michael went on to medical studies and residencies in Boston, New York, London, Paris and finally Montreal, where he practises as a neurologist, living in Westmount with two Steinways in his living room in case he finds someone to play duets with.

I hadn't thought much about the show for many years until I began writing these pages about the past and dug out a recording we made at the time. I no longer possess a copy of the script. Though I can hear lots of flaws in what's on that recording, it also has a persuasive quality and moments that I can still find moving. On the whole the solos and duets work better than the choruses, though one of the most touching moments is the first act curtain in which a love song is counterpointed with a hymn, individual and community making their different statements.

The material of the story came mostly from literature, hints of Synge's *Riders to the Sea,* elements found in books of Maritime folk songs. The action takes place in a seaside fishing village, and I'd never seen the ocean in my life, but I'd lived in a small town on Lake Ontario, and perhaps that made its contribution. Two of the best songs in the show were existing poems, one a cradle song and the other a triolet I'd written in the summer of 1958 while living in a cabin on Stoney Lake where I was tutoring a fourteen-year-old boy who had a multitude of problems which had begun with cancer in early childhood.

> There will be no home for my pilgrim bones
> When I go down with the western moon.
> I have broken no land, cast out no stones
> There will be no home for my pilgrim bones,
> No homeplace, harbour, my labour owns,
> I pass them by too late, too soon.
> There will be no home for my pilgrim bones
> When I go down with the western moon.

Youthful and romantic of course, but in the show, beautifully set to music, it made a convincing song of seduction, with its obvious appeal to Katy, the central character, who has earlier sung a matching piece.

> Nowhere's my home and my destination ...
> I will roam till the stars are mine,
> Until I find the everywhere town I dream of
> And my everyone man, then like my stars I'll shine.
>
> I will go on till I find tomorrow;
> Never stop till I stop to die.
> Forever tonight I dream of a miracle
> Land in the air, a town where none will cry.

That lyric was written for the show, a skilled piece of work of a late romantic sort. I think *Katy Cruel* was part of my lifelong struggle to satisfy both the part of me that loved popular art and the part that loved high art. Did I aspire to write *The Shadow* or 'Mr Arcularis' or pure poetry? All of them somehow. Listening to the recording I think that even the worst lines have verbal energy and musical imagination.

And we had the guts to do it.

With Michael Rasminsky at the piano.
(*Toronto Star:* photo for *Katy Cruel.*)

Eight

So we were married, two young souls contained in the hot, close, all-but-squalid intimacy of a life in a pair of small rooms shared through all the hours of the day and night. At the end of our final university term, we were flat broke, but clever and determined as always, Nancy talked her way into a job waiting on tables – the manager didn't want to hire her, but she simply didn't let him say no – and I found a couple of part-time things, one as counsellor in a day-camp. At that point, there was no news about the Commonwealth Scholarship I'd applied for – I'd turned down other scholarship nominations – so I was checking the want ads, and I found and applied for a job at Maclean-Hunter, as editor of the *Truck and Bus Monthly*. I didn't get it, but I was well-spoken and the company had a program of training promising young men, so they sent me off for a battery of tests at the office of a personnel consultant. The tests took most of a day. What I remember most vividly was that I was to look at a blurry drawing – what appeared to be human beings in some specific but undefined location – and I was to write down what was happening. I made up a story, and it was only after I was done that I realized that what I had recounted was, more or less, the plot of Henry James' novel, *The Portrait of a Lady*. A university acquaintance was going out with the daughter of the man who ran the testing program and I heard that I had done very well, but by the time Maclean-Hunter got back to me I had been offered a scholarship that would take us to England, and told them this – foolishly – before they offered or didn't offer a training position. An unlived life: I've sometimes wondered.

The other unlived life – I've written about this one – was singing. A music student in the University College residence used to have me join his choir somewhere in the western suburbs of Toronto for special services. Once they performed a St Mark Passion, which might (or might not) be by Bach. I started out singing Christus, and got assigned more and more solo parts as choir members backed out – I was Jesus and Judas and who knows who else. Another time I sang solos for a presentation of *Messiah*, and on that occasion the choirmaster of Avenue Road United attended the performance, along with two or three of his professional soloists. At the end of it he offered me a job as the bass soloist at that big downtown church. I accepted, then had second thoughts and said No; singing was hard on my nerves, I wanted to write. Didn't sing much for years after that. What if I had accepted the job...? Well, I didn't.

In September of 1960, Nancy and I got off a boat at Southampton for two years in England, financed by a Commonwealth Scholarship. Having accepted the scholarship, I was to go to Liverpool and do a master's degree at Liverpool University. This was a compromise. I hadn't intended to be a graduate student – I didn't think of myself as an academic – but Nancy and I wanted to travel and took the only means that came to hand. The place I most wanted to go was Africa, and this was in the days when CUSO sent volunteers, but somehow I had never heard of all that.

The always astute Edward Lacey, reviewing my first book, remarked on the effect on my imagination of taking my already northern and Protestant sensibility to England instead of to some warmer brighter place. After a disastrous year in Edmonton, Edward went south. Way leads on to way, as Robert Frost observes, though I couldn't have known, as that first train travelled through the green countryside toward London, that two years later I would have a child and a university teaching job, that Africa had been postponed, probably forever.

The great cities, London, Paris, New York, while they are characteristic of the countries they're in, are not really representative. London is London, Liverpool is England. In September of 1960, the first Commonwealth scholars were given a formal introduction to the country – I think we were at a reception with the Queen Mother – and we had a few days to see London, the galleries and theatres, including Donald Pleasance in the first production of Pinter's play, *The Caretaker*, a glimpse of a whole new theatrical world and of the darkness of an England that lay behind the teashops and the bright green grass. Arrived in Liverpool on a Sunday, we missed breakfast at the small hotel where we were booked and began to learn about the complex rules of the country – not obviously foreign but very strange – we'd come to. It was hours later and after miles of walking around the city that we found a Chinese restaurant where we were at last able to get something to eat.

You have been a child and learned how life is, then you want to see a different world, only to be startled by its difference. It can be such small things, habits, odd rules, stubborn eccentricities, that cause the greatest shock. Shopkeepers couldn't or wouldn't understand us; we took a while to figure out how things were done. A subject of contention with our first landlord was the water heater. The same one served both his house and our flat. It was heated by our coal fire and his immersion heater. Once a week he and his wife turned on the electric heater and expected bath water. In the depth of an English winter, at the edge of the Irish sea, without central heating, the only place we could get warm was the bathtub – we filled it with water and got in together – and the fire that heated the water was burning all the time, and besides, I think I never quite understood the rules, or what an immersion heater was, or even that these English might only heat the water for a bath once a week – that delight in meanness.

In ways the flat was splendid. It was across the Mersey from Liverpool, at the edge of a resort town called New Brighton, which had a few shops selling prawns and some sort of fun fair, though I can't ever remember seeing it open. The apartment was in a sumptuous nineteenth-century house on a hilltop, on a street grandly called Montpellier Crescent. We had two large rooms and the servants' quarters, consisting of two cubicles and a scullery. The grand sitting room had large windows that looked out over the Mersey and the Irish sea. Since our marriage, we'd lived in an attic on Spadina Avenue in Toronto, and then in one room of a summer cottage shared with staff of the Peterborough summer theatre – where we'd been called back just after the new season opened when Bill Davis decided he needed organizational help. Knowing we were moving to England in the fall, we both quit our Toronto jobs and went to Peterborough – Nancy as business manager, while I was to be lighting man as well as being jack-of-all-trades again. The formal sitting room of the flat above the Mersey estuary was unthinkable luxury. Moving in during September we had no way of knowing that the room would never once be warm enough to use. We spent the winter in the tiny sitting room of the servants' quarters, with both doors closed and the wing chairs pulled up to the coal fire.

Nancy hadn't seen her older sister Nora for several years. Nora had left university to move to England and take up an acting scholarship she'd been offered at the Royal Academy of Dramatic Arts. To help support herself she had worked as a companion to the aged mother of Christopher Fry, author of verse plays which were wildly successful at the time and have now largely disappeared, but after her graduation and a successful show of her paintings in a London gallery, she had gone off to Paris to be an artist, and though she soon enough gave it up, she had stayed on there, working at this and that, most recently teaching English to private students. Now, it appeared, Nora had plans to return to Canada for the period we were to be in England. Nancy badly wanted to see her, and so shortly after we arrived in England we contrived a very cheap trip to France for a few days. You took a bus from London to the south coast of England where what appeared to be an aircraft left over from the Second War took off from a hilltop, managing to stay in the air for just long enough to putter across the Channel, where it fell to earth and you got on another bus that drove you to Paris. We had recently been introduced to English food, and I remember that a simple ham sandwich in the tiny French airport was a great treat. In Paris, I met Nora for the first time. Dark hair and eyes like Nancy, but she was taller and had all the presence and force of a fine actress, quite beautiful, though her nose, operated on after a car accident in which it had been broken, still hadn't perfectly healed. Living entirely in French, she was beginning to lose her English idioms. 'I'm not in the bath,' as she put it. Never strong on practical matters, Nora had been unable to find us a hotel room – Paris was full of people there for the autumn sports or something absurd like that. I used a version of my Peterborough technique and simply walked along the nearby streets stopping at every hotel to ask if they had a room, and we rented a narrow chamber with an even narrower bed under the eaves of a small hotel in the neighbourhood, the toilet down the hall the classic two footprints and a hole. However, we were to spend most of our time at Nora's apartment, which she shared – apartments in Paris being scarce and expensive – with Guy Pèchenard, who was landlord, friend, and sometime lover – the only man she ever loved, I suspect. Guy was a doctor, a heroin addict, and a communist, and over dinner that night we had a vigorous political argument, limited by my rather stumbling French and his complete lack of English, but enjoyable all the same – Orwell versus Stalin as I recall.

At Nora's urging, Guy drove us rapidly and somewhat impatiently around Paris, and while we were driving along the Champs Élysées, we were astonished to catch sight of Erna Newman (soon to be Erna Paris) who had shared classes with me for four years and had appeared as a dancer in *Katy Cruel*. She was in Paris studying, was in fact to marry there and live some time in France. Guy was happy to let us off and be free of his duties as a tour guide, and we went to a café with Erna, and she and Nancy talked about how far they had needed to turn up the hems of their skirts to match what was worn on the streets of France and England – two tiny vivacious Canadians learning to show off their legs.

We were soon enough back in New Brighton, but at Christmas, Nancy's father sent Nora enough money to fly to England and visit us. She slept in the tiny, cold, maid's bedroom of our flat for a few days and then we all took the train to London where we stayed in an apartment borrowed from Bill Davis, who was studying at LAMDA but off skiing for the holidays. In New Brighton Nora had picked up a paperback of Alan Sillitoe's *Saturday Night and Sunday Morning* which had pictures from the film on the cover.

'That's Albie,' she said. 'What's he doing on this book?'

Albie was Albert Finney, just then becoming famous – though Nora living in French had heard nothing of it – for his intense portrayal of characters from the working class of the north of England. He and Nora, it emerged, had been lovers when they were both students at RADA. A very stupid man, she insisted, but all the same when we got to London, she toddled round to the theatre where he was playing in *Billy Liar,* went out for a drink and got him to leave free tickets at the box office for us the next night. Nora's older friend Adza Vincent – Christopher Fry's secretary during the time Nora worked for him and now a theatrical agent – was to pop round on her way somewhere, New Year's Eve I think it was.

'We should give her some flowers,' Nora said.

Everything was closed by that time, but we had a bouquet of daffodils, bought in the Earlscourt tube station to brighten up the flat, sitting there in water.

'I'll give her those. She won't take them with her anyway.'

Nora had grown to understand English social gestures, or perhaps she just understood Adza, who swept in, full of her story about how she'd had to go down to the pub to find someone to do up her dress for her. Nora presented her with the flowers, she exclaimed appropriately, and a few minutes later she was gone and flowers were back in water. A satisfying piece of theatre all round. And soon enough Nora had flown away and we were back in front of the coal fire living our quiet life.

Early on I had established a pattern of catching the little electric train into Liverpool, spending much of the day at the university library, reading the plays of Ben Jonson, John Marston, George Chapman, and walking through the gathering dusk to Central Station to catch a train home in the afternoon. No course work was attached to the graduate program, though I suppose I could have audited undergraduate courses, and I was invited (half by mistake I suspect) to use the faculty club for lunch. The university offered two graduate awards called the Noble Fellowships so a couple of other English graduates could be found there. One of them, a Cambridge-trained Scot named John Finlayson, ended up teaching at Queen's when I did.

Our original hope had been for a scholarship to London, and we had always assumed that Nancy would find something to do in or around a theatre, but Liverpool was where I got sent, and after a failed attempt to form some kind of connection with the Liverpool Rep, Nancy was left on her own all day – though she began to audit a university extension course later on. She was later to say that she thought the isolation had driven her mad; she once spent an entire afternoon mending a tea towel that had been burnt by falling on the open flame of the gas stove.

Liverpool was grim, black, ugly, yet somehow a harshly splendid city. In the centre of it were a number of huge overstated buildings, John Brown Hall with its thick classical columns, Lime Street Station, the Art Gallery, all of them black as soot, but with the white markings of years of pigeon shit. The brightest thing in the dark streets – apart from the flagrant green and purple miniskirts – was the reddened cheeks of the men and women, the younger ones a fresh pink, the older ones with the snaking red rivers of broken veins and finally the purple flush produced by years of coal fires in cold houses. Everyone was still burning soft coal, and the fogs still came down and blinded the city. You stood by the window and beyond was nothing but the thick wet whiteness, no shapes, no hint of the direction of the sun or sky. Up and down were equal. One morning, I was at the university library, reading. I looked out the window, and outside it was night. The fog had come down and all the city's smoke was trapped underneath.

The university was at the top of Brownlow Hill. Going up, there were grim new council flats on one side of the road, on the other, rows of brick houses, some of them still derelict, boarded up since they were shattered by bombs during the war. In 1960, that war was only fifteen years in the past. The shell of a bombed church had been deliberately left standing in the centre of Liverpool as a memorial. Brownlow Hill was steep, and on foggy days, you would see men and women with handkerchiefs over their mouths as they climbed while trying to breathe the bad air.

The house where we lived was on the Birkenhead side of the river, but it too was grim, black, a nineteenth-century imitation classic, with a columned porch. The landlord was a little stammering man with a moustache. He had a high-complexioned blonde wife who was left alone in the house a great deal while he was off travelling from town to town in his little car, selling something. It was in the grand front hall of their part of the house that he told me sometime in the spring we'd have to leave. Part of it was the hot water, I think, and then he said that we didn't keep the place clean. Though in his terms that was probably true – the big sitting room never got cleaned since we never went into it – I was insulted and furious, so furious that I moved toward him in a gesture he found threatening, as if I might be about to hit him. Perhaps I might have, but he ran halfway up the stairs and shrilled something at me, and I walked out, back into our own half of the house where all the suppressed rage came out in thirty seconds of uncontrollable animal screams. Perhaps the English madness was catching.

Nancy was pregnant by now. We may have expected problems trying to rent a place when we'd soon have a child, but there were none. The apartment we found was very close by. We rented from a woman named Mrs Prescott. She had the first floor of the house, we had the second, the third was empty. She was a woman of some warmth and charm, well-spoken, dressed in a pink suit, with an appealing smile, but she was showing signs of wear. Her hearing was poor, and she was incontinent and smelled of urine. There was some confusion about keys, which locks were used and which weren't, so we were occasionally locked out. Knocking on the door was useless. Though she was usually settled in her chair in front of the TV, not very far from the front door, she never heard a knock. However a loud thump on the front window might rouse her and bring her slowly on her stiff knees to the door where there would be a good-tempered but mildly addled conversation about just why we were locked out again.

There was something of the theatre of the absurd about it all. We might well have been living in a play by Pinter or N.F. Simpson. In England the theatre of the absurd sometimes appeared to be plain realism. In London we'd met someone – manservant to Adza Vincent – who might have been the model for Pinter's caretaker. His name was Light.

Mrs Prescott was unable to learn or remember Nancy's name. She tried Elsie for a while then moved on to Enid. Finally she settled on Ethel for most occasions. One Sunday morning I met her in the front hall, and we had one of our discussions about the newspapers. She took the *Express* and the *News of the World,* we took the *Observer.* She was worried about why she hadn't found our newspaper when she'd gone out to get her own.

'Nancy already got ours,' I shouted.

'Who?'

'Nancy. My wife Nancy,' I shouted, even louder.

'Is your wife's name Nancy?'

'Yes.' I shouted, triumphant. Finally we'd get it straight. 'Her name's Nancy.'

She stared at me.

'Then why do you call her Ethel?' she said.

'I don't call her Ethel,' I shouted. 'You do.'

Off we went to our Sunday papers.

After a while we got the habit of watching TV with her on Saturday nights, Perry Mason. 'He has nice hands,' she would say every week when a certain introductory shot came on. Sometimes she would offer us a little something to eat – a tin of apricots with two or three spoons.

Our apartment itself was like our landlady, pleasant, even attractive, but deteriorated. Each time a rug had worn out, another had been put on top of it. The living room had carpets four deep. There was no door to the attic above, only an open staircase, and the upper rooms had odds and ends of furniture, the feeling of past lives. Mrs Prescott had a son, somewhere in the Midlands, and a nephew who came every Saturday to take her out for lunch and a little shopping. This house was even closer to the sea than the previous one, and at most times of year it was possible to wipe water off the walls. There was a spare bedroom, and in the summer my parents came to visit and we rented a car and travelled with them.

Our child was due to be born in early October, and one night not long before that, I woke to hear noises outside our bedroom door. It was Mrs Prescott, who had somehow managed, in spite of her age and arthritis, to walk or crawl up the stairs and was standing there breathless and worried. She thought she'd heard a baby cry. No, I said, not yet.

'Well, as soon as ever it does,' she told me firmly, 'you get her to the hospital.'

I promised, and she thumped and bumbled back down the stairs.

When the colder weather arrived, I became aware that she was

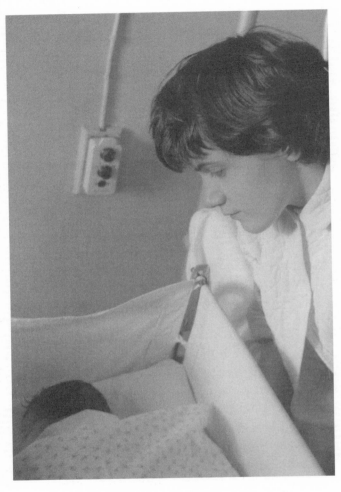

Nancy and Maggie in an English maternity ward.

having trouble with her fire. She had a gas poker attached to a little natural gas outlet beside the fireplace. The principle was simple. You lit it, put it among the chunks of coal, and the flame of the gas would set them alight, but she had left it in the burning coal too long and the metal had melted. Instead of that device, we used firelighters, little blocks of material soaked in some kind of oil that produced a concentrated heat and started the coal. I showed them to her and I think bought her some, but she had little luck. There was nothing else for it but to go down and light her fire for her every morning.

After Maggie was born – it was very English, no doctor and the midwife was on her tea break – we were faced with the problem of washing diapers. What we would do was boil them in a large pail on the gas ring in the kitchen, then rinse them in the bathtub. However the gas pressure was limited. We'd got used to hearing Mrs Prescott's whistling kettle for long periods downstairs before she noticed it or remembered to make tea, but as long as her gas ring was on we couldn't get enough heat to boil the diapers. So when the kettle began whistling, one of us would go down and make her tea so we could turn off her gas and get the diapers to the boil. We then, fearing a recurrence of a little diaper rash, rinsed them so many times that Nancy's hands gave out, and I was left with the job.

It was a long winter. The previous year, though we had been miserably cold, spring had begun to come in March. This year, the pipes were still freezing in April. The next winter was to be even worse, but we were gone by then. In parts of the north of England, it was not unknown for babies to die of hypothermia while sleeping in their cribs inside the house. We had a small paraffin heater – north Americans would call it kerosene, and it was in fact like a large kerosene lamp, with a wick and a chimney – and we carried it from room to room, to whichever room the baby was in.

Shortly after Maggie was brought home from the hospital, she began, one evening, to scream, apparently in terrible pain. It was very frightening. We had no family to consult, but eventually we found the description of colic in a paperback copy of Dr Spock that someone had mailed us. That seemed to be what we were faced with. It helped if I put Maggie in her carriage and rolled it back and forth across the room, so for three hours every night I would do that, first running back and forth, then as she calmed and went to sleep, moving more slowly, and finally sitting and reading, while rocking it slowly with my foot. I read all the *The Rise and*

Fall of the Third Reich doing that. For the rest of the night, she would sleep between feedings.

Beneath us, Mrs Prescott was drifting away. One morning around eight I went down to get the milk and the paper, and found her arriving back at the house. She'd got up hours before – it must have been still dark – and gone off down the street to have her hair done. When she found that the hairdresser was closed, she sat in the train station for a while, and then made her way home. What a fool I am, she said.

I lit her fire every morning and sometimes we made her tea, and her nephew came on Saturday, but it wasn't enough. She probably wasn't eating much, and the starved and frozen brain was growing more confused. There was the evening I found her stamping around the front hall, half frozen and furious.

'What's the rota?' she demanded when she saw me.

I could make no sense of that, but as I talked to her, it became clear that she thought the BBC had taken over the house. She had always been tempted to believe that the people on television could see her as well as she could see them, and now she felt they were in the room with her, taking over, demanding meals and beds, keeping her out of her comfortable chair. Sometimes she would pack up a basket, a few spoons, a magazine, and prepare to set off for someplace where she would be at home.

While she was growing senile down there, we heard odd voices through the wall from the semi-detached next door. The man who lived there was named Basil, and he appeared outdoors, from time to time, wearing a pith helmet. His wife was rarely seen. She had long white hair with yellow stains in it, and only now and then came out of the house to look for one of her cats. The two of them would shout or throw things. Nancy, nursing the baby in the night, afraid that she'd sleep and smother her – sitting up in a kind of dream sleep afraid to relax long after the baby was back in its bed – would hear the noises, and frightened for her new child, she was convinced that the woman in there was mad and was going to break through the wall of the attic and steal the baby. I would get up, turn on lights, go to the attic and reassure her there was no hole in the wall, no one was hidden in the dusty rooms above us.

Nancy had an Irish friend, met when they were both in the maternity ward. Betty was a pleasant lively woman whose husband, Liam, was the archetype of heedless Irish charm. He was a printer by trade, but he didn't work. His father had a printing business in Dublin, and I think a lot of

Liam's time was spent trying to screw money out of the old man. He once got me to forge a signature on something, said it was for the tax people, but I suspect it was to get money from his father. Not long home from the hospital with her new baby – she had an older son – Betty began to find women's underwear around, most of it none too clean. Shocked and betrayed, she was the more shaken when she worked it out that Liam wasn't carrying on with someone who wore the underwear but was wearing it himself. It was not long after we left England that we heard Liam was in Mountjoy Prison, and then he was dead – of a brain tumour apparently.

A winter of cold and madness. (England was Donald Pleasence, with his strange wild voice, pounding his fist into his other hand, determined to get to Sidcup.) Late in March, we ran out of money. I got a scholarship cheque four times a year, but one quarter was a week longer than the others, and what with the baby and the cost of coal and paraffin, we were down to our last bit of cash. By now I had phoned Mrs Prescott's nephew and told him that she couldn't manage on her own any more, and he had come and collected her and taken her to some kind of old people's home. She didn't last long there. She was incontinent, and she upset the others by calling the place the loony bin. So her sister, who lived nearby, took her in, and once warm and fed, her wits came back, and she only remembered the last days in her house as a kind of bad dream. After she was gone, I stole all the coal left in her bin since we couldn't afford to buy any. We ate hamburger one day and sausages the next, carrots one day, parsnips the next, and we made it through until money arrived.

There was another side to England of course, the great culture of Europe. There was the *Guardian,* the *Observer,* BBC radio, including the Third Programme, the movies of Fellini and Antonioni and Bergman, our Christmas in London, days in the old medieval city of Chester, only a few miles away by train, and a couple of trips to the beautiful hills of North Wales. This was the time of Osborne and Wesker and Alan Sillitoe. With a visiting friend, we once drove from Liverpool to York through towns like Bolton, Bury, Burnley, mile after mile of blackened brick houses and factories. I came of ordinary working people, but this kind of industrial waste land was new to me, unthinkable.

We lived in a genteel fringe of Birkenhead, but close by were those who bought from the tallyman – an itinerant salesman who would let you make a purchase and pay later in instalments of a shilling or so, and there were second-hand stores that sold for next to nothing, and those who saved did it at the Post Office; you had to be very well off to have a bank account. By now, we knew these things, and knew how to deal with the newsagent and the greengrocer, and when the postman – who'd predicted that our child would be a girl – the way she's carrying it, he said – had a letter from Canada addressed to someone he couldn't find, he came and asked us who it might be. Two years, the birth of a child, engendered a kind of familiarity and trust.

Our main recreation, until Maggie was born, apart from simply walking and exploring, was going to movies. We had two cinemas available, one a short walk away on the main road through New Brighton, and another a longer walk or short bus ride. They were cheap. In New Brighton you got a double feature for one shilling and sixpence – twenty cents, let's say – and at the other cinema you got the latest of European films for not much more. Or you could go into Liverpool if you wanted more choice. We once went to two double features in a day, one in the afternoon in Liverpool and a second in New Brighton after we'd come home and eaten. We travelled into Liverpool to see *La Dolce Vita*, though most of what we saw of European film was at the *Continental* in our own neighbourhood. I loved the films of Bergman, and though I found the French and Italians more of a stretch, I think now that those puzzling allusive films sank into me deeper than I knew.

Years later I developed a theory that the reason I took to Bergman so quickly wasn't just his Northern and Protestant sensibility but even more the high contrast in the black and white shooting, the dramatic angled light, an equally northern characteristic when you think about it (as I write this I can see slanting November sunlight forming a bright pattern across the floor), and the rather nebulous veiled imagery of a certain kind of French movie always left me a little stifled.

In spite of the time spent at the library and the time spent at movies, I found myself free enough in the evenings of our first winter that I wrote some stories and a full-length play. The play was written for Nancy, with a large part made to her measure and which she did finally perform, though years later. Part of its inspiration was something I'd read in Robertson Davies, probably in *The Table Talk of Samuel Marchbanks*, about those Canadian houses which looked as if the plays of Ibsen or Chekhov might be going on inside them. I hadn't read all that much Ibsen and Chekhov, but I thought I knew what he meant. The play was called, fittingly enough, *A Time of Winter*. I wrote it more or less secretly and gave the text to Nancy for Christmas.

It was during the next summer, when we were settled in Mrs Prescott's raffish establishment, that I took a break from the thesis I was writing and went back to that coffeehouse on Bloor, the pretty girl who kissed her own hand. I'd messed around with the material during my last year of university in a creative writing class given by Norman Endicott, a thoroughly likeable, if perhaps slightly quixotic man, but I'd never made sense of it. I had recently begun reading the novels of Simenon – in translation, though I later read a couple in French – and I had become fascinated by the way he wrote them, in ten days of intense and concentrated work. I decided to do the same with the unrealized material of my story about summer in Toronto, and to develop it at greater length. I worked out a plot, taking hints from some of the characters I'd known around the university. In ten days I completed a draft of the novella called 'The Streets of Summer'.

Though I was pleased with it when I was finished, it was an awkward length, at least for that period in publishing history. In recent years I've gone back to writing novellas, but now publishers are willing to have them stand alone, and three of them have come out in that form. But *The Streets of Summer* had to wait until 1969 to come out in a volume with a number of short stories. Most of those reviewing the book, saw the novella as the best thing in it. 'A splendid story,' Clark Blaise called it in his review, and went on to say, 'perhaps it could be an even finer film.' Nice idea, though it never happened.

So in that English summer I imagined a Canadian summer. Fall came, Maggie's birth, and after that the terror of being a parent to this tiny, bright-blue-eyed, clever, intense creature when I wasn't, in many ways, much more than a child myself, and then the nightmare winter. At last, it was spring again, and the skylarks would hover over the bit of waste land beyond the garden, between the railway tracks and the sea wall, and Maggie was learning to drink from a cup and eat with a spoon. I was twenty-four years old, and we were going back to Canada where – those were the palmy days – I'd been offered teaching jobs and had accepted one at Queen's University.

Nine

The old frame house on Wolfe Island is full of ghosts, my own and those of nameless others. We spend a few weeks there each summer. My last surviving link to Eastern Ontario, where I lived for most of thirty years, it stands only ten feet from the water, facing a large bay and beyond that, the beginning of the St Lawrence River. Across the surface of the water, infinitely variable in the way it catches the light, changing with the weather and the time of day, you can see the city of Kingston. Sometimes the details stand out sharply in the clear air, sometimes you see only shapes in the haze. In summer tiny sailboats appear in the distance, like a flock of white moths. Morning sun casts on the wall the shape of a window, the pattern of the white net curtains. Swallows weave over the shallows with their quick effortless veering flight. Occasionally a fish jumps. A sailboat is anchored in the bay. The ferry comes and goes.

Visitors arrive by boat. In the years when I spent the summer alone here I sometimes watched the ferry a little desperately, hoping to see a familiar figure. Now Judy and I invite friends, sometimes recognize the figure standing on the ferry deck or stepping ashore. I remember Al Purdy striding off wearing his wife's hat, which he'd confiscated because the doctors had told him to keep out of the sun. Don Bailey, reeling from a marital disaster, came for a week and did a little fishing, tried to fly his kite on the end of a fishing line, told his wonderful, intricate, unlikely stories, gradually began to relax. A year later we were expecting him to arrive again when I got a phone call from his son to tell me that Don was dead, found in his apartment when the caretaker realized that the TV had been on for two days without a break.

The ferry to Kingston comes and goes once every hour. If you walk down to the dock, take your place on the narrow top deck for the crossing, you can look east, downriver to the first of the Thousand Islands with their stands of pine and spruce, or west, where your eyes follow the long vista of the lake to the horizon where water meets the sky. As the ferry moves closer to land you see the buildings of Fort Frederick and the Royal Military College on the right, old Fort Henry on the hill behind them. On the left the city of Kingston, a Martello tower, the large, domed city hall, and a block or so away the other dome, St George's, the Anglican cathedral. All of these are built of local limestone, monumental constructions lightened by the sheen and lustre of the pale grey stone. Many of them were built around 1840 when Kingston was expecting to be the new capital of the united Canadas. As the boat comes close to land, it passes by two marinas, and near the shore are hotels and restaurants for the tourist trade. When I moved to Kingston, the waterfront was a place of warehouses, railway tracks, deteriorated factories, sheds, wharves, the marooned remains of an industrial past fallen into desuetude, the abode of rats and rummies.

Starting from the dock where the ferry comes ashore, Queen Street, King Street, Princess Street lead you into the old city, streets and alleys that contain all the stories I lived out, and those I was told, other people's secrets, nightmares, ecstasies, what you ponder to nourish your sense of what men and women are, the complex narrative that shapes itself from gossip and confession into a vision of life. Memories. I can look around me and say, yes, in this building I appeared in a production of *The Threepenny Opera*. In this one I arranged and observed the production of poetry posters. Down this lane is a door and the stairway that led to Tom's apartment where I went to so many parties, once jumped out the second-floor window into a huge snowdrift, Tom's sister-in-law, not to be outdone, hurtling down into the drift after me. In this elegant stone building I once taught classes. Here is a church where I sang. I lived in this house and this one. Just along this street is a room where I made love to a beautiful young woman.

Ten

It was late in the summer of 1962, and I borrowed my father's car to drive to Kingston, make my first connection with the university and rent a place for us to live. I parked just in front of the hospital below the wide green lawn of the front campus. To the right were tennis courts, and at the top of the gentle slope two nineteenth-century limestone buildings. The English department was a block away in a large brick house. I made my call there, then drove downtown and found a cheap, slightly tawdry room in the British-American Hotel.

Before I left the city the next day I had rented a house in Strathcona Park, a suburb at the far end of Princess Street, a plain box-like house, two bedrooms, a yard run wild. We were to live there for two years, the only time in my life that I have lived in a suburb. Maggie, never easily adapted to change, as we were to discover, was still, two months after leaving England, on British or at least mid-Atlantic time. She woke every morning at 5 a.m., and we would take turns getting up with her and taking her for long rides in a stroller. Soon I began my daily trips to the university, catching the bus at a nearby corner, and reappearing on the return route at the end of the day.

It was in the spring of the year that Maggie was badly scalded. My parents were visiting, and the four of us were crowded round the table in the tiny kitchen, Maggie and Sandy, her dog, playing on the floor. At the end of the meal, as the kettle was boiling for tea, either Maggie or the dog or both got entangled in the cord of the kettle and it was pulled off the counter and the boiling water poured out on Maggie's arm. She bears the scars to this day. She was remarkably brave through the trip to the hospital and the treatment, until the point came to leave her for the night. Then she cried and cried. Though the hospital was pretty enlightened, for that period, about allowing parents to stay with their children, they had no facilities for anyone to spend the night. However, for the next nine weeks, we passed a lot of hours of every day in the pediatric ward. Nancy would go around noon, and I would walk across from my office later on. It was an education, seeing all the parents and children who passed through in those weeks. One of the shocks was to discover that a certain number of parents apparently disliked their children – not anger or frustration, just a coldness, an inability to be touched. On the other hand there was a rough-looking couple from the back country north of Kingston whose little boy was in for several days. The mother had startling stories of the misadventures her children had suffered. One of them drank car gas, she said. Her system for very early toilet training was crude, if effective: you just give them a smack and make them stand in the corner. The burly father was a silent man, but there was a quality of warmth about him. *Settle down, boy,* he'd say, as if he couldn't quite remember the child's name, *you just wait here, boy,* but the tone was kindly. Once after Maggie was out of hospital, Nancy saw the little boy on the street with another woman, a more respectable one; nabbed by the Children's Aid, we assumed, and put in foster care, and I suppose they had their reasons. Drinking car gas can't be good for you in the long term.

By now Nancy had made friends with a woman up the street who ran an equipment rental business out of her garage. She had also begun to be active in Domino Theatre, the local amateur group. Had discovered that Beverly Stewart, who had been in the same company of actors travelling back and forth between Peterborough and Port Carling three years before, had settled in Kingston – where she had earlier attended Queen's – and was married to a schoolteacher and had a daughter a little younger than Maggie. The first play Nancy directed, a one act piece, was John Mortimer's brilliant two-hander, 'The Lunch Hour', with Bev and another local actor. It was performed in a small attic space over a store in downtown Kingston, a fine, funny and convincing production. What Nancy now began to discover was that while she might be a capable actress, she was an even better director, and – as she later learned – a superlative producer, since she combined a knowledge of acting and directing with nerve, a vision of possibilities, and a rare mastery of time and money and the handling of delicate egos.

I made friends with a couple of people on the Queen's staff, particularly Bill Barnes, who, in his avocation as church organist, was to get me back to singing in later years, but our social life was increasingly related to the small, feverish world of local theatre, not only Domino Theatre but also the Faculty Players, made up of staff and spouses from Queen's and RMC. Nancy and Bev played the two female leads in a production of *Uncle Vanya*, Nancy as Sonya, Bev as the vamp Yelena. It was the period when How to Play Chekhov was a subject that could be discussed all day and all night.

Years later, walking down a Toronto street one summer night, observing the crowd gathered outside Theatre Passe Muraille, I thought that theatre, with its impossible hours, poor pay, its demand for energy, for self-display, is for most an activity for the years of youth – all that sexual energy, appetite, confusion. There are, of course, those who work at the craft for a lifetime: perhaps I only mean that I drifted away from it.

For some reason all the best male actors in Domino Theatre were insurance agents, and one of them, Deryck Hazel – who before his early death got as far as small parts at the Stratford Festival – lived with his wife, Barbara, and four children at the corner of our street. Theatrical jealousies, theatrical love affairs, competition between the two amateur companies, struggles over a permanent location for the theatre, all these were the stuff of life, with Bev and her daughter, Hollie, Barbara and her children, moving in and out of our daily experience.

When we arrived we had borrowed money to pay the first month's rent and buy a washer and dryer – no more boiling diapers – but we paid it off in a few months by living frugally all that first year – Nancy once saved for a week to buy a small cushion that cost less than a dollar. I found my way around the university and nervously sat in front of my classes – I was afraid that if I stood up I might faint – hoping to teach them something. When I first appeared in the faculty lounge of Kingston Hall, one of the aging academics took umbrage, convinced that this skinny young man was a mere student, but someone set him straight. Though at twenty-four I was too young to join the university pension plan, I was an official faculty member, required to teach four sections of engineers in their first year English course, and to present the poetry of the nineteenth century to forty Arts students, some of them older than I was. This was a difficult assignment since I had only studied the material as an undergraduate at Toronto and was further handicapped by not much liking some of it. I always skipped over Shelley as quickly as possible. I thought him a hateful man and a vacuous poet. They were free to like his poetry, I told them, but I didn't. What most caught my interest from all I taught in that course were Coleridge's conversation poems. 'The Rime of the Ancient Mariner' and 'Kubla Khan' were all very fine, but 'This Lime Tree Bower My Prison', and especially 'Frost at Midnight' gave me a wonderful sense of the poetry implicit in a calm yet lyric account of everyday life.

> Therefore all seasons shall be sweet to thee
> Whether the summer clothe the general earth
> With greenness, or the redbreast sit and sing
> Between the tufts of snow on the bare branch
> Of mossy apple tree, while the nigh thatch
> Smokes in the sun-thaw; whether the eave drops fall
> Heard only in the trances of the blast,
> Or if the secret ministry of frost
> Shall hang them up in silent icicles,
> Quietly shining to the quiet moon.

My reading has always been scattered, headlong, incomplete, but as long as I was teaching poets I enjoyed, my enthusiasm and energy could stand in for a lack of erudition. Look at this, listen to this. I was teaching myself to be a poet. Preparing lectures the night before I gave them. Even in my second year of that course I was often uncertain. Near the front sat an attractive dark-haired young woman who was a very attentive listener, inclined to nod in agreement as she took in what I was saying, all very reassuring until the nodding stopped, and an arm went up. She was a careful listener, for inevitably when she asked a question, I had reached the point where my mouth had outrun my brain, and I often had a difficult time answering her. Carol Anne Matthews (later Carol Anne Wien) took a second course of mine the next year, on the history of the novel, where I was probably more at home. She made a practice, over the years, of turning up when I was giving readings in the various cities where she was living, and thirty years after those first classes I had the pleasure of editing her book of stories, *Turtle Drum,* for Oberon Press. Carol Anne has a memory from those days of Maggie, all bright blue eyes and thick blonde hair, arriving to meet me after class.

As background to the teaching I was doing, I read randomly among books of criticism, and I found myself particularly drawn to moralizers like Yvor Winters and F. R. Leavis. The Protestant heritage I suppose, but I think what I felt was a certain distrust of the merely aesthetic, along with an uneasiness about the merely historical, though that was a significant part of what I'd been taught at university. I know that some of my friends at Queen's were, over the years, impatient with all this moralizing, but I was determined that judgments on the basis of taste were dangerously close to solipsism – what I feared, hated most in those days – while historical exegesis, though it had its points, was not the study of literature but of history. I don't think I ever worked out a fully articulated position that solved these problems, but I wasn't wrong to puzzle over them. You must have architecture before you can have decoration, I might have said. Ethics, politics, theology: they were serious, serious in a way that literature wasn't, though I never found a framework of thought to which I could commit myself: the formidable ideologies of communists and Christians enticed me like wanton dreams, but I could subscribe to neither. I can remember teaching a course in the history of the novel, dealing with *Pilgrim's Progress* and *Robinson Crusoe* one right after the other and noticing how much they were the same story, about a man alone making his soul, journeying toward some spiritual authenticity. The discovery pleased and fascinated me. It was many years later, after a seminar class I'd enjoyed, that I was talking to my friend and colleague Claudette Hoover in her office down the hall from mine, describing the class. 'David,' she said to me, 'you don't want to teach. You want to learn.' It came to me that what she said was absolutely true.

Things I learned: reading I.A. Richards one day I came on a passage that stayed in my mind over the years and influenced the way I thought about poetry. He was writing about the elements that make up a poem and he drew a distinction between Feeling, the poet's response to his material, and Tone, his (implicit) response to his audience. It was the first time I had ever come on a serious effort to define tone in poetry, and what he said struck me as important, an attempt to come at the way poetry occurs in the interstices of what is said, in the space between the poet and the reader. The example Richards used was Gray's 'Elegy in a Country Churchyard'. The conclusions Gray drew in that well-known poem were truisms, Richards asserted, but the power of the poem lay in the fact that Gray knew they were truisms and expected the reader to know it, though both might be touched by the bleak awareness that these were the only conclusions to be drawn. This sense of shared attitudes is no doubt a characteristic of eighteenth-century poetry. It was in Sir Leslie Stephen's biography of Pope that I found, many years later, this suggestive passage: 'Every poet has an invisible audience ... who deserve a great part of the merit of his work.' There's a line in an early poem by Michael Ondaatje about 'virtuoso performances/That presume a magnificent audience'.

At the time I was reading Richards I was teaching the poetry of Wordsworth, and it struck me that Wordsworth, in his early poetry, as part of his break with the past, had deliberately shattered the eighteenth century's tacit understanding between writer and reader, with effects that were sometimes powerful and sometimes unintentionally comic. Tone, I grew to think, was often at the core of a poet's achievement. Once, while looking at John Newlove's poems, I thought to myself that his greatest achievement was his absolute mastery of tone.

A recent thought: an astringent yet light, even airy, quality of tone is part of the achievement of George Johnston's poetry, and in a generally positive analysis of my book *Atlantic Crossings,* Johnston mentioned, with reference to my poetry, 'a no-nonsense tone ... which is not one of its stronger characteristics'. Of course.

One of the fascinations of Margaret Atwood's poems I decided a few years later was a quality of tone which suggested secrecy while in fact revealing, or half revealing, a good deal. (*I'll tell you, but I won't tell you.*) I always associated that quality with the period in the early years of her fame when she complained of women who pursued her even into public washrooms, determined to make contact, to penetrate the veil of secrecy. And by contrast the tone of Al Purdy's poetry suggests one of those guys in a barroom who is determined to tell you more than you want to hear. That intense need to get something across is part of the appeal of Purdy – urgency trumps poise – but with the potential to make him seem simpler and more open than he is.

So all this was just beginning to work itself out in my mind while I was teaching classes and we were setting up housekeeping in the little suburban bungalow. When we moved to Kingston, we had little furniture, a bed, a crib, a few things scavenged from our parents, and not long after we arrived, one Saturday when we were downtown near the local farmers' market, we discovered an antique business, a little place called 'The Trading Post'. Bill McVety and Gordon Baker, who ran it, were pickers, wholesalers almost, of the old furniture of Eastern Ontario. They had a small truck, and twice a week they arrived early in the morning, unpacking what they'd found onto the sidewalk outside the shop, the best pieces often sold quickly to the dealers and enthusiasts who knew when the truck was arriving. Since the store was small, with little space for storage, they sold things cheap and then went out for more. Nancy and I had little enough money, at first, but we found the few dollars necessary to buy a couple of pieces of furniture, and at night, working in the airless basement of our house, I stripped them with paint remover and refinished them. On winter evenings now I sit in front of the fire in a maple ladderback rocker with a seat of woven elm bark, which was bought from the Trading Post for eight dollars, and it still looks very handsome. (I recently had a sort of nightmare involving that chair, about someone who had over-restored it, then lost it – clearly a dream about losing part of myself, what the chair has become over forty years.)

Once we had a car, I began to explore the back roads of the country north of Kingston. I would take Maggie with me, and I would study the empty fields, the birds and flowers, the old stone houses: an accidental elegy, land that was hardly worth farming now going back to rock and trees. Or we took our dog to the park by the lakeshore to let him run, the place deserted except in the heart of summer. One day the Trading Post offered for sale a primitive painting, in oil, but childlike in its awkward portrayal of a figure on old-fashioned skates crossing a lake in a snowstorm, a pack of wolves in pursuit. I bought it, and one of the first poems I wrote in Kingston was prompted by that painting.

> After a night of snowstorms I looked out
> across the field where tufts of grass and weeds
> grow wild between our door and the nearest streets.
> An owl had flown from somewhere in the night,
> an owl that hunted food in the light snow,
> turned, banked, wheeled, hovered and dropped,
> soared once more, hungry and patient, stopped
> only to rest for seconds on a grey bough.
> That morning I knew the mind that saw a boy
> skating across a lake lost in the trees
> while grinning wolves pursued. I seemed to know
> the unskilled fingers that could find no way
> to draw a boy that looked like other boys
> but felt the teeth and talons in the snow.

Though it had always been my intention to write fiction, once we were settled in Kingston I more and more began to find myself at work on poems. At first, I think, the powerful impulse toward poetry grew from the return to circumstances a little like those of Niagara-on-the-Lake, a pioneer community on the shore of Lake Ontario, wild birds, domestic life, ancient furniture. It was also much easier to write short poems in the time available to someone who was earning a living and dealing with children. Children themselves (even aside from the wonderful nursery rhymes one reads them) are poetic, sensual, immediate, inspired.

I got another angle on the Ontario countryside when we visited Nancy's family, who were now living a few miles outside Owen Sound, at one end of a wooded property where Jim Keeling had built an auction barn, in which weekly cattle auctions were held. He was also raising cattle on various pieces of farm land in the district, and early in the morning he would drive from farm to farm checking on the stock, driving his big Lincoln over the roughest tracks as if it were a jeep. Maggie and I were often up early, and he would sometimes invite us to go along with him and his little rat terrier, Nicky. (He was very fond of that not-very-appealing dog, and when it died, he drove it around, dead, for a day or so, unable to deal with it, and finally he told his wife she'd better go out to the car and take a look at Nicky. He couldn't bear to dispose of the corpse himself.)

Another early poem is about an old wagon I observed near an abandoned barn during one of those outings. The land near Owen Sound was better farmland than that north of Kingston, but even so, a lot of the houses were empty. Then there was the morning we drove to a farm along the highway and down a mud track to a distant field. At each fence, I would jump out of the car, hold the gate open as Nancy's father drove through, then close the gate and jump back in. We left the car parked at the far end of a pasture full of grazing cattle and went on foot into the field below, marshy land that was to be filled in for more pasture or a hayfield. Jim Keeling was never without some project for building or improvement. I think he expected to find a bulldozer there at work, but the land running down to the river was empty.

'Dave, would you go back and look up the road and see if the bulldozer's coming,' he said.

I started off. This would have been the summer of 1964, Maggie two years old, Nancy pregnant with Kate. Maggie and I walked up the slope to the fence, ducked under it and proceeded into the pasture far enough to see the road. Nothing coming. By now I had picked up Maggie, still small enough that I carried her easily in the crook of my left arm. As we stood there looking up the empty dirt track, I noticed a brown-and-white cow with big curving horns moving toward us. I checked to see if we had got

95

between her and her calf, but the calf was behind her. Still she came closer, and I made the kind of loud noises you make to try to scare off a large animal. She wasn't scared off. She was coming still closer, was only six feet or so away, her head down. My shouting did no good, and within a second I was knocked to the ground. When I tried to get up, the horns beat me down again, and I fell on top of Maggie, hurting her – her lip was cut – and she began to cry. As I slid to one side, away from Maggie, an unlikely but wonderfully appropriate literary memory came to me, a Hemingway story of a bullfighter on the ground and trying to save himself, kicking the bull in the face, and I lifted my feet and kicked frantically at the cow, pushing her back enough that I was able to stand and take hold of the horns. I bent the big animal's head back over its shoulder, twisting the neck, perhaps hoping to wrestle it to the ground. I realized that I couldn't throw it down. It was too big and strong. But for the moment I was in control.

'Stand up, Maggie,' I said.

Maggie must have recognized that this was serious and dangerous. She stood up without a second's delay.

'Now walk over to the car,' I said, and once again she obeyed.

I was still holding the cow bent double, and I noticed the other animals in the field observing this, including a bull a hundred feet away.

'Now go round behind the car,' I said to Maggie.

Going out of my sight was too frightening, and she wouldn't move. I bent the cow round as far as I could, then let go and ran, grabbing Maggie on the run and hot-footing it to the fence, where I dived through the gap beneath the bottom strand. I didn't look back. When I reported what had happened to my father-in-law, he wasn't exactly disbelieving – obviously it wasn't a story I'd make up – but when we went back up to the car and drove away, the cow ignored us. If you weren't actually there wrestling with a cow to save your life, there was something laughable about it. I think Jim Keeling took the whole thing with a grain of salt until the occasion, a week or so later, when the same cow went for him when he came into the field. The next day it was shipped to the slaughterhouse.

When we got back to Nancy's parents' house, I discovered that I had a scrape across my ribs, where the cow had just failed to impale me on its horn, and though I had been unaware of using any muscular force in wrestling with the beast, my arms ached for hours afterward: adrenalin rising in the face of emergency can do extraordinary things. On occasions when I've told the story, listeners are always tempted to correct me – not a cow, surely, but a bull. No, it was a cow, and she had a calf, which was a safe distance away.

And where would I have been if I hadn't read Hemingway? – a question which is comic at this distance, but was not amusing at all when I had a thousand pounds of horned beast trying to destroy me with those long curving horns. A day or so later we drove back to the safety of Kingston.

It was at the beginning of my second year of teaching that Tom Marshall turned up at Queen's. He had graduated in history, taken a year to travel around Europe with a friend, but at some point he had convinced the English department to accept him as a graduate student so long as he did a few makeup courses. He was committed to poetry, and soon he and his friend Tom Eadie, still an undergraduate, took over *Quarry*, the undergraduate literary annual, and they turned it into a literary quarterly with serious national ambitions. Tom Marshall edited the 1963–64 edition, in which he included a number of francophone poets from Quebec. The large 1964–65 edition, edited by Tom Eadie, contained material by Earle Birney, Fred Cogswell, James Reaney, Al Purdy and Raymond Souster, as well as material by young local writers like Tom Marshall and Michael Ondaatje, also an odd little play of mine called 'The Dreambook'. In the introduction Tom Eadie announced that the magazine had become a quarterly, and the first issue of the quarterly appeared in September of 1965.

The English department had rooms in two old houses on the edge of the campus, and my office was in the smaller of the two buildings, on the top floor. I was there alone for the first year, but then Fred Colwell arrived to take over the empty room across the hall. Alone up there, we could talk back and forth from office to office. Tom, as a graduate student and teaching fellow, shared the back kitchen on the ground floor. Tom and I were both somewhat reserved, but we were both committed to writing and gradually became friends, remained so until his early death in 1993. Certainly there were occasions when he irritated me – in an early letter I described him, in one of his impossible moods as pompous and paranoid – but I gave him a lot to put up with as well, and somehow we stayed friends for many years. I still miss him. When he returned from his trip to Europe, Tom had found an apartment on West Street, the student Bohemia opposite the wide spaces and tall trees of Macdonald Park – the lake just beyond, Wolfe Island visible in the distance – and sometimes I

Tom Marshall, 1969

would come to the park with Maggie and the dog, and would shout up to him, 'Can Tom come out and play?' and sometimes he could. There's a poem that catches some of the innocence of those days when Maggie and I rambled around together with the dog, before her sister Kate was born, or when she was still a baby.

On Saturday mornings, Maggie and I
visit the market and the docks;
as we watch the ferry, the buoys, the gulls,
they dance and try to make a poem,

but Tom has written so many poems
about those gulls, it seems to me
that he must own them by now. Except
that Maggie and I own all the birds

and all the plants and animals
because we know all of their names,
(cowleen, Joe-Pye weed, sparrow hawk),
we learned them patiently, one by one;

for we would not want to live in a world
where we could not call out the names of things.

It was in the spring of 1964 Nancy found in the newspaper an ad for a house for sale. Until then I don't think we'd discussed buying a house, but she must have been giving it some thought. She was pregnant, due to give birth in October, and the rented house on McMichael Street was not one we were fond of. We went to see the place she'd seen advertised, a nine-teenth-century stone house in Portsmouth village.

Portsmouth had at one time been a separate community, on a small harbour just past the old prison, but as Kingston grew, it had been incorporated into the city. It still had its own main street, with a number of stores, Cowan's Red and White, Baiden Hardware, Peters' pharmacy.

A story from later years gives a sense of the place. The mental hospi-tal was just up the hill from the local stores, and a certain number of the inmates – some who probably shouldn't have been there in the first place – were beginning to be allowed increasing freedom. One of them, afflicted with cerebral palsy I suspect, with a normal mind trapped in a crippled and distorted body, gradually found he was able to walk some distance if he used a wheelchair as a walker to support him. I saw him going awkwardly but effectively up and down the streets, and then I discovered that he used Baiden Hardware as his bank. Whenever he laid his hands on some small change, he would drop it off there. Kindly, decent Bill Baiden – who often gave me useful gardening tips – would make a record of it, and if the man wanted to spend some of his money, he would stop in and pick up a quarter or fifty cents and go on his way with it.

Portsmouth in those days was an old-fashioned country village, and only accidentally part of a city. Though the place we found for sale there was an old stone house, it wasn't one of the sumptuous Georgian places that could be seen in Sydenham Ward. It was a rather plain workingman's house, but it had a big yard and an attractive board and batten outbuilding – a small barn or drive shed. Across the street was the Church of the Good Thief, a large limestone construction built, in part, by convict labourers from Kingston Penitentiary, which lies just the other side of the harbour. The church had a wide lawn and a brick rectory.

Neither of us slept well the night after we viewed the house, but by morning we had decided to make an offer. We had no money, but my parents agreed to lend us the down payment, and the rest would be a mortgage. One of the advantages of teaching in those days was that there were a good many extension courses, evenings, summer, in Kingston or sometimes out of town, and I knew I could pay back the down payment by teaching those. So we bought it, and with the help of friends, we got our possessions moved, and we were settled in by the time Kate was born. We lived there for nearly twenty years.

Eleven

An age of poets, a place of poets: the senior faculty at Queen's included two, Douglas LePan, who had come to the university after a career in External Affairs, and George Whalley, the department head who hired me. Malcolm Ross, who had moved to Dalhousie before I arrived, while not a poet, was one of the earliest serious critics and editors of Canadian writing. In the next few years, the poets of my generation and the next began to turn up, Tom Marshall, Michael Ondaatje, Stuart MacKinnon, Douglas Barbour, Gail Fox, Joan Finnigan. Bronwen Wallace and Carolyn Smart appeared and began to publish a few years later on, Steven Heighton later still. Like Tom, Mike Ondaatje was doing a few courses as part of a master's degree. Stuart MacKinnon worked in the library. Gail Fox was married to a young member of the philosophy department. Douglas Barbour was a graduate student, and Bronwen was an undergraduate who went away to study in Windsor and came back with a husband and child and a serious commitment to writing.

George Whalley, though I felt great respect for him, and gratitude that he had hired me, was always something of a mystery to me. George had served with distinction in the second war, in the Royal Navy, on loan from the Canadian forces. To quote the blurb from his collection of poems, *No Man an Island*, 'he saw general and special service in the Atlantic, North Sea and Mediterranean and with Naval Intelligence and Operations of the Admiralty.' Later he served in Canadian destroyers, and he left the navy with the rank of Lieutenant Commander. There were many mythological-sounding stories about the heroism of George's navy career; one suspected they were all true. He was a brilliant and popular teacher, famous for the long silences in his class while he formulated a thought or waited for the students to have one. Though he was always perfectly pleasant to me, I felt that we spoke different dialects. I could never find anything to say to him. In 1971, when my first novel, an eccentric version of a spy thriller, came out, he was passing by my office and came in to say that someone had given him the book for Christmas. He spoke kindly of it, went on his way to the small upstairs room which he kept for his own work, away from the main departmental office. I decided that I would, for once, attempt to talk to him, and I went up there. He was quite willing to chat more about the book, so we did, though I found it still an effort. I talked about some of the characters I'd come across in my research, the famous English spies of the time. My favourite was the wildly eccentric Guy Burgess, and I was talking about him, when suddenly a thought penetrated. George had worked in Naval Intelligence.

'Did you know Guy Burgess?' I said.

George mumbled something polite to indicate that they might have met, and I went back to my own little den. George knew everyone, and perhaps everything.

He was an elegant man, a sailor and outdoorsman who apparently was a brilliant pianist, though I never heard him play. He kept a clean handkerchief in the sleeve of his jacket. Naval officers did that, I learned years later. George wasn't always popular among the yahoos of the university faculty. Some of them called him 'Precious George', but I always regarded him as an extraordinary man, though I never learned – even when I edited a book he put together years later – how to communicate with him with any ease.

However we did share an interest in how a sensitivity to poetry might be encouraged, and I began to teach non-credit workshops that were meant to stimulate English students to find a language for the discussion of poetry. On one occasion I assigned a poem by Edgar Guest, whose rhyming ditties (*Let me live in a house at the end of the road/And be a friend to man.*) were often found framed on the walls of old-fashioned houses. All right, I was ready to admit, this was bad poetry, but how did you say so, prove so and express your critical point? I'm not sure whether it was a useful exercise, but it may have stirred a few thoughts. Another day I assigned an obscure Dylan Thomas poem and demanded that the students tell me what, if anything, it meant. All this feels a long way off by now, but I was young and keen and wanted to be difficult.

Michael Ondaatje was one of the students the first year I taught this course. (Name-dropping: a year earlier I taught David Dodge in a first year English course, and I like being able to claim that I taught the Governor of the Bank of Canada all he knows.) Mike and I already knew each other as poets, and since it was a non-credit course, I didn't have to worry about assigning him marks, a doubly good thing since his handwriting, elegant squiggles inscribed in green with a fountain pen, was almost entirely illegible.

All the local poets had developed some connection with *Quarry,* the new literary magazine. Tom, Michael and I all edited issues. At one point in the early history of the magazine, it became clear that it needed money, and Michael and Kim Ondaatje convened a meeting in the living room of their small apartment to look at funding possibilities. One of the consequences was my creation of three series of poetry posters which were issued, and which actually made the magazine a few dollars.

In 1967 the first and most spectacular series was silkscreened by a local artist and designer, David Brown. He had created a brilliant advertising poster for a production of Pinter one-act plays at the Queen's Drama department. Fred Euringer, who had acted in Straw Hat Players with Nancy and Beverly Stewart, had recently arrived at Queen's to run the drama department, and he directed one of the plays and appeared in the other, which Nancy directed. So we owned a copy of the poster, and very beautiful it was. I went round to David Brown's studio, a bare attic loft over a store on Princess Street, and proposed to him that we do a series of poetry posters. He and the magazine would split the proceeds. He agreed, and I began to assemble the poems. In that first series, there were poems by Irving Layton, George Bowering, Michael Ondaatje, Joy Kogawa, also a short poem of mine. The posters were large and bright and striking, though a couple were pretty hard to read. Layton's poem, for example, was done in red and green of the sort associated with acid rock, and while it certainly grabbed your attention, the effect was more hallucinatory than legible. 'They are expensive,' I said of the posters in a letter to Michael Macklem, '$3.00.' The sixties was the age of poster art, and even at that high price (day return bus fare to Ottawa was $6.95.) the Quarry posters sold. Individuals bought them, and libraries, and I would take a pile of each to Toronto where Marty Ahvenus of the Village Bookstore, then on Gerrard Street, would buy them from me for resale.

The second series, smaller, monochrome and printed by offset, presented poems by Tom Marshall, Gail Fox, Gwendolyn MacEwen and Dorothy Livesay. The Marshall and MacEwen poems were illustrated by drawings by a Kingston artist, Joan Bray, and for the Fox and Livesay poems I took photographs and enlarged them to a suitable size. The Queen's English department by now owned a proof press and a font of metal type, to be used for teaching bibliography, and the texts for all four poems were handset using that type. Gail's poem was about having a child, learning to be what was needed, and the photograph I took of her and her son Jason was deliberately overexposed so that the image vanished into light, the brightness in the blurred background of leaves providing space for the text. The Livesay poem, a response to the 1968 Soviet invasion of Czechoslovakia was a kind of palinode, a rejection of the absolutes of her youthful politics, full of images of hammers and metal, and the photograph I took was of a local junkyard, heaps of scrap, the lines of the poem to be discovered among them.

In 1971, after a year in England, I produced a third series, smaller than the first lot, but once again in colour. My friend Dennis Crossfield was running a silk-screening shop in the Queen's student union, and he and I designed the final set, which he produced. This time there were poems by Dennis Lee, Bill Barnes, Dale (now David) Zieroth, and a little poem of mine about a Kate in a field of flowers on the island of Ibiza.

That's how things went in those years, an extravagant confidence everywhere. You had an idea, and you did it; new literary projects appeared on all sides. There was an agreement that poetry was important. In 1964, McClelland and Stewart published new books by Irving Layton, Leonard Cohen and Phyllis Gotlieb, and they sent the three poets on the road. In Kingston they performed in a good-sized auditorium and afterward Fred Colwell had a party for them at his apartment, the top floor of a Victorian Gothic edifice with a tower on the corner, a round tower room beneath it. Layton and Cohen were bardic among the admiring young women.

Fred's apartment with its odd little tower was a splendid place for parties. All of us were writing a lot of poetry, filling every spare moment with words. One night Tom arrived late, a little spaced out, and handed me a draft of the hallucinatory conclusion to the first part of his poem 'Macdonald Park', which he'd just written. Tom's nearby apartment overlooked the park, which was at the heart of many of his early poems. There is one about the wooden owl over his window. I climbed out on the balcony, hung out over the edge and rapped it with my fingers to prove to him that it was not wood but moulded tin. 'You see, Tom,' I said, 'it's not wood, it's metal.' He didn't change the poem. Perhaps we never quite agreed about the importance of mere facts. When he died, his brother Andrew and some friends arranged for the planting of a memorial tree in that park – though it's on the wrong side, on Barrie Street, not West.

Whenever I'm in Kingston I go round and see Tom's tree – very tall by now.

> In your lost poem they lie
> cut, elms by the courthouse
> in their epoch of disease.
> (All trees attend in their silence
> the flight of a hurtful lover.)

> A new elm risen in your name
> stands three men high tonight
> on the wrong side of the park.
> (You camped eastward, on West,
> now in the obverse of living.)

> In your crazed clairvoyant city
> fearless children climb, who
> explore a geography lost
> on the back of the map.
> (You are nowhere and with us.)

I missed Al Purdy's first reading at Queen's. George Whalley had invited him, and afterward Fred Colwell told me about it. I met Al only a couple of years later, after my first book came out, when I got a call one day in my university office, Nancy reporting that Alfred Purdy and his wife were at the house, to get a book signed. So I drove home, and the book became part of Purdy's vast collection of signed volumes of Canadian poetry, and Al and I took the first steps toward becoming friends.

All this was in the early days of the Canada Council reading program, and a lot of poets were taking their show on the road, getting to see the country by performing their work. The reading I remember most clearly was given by Gwendolyn MacEwen. Kim and Michael Ondaatje arranged for her to read at Queen's in 1966. I admired her poems (in *Canadian Forum* I had read what is still perhaps my favourite, 'Manzini: Escape Artist'), but I sometimes had a sense that I didn't quite understand her exotic spirituality. However when that small, dramatic figure with large eyes outlined in kohl, stood and spoke the lines aloud, I thought, *Yes, of course: I understand perfectly.* Somebody asked George Whalley to write about Gwen's poetry in *Quarry,* and he produced an astute and detailed account of what she was up to – a typically rich and enthusiastic exploration of a poet of a new generation.

When I check the dates on the books of the period, I discover what a short time it was that we were all in Kingston together. By the fall of 1967, Michael was teaching at Western, but he soon invited Tom and me to read there, and he and Kim spent their summers in or near Kingston, so in some ways they seemed never to have left. From 1966 to 1968, Tom was in London to write a doctoral thesis on the poetry of D.H. Lawrence. Perhaps the moves and reconnections contributed to the high spirits of the time, the sense that anything was possible.

My first meeting with Margaret Atwood came about through the Ondaatjes. She and her husband Jim Polk were passing through town and we met for lunch, a polite, reticent occasion, remarkable only because of how different everything was the next time we met, in 1971, when I had invited her to read (a joint reading with John Metcalf – an odd couple, I suppose, but it went well). She was vivid, lively, confident, even confiding; this was a new world, and here was the whole splendid Atwood phenomenon. Nancy and I were living apart at the time, and I had arranged for Peggy to billet at the old stone house in Portsmouth with Nancy, while John and his wife Gale used the bedroom of my small apartment, and I slept on the couch. In the morning I picked her up, and we did the town, so far as you can do the town in Kingston on a weekday morning, bookstores and what have you. We talked about all manner of things, and what I have never forgotten, because it seems so perfectly unlikely in the light of the fabulous Atwood career, is her insistence that she was a low-energy person.

'I have to be careful,' she said, 'or I'll fall asleep with my face in my dinner plate.'

It's fashionable to scoff at the sixties, but the liberation they advertised was, at least in part, real, and in many ways it was a time of radiant possibilities. Certainly so for me. One summer, sitting at a small table in the dark old barn, I wrote a novel, which I later burnt – one of my failed attempts to adapt the thriller form to what I knew or could imagine. Between moving to the old stone house in 1964 and the centennial year, 1967, I wrote all the poems in my first collection, *Figures in a Landscape.* Circumstance had pushed me toward poetry. Part of it was having all those other young poets close by.

The lively poetic universe around me was in tune with the growing excitement about Canadian writing all over the country. In Kingston Tom was usually, in his own reticent way, at the centre of things, observing them with a wry detachment but also with a passionate concern. He cared deeply about poetry and about his own poetry. These were also the years of what he later called – I remember him saying it – 'the great disastrous love of my life'. I don't know how many of his friends were aware of it – I wasn't until long afterward. Not many knew, I think.

It was the summer of the year 2000, a lifetime later, that I went to Ameliasburgh for Al Purdy's memorial service. Before the event a number of us met up with Al's wife Eurithe at their house on Roblin Lake. I walked into the house out of bright sunlight, blinded, and didn't at first see who was standing on the other side of the table. It was Mike Ondaatje.

'Did you get my letter?' he said. 'I wrote to you about Tom's book.'

I had edited a posthumous collection of Tom's poems.

'No, I said, 'it didn't get to me.'

'I never realized he was gay,' Michael said.

In the posthumous collection I had included some explicitly homosexual poems that Tom had kept, mentioned to me in a roundabout way, but never published. I had decided that there was no one to be hurt if Tom came out of the closet at that point.

'He had to tell me,' I said.

So we knew Tom in those early days, and also we didn't. He kept his secrets. (He had his reasons, of course; homosexual acts were still illegal; men often got fired if their homosexuality was discovered.) It was only years later, when I'd been his friend for a long time, that he made it a point to talk to me about these things.

The poems that Tom was writing in those years appeared in his first collection, *The Silences of Fire*, and he never wrote better. I read some of them as they appeared in *Quarry* or *Queen's Quarterly*, and lines still inhabit my mind forty year later, lines that reach toward some inner ecstasy, some Orphic illumination perhaps, while catching at concrete details, dramatic, comic, bizarre.

CHRIST THE ASTRONAUT
BURNS ON THE SKY
NAKED WITH LUST AND PAIN

And across the page from that a poem begins,

I think I am becoming
a tree. At any rate
something slow, lethargic,
vegetable.

Leaps of imagination, sudden shifts of perspective and tone, deadpan comedy. A love poem says, 'I care more about this/arrangement of words than about you.' Dreams link to images of apocalypse, the attempt to locate the intensities of a personal life within the strangeness of history and a crazed and dangerous present. The poem about the wooden (tin) owl is placed on Tom's twenty-eighth birthday, which would make it April of 1965 – we were within a week of the same age. Probably it was that summer that I climbed onto his balcony and rapped my knuckles on his guardian spirit. 'Poem on Good Friday' is a lyric and philosophic poem with the inevitable gulls. ('But Tom has written so many poems/about those gulls, it seems to me/that he must own them by now.'). Its memorable conclusion:

The mind sets. But the heart,
luckily intractable, rebelliously will not give up.
The mind learns treachery will be the thing,
the value and virtue of fragility. Finally
only tension is creative. Gull-cries
echo in the marriage-bed. All quest,
all questioning affirms, announces,
the answer to desire is desire.

Some of these poems appeared in Tom's first book, *The Silences of Fire.* He went on to write *Magic Water, The Earth Book,* and *The White City,* and then to put the best of the poems from this quartet together in the large collection *The Elements,* published by Oberon Press with a superb drawing of Tom by his friend Klaas van Weringh on the cover. It's a book that ought still to be in print and widely read. But death intervenes, and hundreds of new books, and every year dozens of young graduates of creative writing departments begin to send out poems, and the past grows vague and lost.

While Tom lived alone high over the park, Michael Ondaatje had young children, as I did. He and Kim lived in a third-floor apartment, and I remember annoying him when I climbed the two floors of wooden stairs that led to his apartment door to discuss some project, *Quarry*, or perhaps the posters, at an early hour when my children were up and ready to play in the park, and his were not. Michael had come, of course, from a world brighter and more exotic than Kingston, and the individual poems of his I remember from those early days were astonishing for their speed, their ellipsis, energized by odd angles of vision, startling images.

Catch, my Uncle Jack said
and oh I caught this huge apple
red as Mrs Kelly's bum.
It's red as Mrs Kelly's bum, I said
and Daddy roared
and swung me on his stomach with a heave.

The first poem in his 1967 book gives a kind of key in the line I quoted earlier, about 'virtuoso performances/that presume a magnificent audience.' A poem near the end of the book concludes with another suggestive phrase, 'I prize pain like this.' (I could argue that all Michael's books are studies in the architecture of pain.) His early poems evoke an extravagant, oblique, inward universe, prickly with startling detail. With my friends writing like that, how could I not be impelled to write more poetry?

Though there was not much of the secular mystic or the virtuoso of pain in me: what there was, as Tom wrote in a critical book years later, was a struggle between the bourgeois and the arsonist, a selfish, hungry, driven man trying to be a decent husband and father. It was my nature to battle with the complications and blessings of the quotidian. There's a poem in several parts called 'A Shaker Chair' which is about the attempt to behave decently, about ownership and hunger and vision. How can we live in the difficult world? What was I to make of my fascination with the communist, celibate Shakers, the purity and beauty of what they created? Links of memory to both Tom and Michael: I remember Tom once half jokingly referring to my maple ladderback as a 'Shaker chair', and Michael, prompted by that poem, sent me, by way of Christmas card, a tiny pamphlet called 'A Shaker Order of Christmas.'

The circumstances of writing 'A Shaker Chair': with a house and a mortgage and two small children, I was always on the lookout for ways to make a few extra dollars, and one of these was to serve as an examination proctor. You handed out the exams and the booklets in which the exams were written, and you sat quietly and observed for three hours while the students did their work. Sessions went on over three or four days. While I was sitting quietly, observing, I took out a pen and began to draft a poem. Three hours of quiet in a bright classroom was a perfect circumstance for poetry, and by the time I was finished earning my few dollars for the sessions assigned, I had in hand a draft of the poem.

While I was teaching and writing poetry, I also began to review new poetry for *Queen's Quarterly*, seven new books in one article, four in another. This gave me a chance to articulate my responses to poets as varied as Irving Layton, D.G. Jones, Alden Nowlan, and Margaret Avison. At the time there was a debate going on between those poets, primarily on the West Coast, who had been influenced by the theory of Charles Olson and Robert Creeley, some of it mediated by Warren Tallman, an American critic teaching at UBC, and poets in the rest of country, who might be reading America poets – Purdy reviewed James Dickey for *Quarry*, Avison was in close touch with Denise Levertov – but didn't subscribe to the Black Mountain theories. Dorothy Livesay did, and in reviewing her book, *The Unquiet Bed*, I set out to confront the new orthodoxy:

'Eastern' poets as diverse as Layton, Gustafson, Dudek and Purdy have recently flung a few stones in the direction of the black mountain of recent American poetic theory that seems to loom over Vancouver.... The first thing that strikes me ... is that the poets are working in a visual tradition while talking a lot about sound ... the second, related reaction to what I know of the 'Vancouver school' is that it is imposing an abstract and dangerous vocabulary on poetry. To quote Warren Tallman in *Canadian Literature:*

The student who wants to write poetry needs to know what is implied and demanded by four degrees of stress, four degrees of juncture, the tone leading to vowels, composition by field, and a host of other practices that call for linguistic definition of what is happening in the poem.

The only example I have run across of poetry analyzed in terms of this vocabulary is in an essay by Dorothy Livesay on the poetry of Louis Dudek. In that case it seemed to me that the analysis might well be rewarding, but that the vocabulary was an arbitrary device to provide a means of communication about the textual detail of the poem that might be achieved by a variety of means ...

The erection of a schematic technique for poets whose method of presentation is predominantly visual seems to me to lead, in practice, to ignoring the structure of speech, its tone (in the old sense), and the sense of an imagined verbal context in which the poem occurs, and to an ignoring of the plastic qualities of language in order to apprehend its tactile qualities. There is a paring away of the social function of language in an attempt to give it a purely artistic function. This may be a useful strategy, but its limitations are obvious and decisive.

I was thinking as hard as I could about the issues as I understood them. Many poets, of course, have had crackpot theories (Gwen MacEwen was fascinated by theosophy) and found them a way of 'making it new' but the value of crackpot theory is as scaffolding, a way of climbing higher, and they are important for the way they allow a poet to achieve a unique voice. Followers are likely to be only that.

Of the West Coast poets of that period, the one whose work has probably lasted best is George Bowering, and though he may have been influenced by Tallman and his theories, he is most remarkable for his mastery of intricate, almost baroque rhythms, and an imaginative energy and daring. (And I've heard him claim that his favourite poet is HD.)

Though I was busy, energetic, productive in those days, I was thin and getting thinner. I couldn't sit in the bath because there was no flesh between my pelvis and the tub. My family doctor weighed me and found I was down to 125 pounds. Sent for tests, I discovered that I was diabetic, though not seriously afflicted. I don't think that was the reason I was so thin. It was the arsonist burning my flesh.

A little prose poem written at that time, in the fall of 1966, I think, when Kate was two years old:

The earth by our front door is
barren. What I plant dies, even
nasturtiums, even marigolds that run
wild at the back of the yard.

Grass will grow anywhere. Dark on a
cold day, Kate comes and I come to plant
grass and Kate to throw seeds out to

the wind. The seeds of grass are light
and thrown, blow across autumn easily.

Her suit is pink like the insides of
things, of the mouth. She is pink
mischief among my planting, Kate and
the dark wind.

We are all light as blown seed. But
it grows anywhere. Young we are
soft as the insides of things. The
earth at our door is barren.

The world of day-to-day fact with all that assaults it and the
tenderness within it: I'm still committed to those lines, but looking back
now, I wonder about the last sentence. Is it the embodiment of an enduring pessimism, or something more personal? Nancy and I were beginning
to have our separate lives. I was away much of the day at the university;
she was away most evenings at rehearsals for whatever she was acting in
or directing, or one of the experimental sessions of improvisation with
young actors, some of them shared with her friend Jim Garrard, who was
later to found Theatre Passe Muraille in Toronto. She created shows for
Domino Theatre's experimental Studio Night. One summer she founded
a new theatre company and did a short season of contemporary plays at
the Grand Theatre. I didn't expect her to be a literary wife who appeared
at every poetry reading, and though I usually went to her performances,
we were beginning to have different friends. Nancy's double life might be
represented by that fact that at home during the day with the children she
didn't smoke. At night, at the theatre, she might go through a whole pack
of cigarettes. Often in the evenings I was alone in the house, the children
asleep, writing poems as I waited for her to return. We shared an intense
commitment to the children and a domestic life in our old house. I think
we were both in pain.

Nancy's theatre work, especially the experiments with young
performers – things like presentations of the poetry of John Lennon, the
dramatizing of poems written by street kids in New York – brought new
people into our lives, young political activists, bohemians. Suddenly
Patrick was always around the house. Patricia Dinely was her real name,

but someone had rechristened her Patrick, and it stuck. She came from a large Catholic family, didn't get on with her mother, and had been hanging out with some of the more bohemian students around Queen's. (Tom, who knew these people, described one of Patrick's older lovers as a satyr.) She turned up at one of Nancy's sessions, and though I'm not sure she ever appeared onstage, she appointed Nancy her friend, substitute mother perhaps, and moved into our lives. Tall, handsome, witty, a fast-talking, smart-mouth woman with a weakness for pills and bad men, she attempted suicide two or three times while we knew her – her description of one of the more dramatic attempts found its way into one of Judith Thompson's plays years later. Patrick had taste and imagination and was always engaged in turning her latest apartment into a something perfect, and she had wit enough that she could do it cheaply, balloons, coloured paper, bits and pieces that she'd shoplifted. She liked to explain how sometimes she stole just for the high, picking up an ornament from one store and leaving it in another where it didn't belong. When the room she was decorating was perfect, she knew she was ready to walk out the door and never come back. Hers was a character in the Sally Bowles, Holly Golightly mould, obviously. Years later she asked me why we had never had a fling or even approached it. I could only say that I was never tempted. And a damn good thing. Life was chaotic enough.

I ran into her one night in 1969 at a party at Tom Marshall's dim, mysterious place in the Annandale apartments in Kingston's old Sydenham Ward with her latest beau, a tall, dramatically dark young man named Christiaan. Soon they were saving up for a trip to Europe: they went together and came back separately, then got together again for a while. I think they were living together – combatively – when Christiaan appeared in a class of mine a couple of years later. Wrote a good essay on – of course – Leonard Cohen. (A friend of Patrick's had been one of Cohen's army of lovers. In Kingston everything connects with everything else.)

There was the Sunday afternoon we got a phone call from the Don Jail. Patrick was locked up there and had asked the authorities to get in touch with us. Through a mixture of luck and experience Nancy found a Toronto criminal lawyer who was at work on Sunday, and he agreed to go to the jail and see what he could do about getting her out. Nancy drove to Toronto to meet with him and visit the jail.

Patrick's most recent man (a former student of mine) had been involved with a group in Kingston who were importing substantial quantities of marijuana. None of them, I think, had an earlier criminal background. Foolishly they had tried to deposit a very large chunk of cash in a Toronto bank. The bank called the police. The police arrested them and searched their hotel room. Even more foolishly, they had kept careful written accounts of all their dealings. Patrick, though she certainly had what's called guilty knowledge, was not part of the business. However she had the same initials as one of the characters recorded in the account book, and police took her to be the leader of this smuggling operation.

Alan Gold, the bright young lawyer Nancy had contacted (I'd years earlier met him at Queen's, taken him into the prison for a discussion with a group of inmates – in Kingston everything connects), got Patrick out on bail, part of the stipulation being that she had to live at our house for a while, and he eventually managed to establish that she was not the person in the written records and got her off. The men arrested in Toronto did some time, but their main Kingston colleague avoided arrest and invested his money wisely.

In later years Patrick moved to Toronto and largely disappeared from our lives, though Christiaan remained a friend. In the meantime she had been the lover of another former student of mine, who was later to be arrested for conning old age pensioners – the bank-inspector swindle. The lowest of the low I've always thought.

Patrick

Twelve

From a distance, with its red roofs and pointed turrets, Collins Bay Penitentiary looks like a fairy tale castle. It's a piece of nineteenth-century fake Gothic that more than one person has called Disneyland. Around are open fields, farmland in the middle of suburbs and malls.

When you went inside, your identification was checked and you walked down a long bare corridor and reached a barrier of narrow rectangular steel bars, which were controlled by the guard who was behind you in the cage by the front door. You waited for him to press a button and for a section of the bars to slide sideways. You walked in and turned to the left. The gate closed behind you with a chilling metallic slam. Ahead was the prison gymnasium, and in the evening it was crowded with men in drab grey clothing, mostly sitting at tables to play cards. Hard men killing time. There was a television room just adjacent. To the left was a corridor that led to the schoolroom.

If you lived in Kingston, you couldn't ignore the prisons, which were all around you. From 1964, I lived just a few blocks from the high walls of Kingston Penitentiary, the same building Dickens had visited in 1842. Across the road from it was the Prison for Women. I passed every day as I went to work. I saw the guards on the walls of KP with their guns, sometimes a man arriving in handcuffs, crossing the road with the baby steps dictated by leg irons. Living a quiet domestic life, you couldn't help being aware that near you very different kinds of people were living very different existences.

In 1967, I began to go into Collins Bay Penitentiary to run a book discussion group, doing it partly out of curiosity and the desire to learn something new. Five years later, at the end of the most chaotic years of my life, it often seemed to me that I no longer knew anyone who hadn't done time.

What happened in those years wasn't just a part of my personal history. The world was stood on its head, for a while, and the most unlikely things happened. The prisons and the university and the small city of Kingston were wound together like a pile of tangled rope full of awkward knots and strange twists. It was the time of men with long hair and women with bare breasts, of Woodstock and the Vietnam War, the draft dodgers and deserters, of an outrageous political idealism and sexual exhibitionism. The prison system, in some ways rigid and unchanging, was in others a mirror of all the things that were happening around it. I remember, early on, a chaplain telling me that a policy memo had arrived from Ottawa, and that it seemed to open the possibility of all kinds of changes in how men in prison were treated. Something called the 'temporary absence' was invented to try to reintegrate men serving time into the community. There was to be more parole. More contact was possible between the prisons and the community. There were successes; two of the men in my first group were among them. They got out, stayed out, learned new things, built new lives, even – to use the old phrase – contributed to society. But a system, any system, is only as good as the judgment of the people running it, and this one created a good deal of chaos in the life of Kingston and it made some terrible mistakes. It's not always easy to understand that a co-operative, polite, artistic man is inhabited by a monster. Is a monster.

It was early days for the new ideas when I first walked in the doors of Collins Bay Pen. Anything new, any promise of change, is appealing to men doing time. You do time by the day and by the year, one of them said. The pattern of the days is always much the same, and when I began the book discussion group, taking it week about with my colleague Fred Colwell for the first while, there was a flurry of interest, but after a while, it settled down to the smaller number who regularly read books and enjoyed talking about them. The others went back to playing cards in the gym, or watching television, or just sitting in their drum and waiting for the minutes to go by.

The weekly group had been organized by Ron Nash, the prison's Protestant chaplain. He'd come to the ministry late, and he had some experience with the outside world, and he arrived at the prison with new ideas at a time when new ideas were acceptable. He would buy copies of the paperbacks I suggested out of the chapel budget and they were available for the men to take out and read. It was simpler than trying to work through the bureaucracy that ran the prison library and the education program. If you did things through the proper channels, they could take forever.

The discussion group was exciting because these men weren't

preoccupied with courses and marks and knowing the right answers. Once, toward the end of the year, I took in a story I'd written, and by the time they'd done with it, I was exhilarated and exhausted.

There were two men in the group who were particularly bright and challenging. One of them was an American, doing life after a shoot-out with the police in a Vancouver hotel. He came of an educated middle-class family – his father once sang in the chorus of the Metropolitan Opera – and he had been a university student when he made the wrong connections and began to move in a world of hot money and guns and stolen credit cards. His job in the prison was chapel clerk, probably the best job in the place, at least for someone who wanted privacy and quiet and a chance to read and think. Eric knew something about everything. It was Eric who first told me about a famous psychological experiment in which ordinary men and women, assigned to play the roles of prisoners and guards, began to take on the characteristics of the roles they were assigned. Eric knew what all the authorities thought, but it was never easy to find out what he thought. A lively sense of humour, a fund of information. He watched and listened and asked himself questions. It was Eric who once asked me why I thought rebellion in the prisons so often centred on food – a change in the number of hot dogs could lead to a riot. He'd been eating the food for years at that point, and it wasn't too bad, just institutional cooking. He'd figured out that it wasn't really the food at all. It was a symbol of something else, though he left it for me to say what. A few years later, Eric got day parole to attend Queen's University – he was in a class of mine – and later he did a master's degree. In criminology: he had that kind of mind.

Then there was a very short, very broad-chested, hard-looking guy, a little younger than I was, prison number 3274, who sat close to the front, always pushing, always full of jokes and wisecracks. I think he frightened me a little at first. He too had read a lot, but if Eric hid himself behind his information, Don Bailey was always out in front of his. He said what he thought or felt.

Here's Don's account of our first meeting, written in his book about his friendship with Margaret Laurence.

'Then I discovered that a professor from Queen's University was offering an informal literature course. I enrolled and met David Helwig. The first night ten inmates shuffled into the prison school room and a rope-thin, bearded man with glasses handed out mimeographed copies

Don Bailey, 1993

of the lyrics to the Beatles' song, "Lucy in the Sky with Diamonds". He claimed it was a poem and then stunned us all by singing the words in a rich baritone voice.'

Did that happen? I can't remember it. I certainly didn't have a beard, not until a year or so later.

Or is it, as Don used to say about his stories, what should have happened?

It makes sense, in a way. I was interested in the metaphoric, consciously poetic quality of the lyrics of the Beatles and Bob Dylan – surrealism for everyone – and I have always been unafraid to sing; in some ways it was always more natural to sing than to speak. I was capable of a certain audacity, and I thought that shock was a useful teaching device.

Whether or not that happened the first night in the prison, I suppose something like it happened as the weeks went on, though it's vanished from my memory. The anecdote certainly embodies Don's sense of who I was, why I mattered to him – that I was as wacky as he was, maybe.

Is it a strange thing that we would become close friends? I was a rather reticent and austere university teacher, and he was an imprisoned bank robber, a hustler who liked to say out loud whatever came into his mind, an abandoned child who'd made a life by challenging circumstance and refusing to lose. The friendship happened, though at first I couldn't have guessed that it would. Over the years I've learned that I like men who wear their weaknesses on their sleeves, though I don't always take to them right away. That Don had talent enough to become a writer probably made some difference. It gave us a world in common. At first the poems and stories he showed me were oddly mixed, intriguing but incoherent, but he had, once there was a hint of a possible audience, a huge energetic hunger that produced new work every week. Within a year of the time I met him, while still in prison, he produced a powerful story called 'If You Hum Me a Few Bars, I Might Remember the Tune', which became the title story of his first book.

It wasn't many months after I started teaching that Don was transferred to the prison at Warkworth, and a year later, when he got out on parole, I was on my way to England for a year. So there was a long period when we didn't see each other, though we wrote letters. Not long after I got back to Canada, my marriage fell apart. By then Don was settled in Toronto, was writing for *Saturday Night* and the CBC, and, after leaving a marriage that hadn't survived his years in prison, he'd met and fallen for

Anne Walshaw, a woman I'd taught back when she was a student at Queen's. (Strange that I knew them both before they knew each other.) I needed love and comfort, and with Don and Anne I found it.

In the years after Don got out of jail, we always lived in different cities, but we managed to see each other often enough to remain close friends. He stayed with me on trips to Kingston. I stayed with him on trips to Toronto. I remember arriving at his apartment in 1981. Anne's breast cancer had recently recurred. It would kill her within a few months. I came in the door beside the stairs leading up to their apartment. Anne shouted down to me from the top floor. Don was out, and she was in bed watching TV. I went up and sat with her and what we watched was the television coverage of the release of the American hostages who had been held in Iran.

The next time I was due to visit Toronto, I called Don. Anne had collapsed and been taken to hospital by ambulance. Her condition was desperate, and while I went to the hospital with Don, met her parents, I didn't go in to see her; she was beyond friendly visits. I was back a few days later to be one of her pallbearers. I remember that as we escorted the body out of the church I saw Margaret Laurence in a pew near the back. She had been very close to Anne – they were friends, next-door neighbours on the Otonabee River, and Anne had lived with Margaret in Lakefield during a period when she and Don were on the outs. As the body passed her, Margaret's face, now heavy with flesh, was shaking – like mud in an earthquake is the only way I can describe it – a terrible, involuntary trembling, as she tried to control herself, not weep, not howl. In her autobiography, *Dance on the Earth*, Margaret talks about how the death of a young woman friend brought back to her all the losses of her early life. She doesn't name the young friend, but I can only assume it was Anne.

Don and I supported each other through a lot of good times and bad. A year or so before his death Oberon Press asked me to edit a book of his selected stories, and in the spring of 2003, it won Manitoba's Margaret Laurence Award for fiction. Cheerful news, but then he was hauled into court once again facing various ugly accusations made by his vengeful ex-wife and designed to spring loose more child support from his by now non-existent income. Blood from a stone. Days after that he was in a serious car accident when another driver went through a stop sign and drove directly into the side of Don's car. Then he was assaulted by the police who'd been told he was harassing the ex-wife – he'd been trying to postpone a court date since he was too banged up to prepare.

A couple of months after that I had another letter. He was on top of the world again. In defiance of a back due for surgery and an ankle that had never recovered after a previous car accident, he'd been kite-surfing on Lake Winnipeg, and he had a new lover, a woman who'd reappeared in his life after twenty years. He proposed to bring her to Wolfe Island with him. Nothing could stop him, it seemed. He'd bounced back one more time. Then I got the call from his son Daniel.

Teaching at the prison changed after Don was transferred from Collins Bay; soon one or two others left and discussing books no longer worked, so for a while I took in interesting people that I could recruit, law students, medical students, a woman activist to let them hear how she understood the world. I wrote a poem about that visit.

Because you are a woman
and among lonely men
they can, for this once, give
a pure love, the gift
of their awkwardness,
wanting you not to go
while the guards are flashing
the lights, thinking
we've stayed too long.

That poem goes on to talk about the bits of paper the men would hand me, their poems or thoughts. I worked it out later that even poems were probably included in the list of contraband I wasn't supposed to take in or out of the prison. These rules became much more crucial as the years went on and more and more people went into the prisons and more and more illicit things got lugged in. Some of those who came to the prison thought of criminals as romantic figures and wanted to be on their side. I don't think I ever made that mistake, though I always assumed that among several hundred misfits, there would inevitably be a few with a talent for freedom.

Thirteen

A lot of good things happened to me in the year of the centennial celebrations. The Eastern Ontario Drama League Festival was hoping for a
full slate of Canadian plays – there weren't many around in those days –
and Domino, the local little theatre, agreed to produce the script I'd
written in England, *A Time of Winter.* It played for a week or so in
Kingston and then was repeated in the festival, with Nancy in the part I'd
written for her. She won the EODL's best actress award and received it on
the last night of the festival looking sexy and theatrical in a skimpy, dark
blue, loosely crocheted minidress hanging on tiny straps from bare shoulders. It made for a great picture in the paper.

By the end of 1967 my manuscript of poetry had been accepted by
Oberon Press, and I'd won a Belmont short story award for 'Something
for Olivia's Scrapbook, I Guess,' which appeared in *Saturday Night* and, a
few months later, in Robert Weaver's second *Oxford Book of Canadian
Short Stories,* with the likes of Margaret Laurence, Mordecai Richler and
Alice Munro. My Belmont Award (given by a tobacco company – all the
company guys are self-consciously holding cigarettes in the photographs
at the award ceremony) was given to me in Montreal, and I felt at the time
there was something a little strange about the details, but it was only
months later I heard the whole story. What had been offered by *Saturday
Night* in the original announcement of the contest was a first prize in
English, a first prize in French and a prize for a writer publishing fiction
for the first time, but I somehow won a second prize, and a Toronto journalist named Phil Murphy, who was receiving his first publication as a
fiction writer, was given the first prize. Something a little insulting about
that, I figured, but I took my five hundred dollars, bought a black leather
suitcoat and went home happy enough.

The story appeared in *Saturday Night,* and I heard from Bob Weaver
that he wanted to use it in the Oxford anthology. (CBC TV bought it to
adapt – very badly, though at least one other story of mine was done
much better a year or two later.) The story behind the awards came from
Bob Weaver at the launching of *Figures in a Landscape* in the spring of

1968. He told Nancy and said she could use her own judgment about whether to tell me.

The judges for the contest were Arnold Edinborough, the editor of *Saturday Night*, and the novelists Brian Moore and Marie-Claire Blais. According to Bob Weaver there was a disagreement about my story between Edinborough and Moore. Moore liked it and was convinced that it was the clear winner. Edinborough, boss of the magazine running the contest, liked it less, but Moore, as the outside judge and a man with a substantial international reputation, insisted. I was to be the winner. (Weaver's story gave no indication of where Marie-Claire Blais stood in all this.) After the discussions, Moore left town, to be notified belatedly by telephone that things had been magically rearranged, and my story was to have second prize – though there was no second prize. Weaver, having heard all this from Brian Moore, mentioned to Edinborough that he liked 'Olivia's Scrapbook' a lot and was using it in his anthology, and Edinborough – having cost me five hundred dollars and hoodwinked Brian Moore – allowed that perhaps he had changed his mind and now liked it best too.

Fortunately I never found myself having professional dealings with Edinborough. The next time I appeared in *Saturday Night*, Robert Fulford was the editor. The Olivia story did me a lot of good – twenty years later Keath Fraser mentioned reading it in the magazine while he was in graduate school and thinking it exceptional among Canadian stories of the day – and earned me some money. I remember once getting a letter and photographs from some high school students in the Niagara peninsula who had done a classroom dramatization.

The germ of the story came from a newspaper clipping about a young girl from Muskoka lost (or was it found?) among the hippies of Yorkville. I didn't know much of Yorkville first hand, but I had been doing a poetry workshop with a group of dropouts, students, political activists, some of the same people Nancy was working with in theatre. The workshop was held in a dim cellar of an old stone building near the Kingston waterfront. You came in a low back door – an unlit cavern off to the right – and crossed a patch of mud to a small space with rough wooden flooring. The whole place had something of the aura of a ten-year-old's clubhouse, and the kids who came were a mixture of the angry, the idealistic and the terminally vague. They were the dope-smoking generation, but not without innocence and concern. Much fluster when it emerged that the bikers of the local chapter of Satan's Choice had used that underground clubhouse for a gang-bang. The hippies got thrown out not too much later, and I wrote a letter to the newspaper on their behalf.

Two of the people who came to that workshop, the organizers maybe, were a couple, Dennis Crossfield and Joan Newman. (It was Joan who came with me to the prison discussion group.) At that time Dennis was in the midst of his shift from biker to political activist, going on to become an expert on the renovation of old properties and a skilled tradesman. I stayed in touch with him over the years we were both in Kingston, and with Joan until she moved on, to Sudbury and then to Ottawa. At the University of Manitoba, Joan, a very beautiful young woman, had been elected Miss Freshie, but by her graduation she had been radicalized, as the current phrase went. She was one of the first people to join the Company of Young Canadians – that home-grown, home-based version of John Kennedy's Peace Corps. She was also one of the first to quit because the company wasn't radical enough. She has, from what I hear, never lost her fire. A few years back she published *The Phone Book,* a study of the abusive labour practices of Bell Telephone.

So if I didn't know Yorkville, I knew the kind of people who ended up there. The little deaf-mute girl who is the catalyst for the events of 'Olivia's Scrapbook' grew out of my sense of the back country north of Kingston and the people Nancy had seen as she was growing up in the lumber camp. What made the story work, of course, wasn't so much its subject matter as the narrative voice, the rueful, pained, comic perceptions of the unnamed narrator – one of the reasons that Carol Bolt's television script didn't have much of a chance – a drama has no narrative voice to support it. When, a few months later, I got a call from Peter Sypnowich at the *Toronto Star*'s Entertainment section asking me to write a Christmas story for them, I plagiarized myself and returned to that voice – though with some of the edges rubbed off – to tell a Christmas story called 'One More Wise Man', not a bad story, I think, and it was republished thirty years later in a book of Christmas stories from Goose Lane. Looking back I've sometimes thought I should have used 'Something for Olivia's Scrapbook, I Guess', or at least the voice, the narrative sensibility, as the beginning of a novel, but instead, when I came to think of a novel a couple of years later, I lurched in another direction. I have always, it seems, proceeded by lurching.

The poetry manuscript I'd put together had been turned down by McClelland and Stewart (though they were still considering the novel I later burned), and I was thinking about where else to send it in the summer of 1967 when I wandered into the main office of the Queen's English department and saw that a new outfit called Oberon Press was soliciting submissions. Their announcement was beautifully designed and printed, and they were close by, in Ottawa, so I shipped the manuscript to them. I got a rather odd response to begin with – by telegram – but then I got a letter from them saying that on the recommendation of an outside reader, they were prepared to publish the book. The explanation for the telegram: the press had been founded by Michael and Anne Macklem, but when my manuscript arrived, they were in England, and their son Tim, sixteen at that point, had been left in charge. He wanted to be quick to acknowledge what I'd sent but didn't want to give away the fact that I was dealing with a teenage boy, so he was rather abrupt and signed the telegram with one word, *Macklem*. The outside reader who recommended the book, I learned when they sent me his editorial notes, was George Johnston. I'm not sure whether he was selected because he was in Ottawa or because he seemed the most appropriate reader for the manuscript. Either way I'm pleased that George Johnston, a good man and a fine poet, had something to do with my arrival on the scene.

Fourteen

No surprise: the palpitations I experienced on that May night in Ottawa have returned as these pages were being written: episodes of atrial fibrillation in August, September, November, December, with medication to slow the heart rate and an anticoagulant to prevent the formation of clots in the atrium, lest they travel to the brain. *In your work, you need your brain,* my doctors say; not a very funny joke, but well-meant. Tests begin, the search for underlying causes, dangers. Apart from the threat of clotting, the episodes are almost inconsequential, without any uncomfortable symptoms – I could go on for many years like this – and I'm able to carry on with my usual activities, except that my usual activities all seem gratuitous and arbitrary when a crucial organ of the body is showing signs of wear. I am invaded by these odd irregular patterns of movement in my chest. Who is doing this? The body, my own body, does it to me. A line I wrote a long time ago: *I am my heartbeat.* And so: do I care to read something serious and enlightening? does it matter if the dishes get done? is it important to write another book, another poem? I lie about skimming a thriller, listening to the quiet chaos behind my ribs.

Glad of heart. Hearty. With a full heart. I knew in my heart. Sick at heart. Heart-broken. His heart wasn't in it. Heart to heart.

I lie awake in the darkness, aware of the arrhythmia, waiting for it to end, and I repeat the words and phrases to myself. You could organize a book around them. *What I knew in my heart.* On the doctor's wall I've been shown a coloured illustration, and he points out the places where trouble occurs. At the farmers' market, one of the sellers has a large beef heart for sale – we had them in the butcher shop when I was sixteen. The heart is a dark, thick piece of muscle with a complex electronic trigger that regulates the beat, say a million and a half beats so far in my life. When the heart stops, the life ends, and every day thousands of lives end. I am trying to tell my story.

Take heart. Set me as a seal upon thy heart. Faint heart never won fair lady. Pure in heart. It does my heart good to see you.

Fifteen

Oberon Press was founded and fashioned by Anne and Michael Macklem, who published more than twenty books of mine. *Figures in a Landscape,* my first – a collection of poems which also included three plays so that it ran over two hundred pages – was only the second book they put out, the first Michael's biography of Bishop Fisher, a Roman Catholic martyr of the sixteenth century. They approached my book with immense enthusiasm, sent out single poems as flyers, held a small launching party for the book in Toronto, pushed sales as hard as they could. They let me know the number of copies shipped on almost a daily basis. Michael wrote individual letters to those who had been involved in the production of *A Time of Winter,* since the text of the play was contained in the book, and to others he thought might buy it. He encouraged my parents to sell copies in their antique shop. He accepted and dealt with my barrage of suggestions. He contrived to get a window display at Smith's bookstore in Ottawa. Peter and Carol Martin's Readers' Club of Canada made the book a dual selection, with Eli Mandel's *An Idiot Joy.* As a result of all that and some good reviews, which he also exploited, this first book of poems by a young writer sold something like fifteen hundred copies. Reissued without the plays and with added poems, as *Sign of the Gunman,* it sold another thousand.

Michael Macklem was, and is, a fiercely driven man, who has always approached the world as a battle in which every day a few inches may be gained or, more likely, lost. Comprehensible I suppose: when he was born, because an older brother had been found dead in his crib, the thymus gland swollen, Michael was given massive doses of x-rays to shrink the thymus gland, and these affected the thyroid nearby so that he was until adolescence, in his own words, 'a fat little porker'. (The doctors expected the therapy to make him impotent. It didn't.) As a small boy, he was brutalized by bullies at Upper Canada College. His mother was a clever and formidable woman who, left a widow with two young sons, married a rather shy lawyer and, after the crib death, gave birth to one final son, Michael. While Michael was pleased to assert that his father, whose business included a lot of money-lending, never foreclosed a mortgage during the Depression, the man understood money and he made quite a lot of it – though I believe they were people of means even in earlier generations. This has allowed Michael to run Oberon for more than thirty-five years without ever paying himself or Anne a salary – that's a gift to Canadian writing, as I calculate it, of well over a million dollars.

Pieces of the puzzle that is Michael: 'I identify with no class,' he wrote to me in a letter. 'In my family we call this affectionately (I hope) my Prince-of-Wales syndrome. Royalty doesn't identify with classes. The funny thing is at some deep level of my mind I really, really believe it. That is why I go about angry so much of the time. Other people don't.' In spite of this view of himself, he was perfectly delighted when I told him his voice on the telephone sounded exactly like the dial tone on the CBC phone system. His letters to me are full of accounts of disaster, a fall from his bicycle when he tried to take a corner too fast, a whole sequence of car accidents over the years. In a Maritime restaurant a fishbone caught in his throat and created panic when for the longest time it couldn't be moved. He once embarrassed Anne by fainting after drinking scalding tea on a torrid day while watching the Oxford/Cambridge boat race on the Thames. He was attacked by pirates on Lake Muskoka.

Only Michael could be attacked by pirates on Lake Muskoka.

I don't mean to make light of the incident. The drunks who assaulted him and Anne and his two sons in their sailboat were intent on doing serious damage to the boat and perhaps to the three of them. It was a pitched battle, and it must have been terrifying. Still, a shipboard assault in the middle of Lake Muskoka?

On the other hand I was once attacked by a mad cow.

Perhaps that's why we got along.

Years later I read in the Kingston *Whig-Standard* an account of a certain Peter Macklem who sailed about the area in a tiny boat, confronting large ships and insisting on his right of way. When I mentioned this to Michael he explained that the man in question was his first cousin who was exhibiting the typical family aggressiveness.

'As to the family aggressiveness,' I wrote back, 'it strikes me that there is something daring, but eventually safe about challenging a large boat. The captain is almost certain to make way for you. You, on the other hand, would be much more likely to challenge a large and *imaginary* boat, and the commanders of imaginary boats are unmerciful.'

What Anne and Michael had in mind when they founded Oberon was something like what Leonard and Virginia Woolf did at the Hogarth Press, and in their first years what they accomplished was very brave and exciting. By 1972 they were publishing Raymond Souster, Hugh Hood, Gwendolyn MacEwen and John Mills, as well as an important art book about a British painter in early Canada. They published *FPG: The European Years,* the book in which Douglas Spettigue showed that the early Canadian novelist Frederick Philip Grove had an earlier literary life in German as Felix Paul Greve. A year or so later they brought out a beautiful hard cover of John Glassco's important translation of the *Complete Poems of St-Denys Garneau.* Those last two books were among the ones I had a hand in bringing to them, picking up information in the halls of the Queen's English department and passing it on.

I don't think they had planned for Anne to be Oberon's main salesperson, but she proved to be good at it. Michael, I gather, wasn't. I remember a story of Anne's about how she went to a Toronto bookstore with copies of *Figures in a Landscape;* the manager expressed some interest but said that earlier some perfectly disreputable person had been in the store trying to sell him the same book. 'Oh,' Anne said innocently, 'that must have been the poet.' Having at that point never met me, she was prepared to make free with my character. I suspect that was Michael's last attempt at bookstore sales – except on the telephone, where he is apparently very successful.

There was a growing market for Canadian books then; small press books by Canadian authors were reviewed in the newspapers whether or not they had won awards – in fact there were few awards – and apart from McClelland and Stewart, there were no big press campaigns at the beginning of each season. Certainly Jack McClelland's gift for PR helped along some of his authors, and in many ways it helped make all the new Canadian writing fashionable. Canada had reached the stage in its development at which readers wanted to read Canadian books, and they went out and found them. Poetry was in vogue. Nationalism has its limits, of course, as a source of artistic values, but writing is easier if you no longer believe that all the action is somewhere else.

From the beginning, Michael Macklem, a sometime academic whose training in publishing came mostly from the years he spent working for *Encyclopedia Canadiana,* designed the Oberon books. In this area, as in every other, he had his eccentricities – he decided he didn't know how to design tables of contents so he dropped them from their books – but many of the books were very beautiful, and he was, I think, the first designer to make a practice of using existing works by contemporary Canadian artists on most of the covers. The best of Michael's designs are clean and sharp and inventive, and while writers have sometimes complained that the tone of the cover is unsuitable to the work, his use of existing art or inventive typography avoided the kind of wildly wrong-headed designs that commercial artists sometimes come up with. (The all-time worst of these was inflicted on my old friend David Lewis Stein in 1964 by McClelland and Stewart. His first novel was called *Scratch One Dreamer,* and on the cover, a photographed hand is seen, scratching across the lettering, as if across skin, obviously the work of a designer who didn't go to the races and had never heard the colloquial use of 'scratch' and of editors who must all have been deeply asleep during the whole process.) In all the hundreds of books Michael has designed, I'm sure there is not a single design that could be called stupid or vulgar. I have heard writers complain of an excess of good taste. My only personal complaint is that Michael likes the work of Mendelson Joe a lot more than I do, and I think Mr Joe has appeared on at least one too many of my books.

In the sixties and early seventies it was refreshing to see books that were designed by someone who had read them, who was committed to what was written in them, who cared. Though Michael and I met often over the years, it was often easiest to communicate with him on paper – he was more relaxed and less likely to feel he was under attack. At first our correspondence was very formal. He was Dr Macklem (Princeton PhD, taught at Yale) and I was Mr Helwig, but we soon thawed and the letters became relaxed and even genial. (There's a photo I took of Michael in later years, sitting at his office desk. Anne took one look at it and said, 'You've never looked that genial in your life.') It was, I think, just after the launching of *Figures in a Landscape* that Michael and Anne visited us in Kingston on their way home from Toronto. They were carrying with them a number of brilliantly inventive collages, illustrations to a version of *Cinderella* which Alan Suddon, who worked at the Toronto Public Library, had made for his children. He'd never quite finished, but Anne and Michael offered to publish them if he would complete the missing ones, and in 1969 the book came out with a bilingual text (another Oberon innovation, I suspect), the English amusingly recounted by Michael – though he gave himself no printed credit – and the French translation by Claude Aubry. A remarkably beautiful and charming book, and over the years I have given copies to many friends when their children were born, and managed to scrounge up copies for my grandchildren, though the book is now out of print. The high cost of colour printing was spread by co-publishing the book with a small English publisher, Dennis Dobson, and for a while all Oberon books came out in England through Dobson. I believe the arrangement ended when Dennis Dobson died.

In the mythology of the time, it is the House of Anansi that gets the most attention, as the place of discovery, bravery, new things – deservedly to a large extent – books by Atwood, Purdy, Ondaatje – but it strikes me now that it also happened because Anansi, like Coach House, was in Toronto, close to the newspaper journalists who make the choices about what's important, and partly because Dennis Lee and Dave Godfrey had an instinct for discreet self-promotion. In the early days Michael promoted himself to some extent, partly because he was the author of a successful Oberon book, but as the years went on and he was busier and more embattled, he more and more went into hiding. I've always remembered an occasion in the 1980s when Sandra Martin had arranged a Harbourfront launch for the current edition of *Best Canadian Stories*. Michael came down from Ottawa to sell books, and the journalists there were quite excited that he was actually to be seen in public where they could take photographs. The Invisible Man appears.

The first five years at Oberon, with all their very real problems, had a kind of innocence based on hope. Michael handed money to writers who never produced books. He sent a cheque to one who was having trouble buying groceries. Michael and Anne began to make their annual trip from coast to coast selling books; Anne knew personally every librarian and bookseller in the country. More and more writers felt that Oberon, with its handsome books and its hard work on sales was the place to be, but by the late seventies, there was increasing financial stress. 'Our year ended on 30 November, Michael wrote to me in 1976. 'Sales were up 15%, profit down 50%.' One of Oberon's economies had been to print books in England, Ireland and Hong Kong, but the Canada Council was insisting that books they subsidized must be printed in Canada. It was one more difficulty added to the impossible task of creating books for the small and widespread Canadian audience. All the same, when the House of Anansi came up for sale around that time, Michael considered buying it, at least went so far as to examine the books.

London, 1969: Maggie (top) in her school beret and Kate (bottom).

It was in 1969, the same year they published *Cinderella*, that Oberon put out my stories in *The Streets of Summer*. Roy MacSkimming at Clarke Irwin had written to me suggesting that I send them something for their series of anthologies of new Canadian fiction writers – John Metcalf, Clark Blaise and a number of others first appeared in that series – and Michael and I wrote back and forth about whether I should send them something, but in the event, he read the novella I'd had on hand for several years and made that the core of a book of stories. *The Streets of Summer* appeared in England through the Dobson connection and got a nice short mention in the *New Statesman*. By the time that review appeared I was in England to write a novel. I had taken a sabbatical from Queen's on half-salary, and applied to the Canada Council for an arts grant, which I received – the only Canada Council grant I've ever had, though of course like everyone I've been published over the years by houses with Council support.

We flew to England, by way of Ireland, at the end of the summer in 1969. Nancy, Maggie and Kate stayed in Ireland for a few days with Betty Kilmartin, the woman Nancy had met in a maternity ward, while I flew on to London, stayed in the YMCA and found us an apartment, the second floor of a brick house in Kew, on Mortlake Road. After a bit of searching around the neighbourhood – the first school we tried was full – the children were enrolled at St Luke's Church of England school, a small, stern-looking building behind a brick wall. One imagined fierce Victorian attitudes, but in fact the teaching was modern and enlightened. Maggie, in particular, found she fitted in well with the English schoolchildren, and she is still in touch with friends from that class.

We had barely settled in when Nancy received a telegram one Saturday morning and learned that her mother – a woman in her fifties with no very obvious health problems – had dropped dead at a Red Cross conference in Toronto. So Nancy flew back to Canada for the funeral, and I stayed in London with the children, writing poems, working on the novel. I'm certain I didn't understand how deeply Nancy was affected by that sudden death, how she was possessed by her sense of the unhappiness and incompletion of her mother's life. Do we ever understand these things about other people? After the funeral Nancy returned to London, and we went on with living.

England was both delightful and grim. Each day one of us walked the children back and forth to school, over a pedestrian bridge by the station at Kew, past a little cluster of shops, perhaps stopping at the candy store if we were on the way home. On weekends we visited Kew Gardens, Newens' bakery and restaurant just opposite, or we took the train one stop to Richmond for shopping at the Co-op or to feed the pigeons on the Green. Once we went to Richmond Park and helped Maggie make a plaster cast of the hoofprint of one of the deer. Kate, in her first year of school, was learning to read. We went to Portobello Road looking for Paddington Bear. We met a few parents of other children at the school, a police detective and his wife, took tea at what appeared to be a kind of commune or group home, a few families living together in the orbit of a woman psychiatrist – a middle-aged woman with a European accent who made me think of Mother Sunshine in Doris Lessing's novel, *The Golden Notebook*. With gas fires we managed to keep reasonably warm, but the winter was grey and dismal, and since I was to get a few hundred dollars for two stories purchased for adaptation by CBC TV we bought ourselves a week in Ibiza, sunlight, flowers, the ancient white city on a hill.

The novel I was working on. *The Day Before Tomorrow,* emerged as an awkward, struggling thing. Some of its pages have life to them, but it was a wrong-headed attempt to capture what I only half understood, the nervous, vivid spirit of the times. (Though I may sometimes have been in danger of being swept along by the political headlines of the hour I wasn't altogether without penetration. In the middle of all the loose talk about revolution, I remember saying that the only truly revolutionary action around was the women's movement.)

In 1968 the students in Paris rose in rebellion: IT IS FORBIDDEN TO FORBID was written on a wall somewhere; I was spending my spare hours teaching in a prison. The 1968 election campaign: I went around shouting at my friends that they must not vote for that man Trudeau, who was presenting himself as a stylish version of *le roi nègre,* but he won anyway. The Prague Spring was put down by Soviet tanks. The Vietnam war hovered over everything. (I appeared in an American Best Poems anthology alongside Senator Eugene McCarthy, the man who won the New Hampshire Democratic primary and caused Lyndon Johnson to decide not to run for re-election.) Martin Luther King was shot. Bobby Kennedy was shot. I listened to the rough, passionate voice of Joe Cocker singing aching songs, to the paranoid jeremiads of Bob Dylan. The Democratic convention in Chicago broke out in demonstrations and what was usually described as a police riot. Draft dodgers and deserters were beginning to cross the border. A colleague at Queen's dropped hints about why her partner had left the U.S. as a matter of some urgency. Bronwen Wallace was patrolling graveyards looking for identities that might be stolen for deserters. In 1969 I published an article in *Queen's Quarterly* suggesting that the solution to the university problem was to stop granting degrees, which were only a means of commercial certification. While we were living in Kew, squatters took over a grand house on Piccadilly – I was using a group of squatters in the plot of my novel – and I went down and took some striking photographs.

Many of these events found their place in poems, but I wanted to reflect them in a novel which would be about something larger than personal life. I went back to the stories I'd read about the English spies, Burgess, Maclean, Philby, and decided to contrive a novel about a Canadian foreign service officer who becomes a Russian agent. (I knew about the Herbert Norman story, but I deliberately ignored it.) The spy story was probably not the right framework for the pained, inchoate vision behind it, but there was something about the secrecy, the doubleness, that gripped me.

Doing research for the book I spent an evening at the Macklems' in Ottawa having dinner with Michael Shenstone, a foreign service officer who clearly thought my idea ridiculous. In London, I boldly wrote to the Canadian High Commissioner, who agreed to see me, and we had tea in his vast, rather grand office.

From a letter to Michael Macklem: 'I wrote to the High Commissioner a couple of weeks ago, mentioning Mike Shenstone's name and asking to talk to someone at Canada House. Yesterday I spent an hour talking to the High Commissioner himself. He was very pleasant and seemed quite intrigued by the novel. He got quite involved in all the problems of who might or might not do what. He believed in the idea much more than I felt Mike Shenstone did. He had to go to a reception before I had got all the details I needed, but told me to phone or write him if I had any more questions.'

The High Commissioner's name was Charles Ritchie. I didn't know until *The Siren Years* was published in 1974 that this pleasant diplomat who gave me tea was the intimate friend of Elizabeth Bowen and other literary figures. He was to become famous as a stylish and ironic diarist, and when his diaries of his years as High Commissioner in London were published in 1983, I was relieved not to find a portrait of that callow, ambitious young writer with a half-grown beard.

So I did my research, wrote every day and sent a draft of the book to Michael Macklem at Oberon. He wasn't enthusiastic, but arranged for an astute outside reader to do an analysis. I revised, reconstructed, and Michael tried it on more readers. I did even more revision, struggling to impose form on an emotional and intellectual chaos. It improved with each revision and finally Michael agreed to do it. Olwyn Hughes, Tom's literary agent and sister of the poet Ted Hughes, had liked *The Streets of Summer* and agreed to represent me in England, but she was lukewarm about the new book and made only one token attempt to sell it. When it came out, in 1971, it got a splendid review in the London *Sunday Times*, and a letter from another London agent who wanted to represent me, but it was otherwise ignored in England. In Canada the reviews were respectable, and it came out in a cheap paperback as *Message from a Spy*. A few years later, Tom Marshall, in his critical book, *Harsh and Lovely Land*, gave an astute and balanced account of the book's strengths and weaknesses. 'The book comes most alive,' he writes, 'when it is given over to the journals of John Martens, the diplomat, who becomes a spy ... The journal is lively and aphoristic – the self-portrait of a disturbed and brilliant man driven to desperation and paranoid fantasy by his son's death, his wife's consequent total sexual withdrawal, and his notion of entering history ... Here the bourgeois becomes the arsonist.'

Those journals of John Martens, I realized not long ago, have close links with a book I wrote ten years later and another that I wrote twenty years after that. In *The King's Evil*, published in 1979, the main character, a fat man who calls himself Dross, keeps a journal while living through a breakdown brought on in part by death and abandonment. He is madder than John Martens – and the book is the better for it – but he too links personal and historical truth and composes sharp little verbal formulas, aphorisms to keep off chaos. Finally in *The Stand-In*, a novella that appeared in 2002, a nameless, embittered, solitary retired professor gives a series of wandering anecdotal lectures in which he tells what he knows about the history of art and drops hints about the story of his life, its betrayals and his impulse toward revenge. It is the most formally satisfying of the three books, and the funniest.

So today I sit down to write about the past, and I recognize patterns lying behind the old books, unseen when they were written. If we knew what we were doing, perhaps we wouldn't have the nerve to do it. And whose voice is it in those books, pained, suspicious, histrionic? Well, it must be mine, in some way, though it seems a long way from the man buying groceries yesterday in the general store, the man in the poems. Other novels are told in very different voices. All writers do this, I suppose. Many years ago I ran into Margaret Atwood at Longhouse Books and we went out for coffee. She had just published the S twins, *Surfacing* and *Survival,* and I remember talking about the difference in her two voices. *Surfacing* was narrated by some inner voice, an Atwood persona familiar from the poems, dreamy, brooding, untouchable. The voice in *Survival* was the cheerful, quick-witted Peggy who was sitting across the table, about to make some snappy retort. Do we possess these voices or are we possessed by them? (That may have been, more or less, the snappy Atwood retort.)

While I was living in England, the world went on in Canada. *Maclean's* wrote asking me to write a poem for a symposium on nationalism, and I wrote a short poem called 'Considerations'.

Any country is only a way of failing,
and nationality an accident of time,
like love.

        That I was born
in Toronto in an April snowstorm
makes nothing certain.

           That I remember
ducks flying in the winter twilight
of Lake Ontario means only this,
that I was there, and I remember it.

Still, to have a country is to have
a way to encounter history in the streets
of a burning city whose fire is our own.

That we have less killing, more absurdities,
some luck, a bit of time,
and memories like those winter ducks
is about as much as a man can ask for,
a place to start.

The poem has made a habit of reappearing. It was selected for the *Oxford Book of Canadian Poetry* and has been quoted in such unlikely places as an essay on sub-Saharan African politics and a speech by Adrienne Clarkson when she was Governor General.

It was an age of poetry, as I've said: in 1968 I wrote a poem about John Diefenbaker that appeared in the *Star Weekly*. Though the poem was not written against Diefenbaker, it got me some angry responses from Diefenbaker loyalists. The poem about nationalism was commissioned by *Maclean's*. Not long after I returned to Canada a new poem appeared in *Saturday Night*. Poetry was assumed to be current, lively, of interest, and this suited me perfectly. 'Posterity is all very fine,' I said in a letter, 'but I want to know I'm speaking to someone.'

Also during those months in England, the CBC bought two stories for television adaptation, and a play of mine was produced by Theatre Passe Muraille. This was in the early days when that theatre was an idea, not yet a building, and a kind of adjunct to Rochdale, where Jim Garrard, back in Canada after a spell in England and France, was one of the building's resource people – the King of Rochdale was how he saw it. I'd written a play called *The Hanging of William O'Donnell*, a story derived from the western Ontario legendary history of the Donnelly family. James Reaney was later to create a very successful trilogy of plays out of the material. I have an unplaceable memory of James Reaney telling me he had seen my O'Donnell play, but since I can't quite locate it in place or time, I'm prepared to believe it was a dream. In ways the whole play seems like something dreamed. I never saw rehearsals or production, and I never looked back at it. I think it was a brave attempt, but muddled and highly imperfect, both too literary and too melodramatic. It had some inventive material – what I remember best is a travelling entertainer who showed slides of the Holy Land and lectured about them. The production was, I gather, 'experimental', the parts traded back and forth from actor to actor. Nathan Cohen, the grumpy *Toronto Star* reviewer hated everything about it. The *Globe* review was interested, but said of the production that I was out of the country and unable to defend myself. Jim Garrard, Theatre Passe Muraille, and the play's author all went on to more successful endeavours.

I also, in the months when I was writing *The Day Before Tomorrow*, got involved in another project that probably had a greater long-term effect than the publication of my first novel. I had recently written a story about a black activist in Canada, his involvement with a Canadian woman and his refusal of a sexual relationship because she was white. I had caught on fairly quickly to the separatist implications of group loyalties – all real feminists must be lesbians *etc.* The story was, in some ways, journalistic, a commentary on the current news, and I never published it in a book since it didn't seem to go a long way beyond that, but it was successful in its own terms, and it was meant for a general audience, not the narrow readership of literary magazines. Bob Weaver bought the story for CBC *Anthology,* but that too had a small specialized audience. There was no forum for fiction in Canada except the literary magazines. *Maclean's,* which had once published fiction, no longer did. *The Montrealer* had disappeared, as had Stephen Vizinczey's short-lived magazine, *Exchange.*

I decided that Canada needed an annual collection of new and previously unpublished stories that would be open to fiction of all sorts and might find a larger audience than the little magazines. Tom and I discussed by letter the idea of doing something through his Quarry Press and I broached to Michael Macklem the idea of Oberon doing distribution. His response was that he'd rather publish the book than merely distribute it, so we agreed to that. I got a bunch of addresses from Robert Weaver, and Tom and I began to get in touch with writers and tell them what we were doing. Mordecai Richler, who lived just a few miles upriver from Kew, sent a pleasant note to say he couldn't afford to offer us a story but why didn't he and I meet for a drink, so we did, at a pub in Richmond, halfway between my place and his. He arrived with a heavy bag of groceries from the Co-op; apparently the Richmond branch had a better selection of cheeses than the one near his home in Kingston-on-Thames. His advice was to have the book published in cheap paperback format on the newsstands. He told me how many copies of some serious American anthologies had been sold in Canada in that form. I agreed with him, was a bit obsessed in those days with getting books sold, but I was unable to make such a cheap edition happen. But the book sold well even in its form as a literary paperback.

Tom and I put the book together after I got back to Canada. The splendid title – *Fourteen Stories High* – was his, and when the book came out, it sold well enough that the plan to make it an annual went ahead. *Fourteen Stories High* included stories by some older writers, Hugh Garner and Norman Levine, and by a number of writers that belonged to our own generation, including George Bowering, Marian Engel and Alden

Nowlan. It gave Don Bailey his first book publication, a fine story about fathers and children called 'A Few Notes for Orpheus.' At a conference in the fall of 1970 I heard Rudy Wiebe read his moving and inventive story 'Where Is the Voice Coming From?', and I was able to get that too for the book. Over the next few years *Fourteen Stories High* sold more than four thousand copies in Canada, pretty good for a literary title in those days, and at one point Michael Macklem asked me if I had known it would sell so well. I had to admit I had no idea.

After we did that book Tom was ready to retire from editing stories, so for the next four years I did the annual with Joan Harcourt, former wife of my friend Peter Harcourt who had returned from England to create the Queen's Film Department. Joan made her living by selling her editorial skills to various departments within Queen's University. My original idea, that the stories must be previously unpublished, led Hugh Garner to a couple of fits of irritability, but the idea of increasing the number of markets for good stories was, I still think, a sound one, and the five collections introduced a number of new writers, first publications by Merna Summers and Margaret Gibson, early stories by Elisabeth Harvor, Dale Zieroth and others. We got previously unpublished stories by Margaret Atwood, Timothy Findley (Tiff still had no Canadian publisher at that point) and Alice Munro. I got the story from Alice at a meeting of the Writers' Union; I didn't expect to, but when I asked, it turned out that she had a new story that was, she felt, a little too close to home in its portrayal of her father's second marriage. I promised that the anthology would never reach Wingham. We both knew that wasn't literally true, but clearly it was a book she wouldn't have to present to the family. (I'm not sure that the story – 'Home' it was called – has ever been reprinted in a book.)

Each autumn the new anthology appeared and was given serious reviews in most of the Canadian newspapers, as a significant event, a way of taking the temperature of Canadian writing. When I went to the CBC in 1974 I felt that for reasons both of time and propriety I would have to stop editing the series, and I recommended to Michael that John Metcalf take over. John and I have disagreed amicably about many editorial matters over the years: I sometimes imagine a spectrum with, at one end, writers that only John could love, and at the other end, writers that only I could love, but with a large range in the middle of writers that we both have admired and published. When John took over the Oberon annual, working with Joan Harcourt at first and later with Clark Blaise and Leon

Rooke, he decided that the anthology should include selections from the magazines and be retitled *Best Canadian Stories* – which would surely be a boon to sales if nothing else. Much had happened in the previous years. Probably by 1975 there were so many active Canadian writers that his position was appropriate. Oberon Press alone issued more than twenty books that year, including, among many exciting things, Hugh Hood's *The Swing in the Garden,* David Adams Richards' first novel, the Glassco translation of St Denys Garneau, the *Selected Stories* of Norman Levine, and George Johnston's translation of the *Faroe Islanders' Saga.*

Sixteen

In the summer of 1970 we returned from London to Kingston, and Nancy, probably impelled partly by the sense of desolation and anger left by her mother's sudden death, fell suddenly and intensely in love, and in the early fall she moved out. My father and Michael Macklem both drove to Kingston to offer their moral support. Tom got me drunk, which prompted a long hysterical scene in the midst of which the dog killed the guinea pig. I settled down with the children in the old house at Baiden Street. Perhaps I was relieved, in a way. When the worst has happened, you pick up and start over.

A collection of poems published in 1972, *The Best Name of Silence,* serves as a journal of the time, though the poems aren't limited to their occasions. They have a greater hardness and polish than the earlier books, and are, though they appear more personal, more detached and accomplished than the novel I was writing at the time. The book opens with poems written in Kingston before we went away, then a group from London and Ibiza.

> A snowflake trembles at the edge of darkness.
> The railway station is bare and cold.
> I wait for the train to come toward me.
> It will cross a bridge over the river.
> The train rattles. Clouds are silent.
> Snowflakes melt as they strike the water.
> The river runs on toward the sky.
> A man walks slowly in an empty street.

I had been reading Arthur Waley's translations from the Chinese. The pages go on, back to Kingston, poems written around, more than about, the break with Nancy, the arrival of a 'lady in a blue photograph'. In the chaos of the succeeding years Nancy once said to me that when we were apart it never took me more than six weeks to find someone else. I think she meant to be sarcastic, but to me it was no more than good sense.

Married at twenty-one, and closely bound up in that marriage, I was pleasantly surprised to find that the world was full of beautiful women who were prepared to show an interest.

Catherine, the young woman in the blue photograph, was engaged to be married, but her fiancé was away for three months on a medical placement in Newfoundland. When he asked her what she was going to do while he was away, she said, 'I'm going to get to know David Helwig.' She did. Tall, striking, of an exotic beauty – a streak of white hair at twenty-one, huge blue eyes beneath a high, domed forehead – she had a difficult recent history and was struggling to live out the life expected of a doctor's daughter by the highly respectable family she came from. Myself, I was a little desperate, in need of rescue, and this shining young woman lifted me out of my melancholy.

The fall of 1970 was an eventful one, in every way. In England, I had felt isolated from the world of other writers and decided to change that. In September Tom and I drove down to Ameliasburgh where we spent the afternoon and evening with Al Purdy and Eurithe, who were welcoming and kind about my somewhat precarious emotional state. Al played his favourite recordings, Burns' 'Ae Fond Kiss', Kenneth McKellar singing about the Bonny Earl of Moray. He told me how he and Eurithe had once separated but ended up back together again.

The house at Ameliasburgh was the A-frame they had built themselves in 1957, on the flat, grassy shore of Roblin Lake. You drove down the main street of the village of Ameliasburgh – A-burgh as Al always called it in letters – proceeding past the octagonal house, the church with its slim shining spire, then you turned left and went round the end of the lake, left again to their driveway. The house was pretty isolated in those days, though as the years went by more and more of the lots nearby were sold and houses or cottages built. Since the choice of bathrooms was between an outhouse and a not-very-efficient chemical toilet, a multitude of visiting poets pissed on the back lawn. I once swam naked off the little dock beyond the young weeping willows. On my first visit, Tom and I stayed over, sleeping in the loft of the A-frame. Later in the autumn I made the trip again, with Tom, Catherine, a friend of hers who was writing a thesis on Al's poetry, Don Bailey and Anne Walshaw. That visit was the occasion when Don managed to fall into the water-filled hole that had been dug for the foundation of a new extension. I was out walking the country roads with Catherine at the time and only heard about it afterward.

Al at Ameliasburgh, 1970.

The Purdys seemed prepared to welcome any number of literary guests, though Al could be prickly with those who rubbed him the wrong way. Eurithe was often absent with the car, doing some kind of business, or now and then looking at properties; she had a weakness for real estate. Eurithe was a teetotaller, and I remember at least one occasion when she walked into the house, looked around, and said in a steely voice, 'Well, what time did the drinking start today?' Though in my experience Al was largely unchanged by the quantities of beer he put down, I think Eurithe was happier after a doctor, concerned about peripheral neuropathy in his legs, told him he'd have to stop drinking, and he did.

I visited at Ameliasburgh many times over the years. The house was expanded to include a new dining area with an adjacent living room. Out the back stood a one-room shed in which Al worked, and where he stored his large library of Canadian books. He once showed me a copy of the poems of Louis Riel which he'd picked up somewhere. He and Eurithe like to spend time book-spotting in second-hand stores. He knew what was what, though a couple of Kingston booksellers complained to me about the prices he asked – more than they would have paid anyone else. The house grew more accommodating as the years passed, the trees on the lot grew tall. Eventually Al spent only the summer months there. My visits to A-burgh over those years were most often with Tom, until his sudden death. I was the one who called Al to tell him the news I'd just received. He was fond of Tom, and I knew he'd want to know. When I told him, he wasn't silent or sad or thoughtful as most might be. He shouted – and it was loud – just one word, 'No!' I remember the first trip to his place afterward, scarcely out of the car and sitting down when Al said in his blunt fashion, 'Well, I guess we're here to talk about Tom.' He was a big man, affectionate, malicious, opinionated, widely read in an eccentric way, and what he cared about most was poetry. When you arrived he'd pull out a poem he'd just written, or somebody's poem he'd just read, demanding to know what you thought of it. Or he'd talk about where he and Eurithe had just been or where they were about to go in search of new places, new poems. Rangy, carelessly dressed, outspoken, observant, in love with contradictions and complications, he was good to me, and at his memorial service I quoted one of the lines from his beloved ballad about the Earl of Moray: 'he was a braw gallant.'

In early October of 1970, not long after the trip to the Purdys', I went off to Ottawa for the weekend conference of the League of Canadian

Poets, which had been founded not too long before by Raymond Souster and Douglas Lochhead. It was at one of the evening parties that I found myself sitting on the stairs chatting with Sheila Fischman, who was there with Doug Jones.

'You know, David,' she said, 'I think you and I have something in common.'

'What?' I said, having no idea.

'Growing up Jewish in a small town.'

Sheila, it turned out, had attended University College when I was there – though we never met – and since most of my friends were Jewish, she'd made the natural assumption.

One of the many writers I encountered at that meeting was George Jonas, and he was carrying with him a half-hour film script which I had written in England and submitted to the CBC. Robert Allen had written to say he liked it but could see no place for it in their schedule. Now it appeared George was going to produce it for something called *Program X*. 'A Day That Didn't Happen' the script was called. It was a story about a man and a woman, friends in childhood, lovers, then only friends again. It played with time and sequence in a way that is natural in film, where time is perfectly fluid and can run both ways. The inventive structure was partly inspired by things I'd seen on the BBC while we were in London. George and I did a little script editing while we rode on the poets' bus from one event to another. Two weeks later the script would go into production.

It was the Friday of that Ottawa weekend that James Cross, the British High Commissioner, was kidnapped by members of the FLQ in Montreal, and suddenly there were soldiers in the streets of Ottawa. The air seemed sharper and brighter. Al Purdy wrote a poem about it all. By October 16, I was in Toronto observing the shooting of my script when I heard the announcement of the War Measures Act. I remember clearly members of the film crew scoffing at Tommy Douglas and David Lewis because they dared to question the draconian powers the act gave the government. I was and remain on the side of those who asked questions about the necessity of this response to the 'apprehended insurrection'. The public wanted reassuring gestures, no doubt, as a child wants reassuring gestures from a parent, but citizens are not altogether children, and the forces of law are not our mummy and daddy.

The leads in the little CBC film were two admirable performers,

Colin Fox and Patricia Collins, and it was efficiently directed by Rudy Dorn, but when I saw it completed, months later, it seemed to have collapsed into competence. There was a kind of poetry in the script that never got realized. After the day's filming George Jonas took me out to dinner at Three Small Rooms, the fashionable little place in the Windsor Arms, and we talked about what was possible in the creative use of poetry on radio. Poetry as narrative music. In response I created a short radio piece, 'Song for a Lady', and a few months later a poetic entertainment about sexual intoxication based on the Bluebeard story and called 'The Best Name of Silence'. I loved that poem, still do, and George produced it with Colin Fox breathtaking as Bluebeard. I enjoyed working with George, and he got to tell me about the brilliance of his friend Stephen Vizinczey's book *The Rules of Chaos,* a witty primer of a certain kind of anarchism which he loved to quote.

Not long after the filming in Toronto I was on my way to Fredericton for a conference of prose writers and critics organized by Kent Thompson. (On the way I visited Bill Davis in Montreal, where he was teaching at the National Theatre School; he was in the middle of trying to get a divorce from his second wife but since *les ordres,* his lawyer was in jail. Everything was strange, chaotic, important, that fall.) The other writers invited to the conference at UNB were Hugh Hood, Dave Godfrey, John Metcalf, Robert Kroetsch and Rudy Wiebe – no women I notice now. Each of us read a piece of fiction, and some of the critics commented or read bits of critical writing. It was invigorating to spend time among serious writers. I was meeting a lot of them in a hurry. I read a story called 'Red Barn, Interior' and John Metcalf expressed his great enthusiasm for some white china cups that were described in it. I half suspected he was having me on.

The first night of the conference a number of writers had gathered in the basement bar of the Lord Beaverbrook Hotel. The strangest feature of this bar was the urinals in the nearby toilet. They were filled with ice cubes, and after a few bottles of beer, I found staring down at them an unsettling experience. The singer who was performing that night was pretty, and the writers were variously and boisterously lustful about her from our table some distance away, until I was prompted to walk up to the stage between songs and ask her if she would have a drink with a table of lascivious literary gents when she took a break. She would, and it emerged that the guitarist playing with her was her husband and that in the daytime she was – what else? – a graduate student in English literature. I spent some time talking to the two young people and they invited me to meet them after the show the next night.

That turned out to be a useful engagement. Saturday night, John Metcalf, Kent Thompson and I had been invited to dinner by Alden Nowlan. Started out as a perfectly jolly gathering, Alden beginning the cooking while Claudine was still at work, his response to us charming and hospitable. Ray Fraser and his wife arrived. As the evening went on, Alden, not uncharacteristically I gather, got first drunk and then angry. He began talking about himself in the third person, mumbling half-incoherently about 'the Nowlan'. His biographers have told the story of the later events – which led to the end of whatever friendship had existed between Alden and Kent Thompson. It was still early in the night when I decided that this was turning out to be boring and unpleasant and said, truly enough, that I had an appointment downtown with the two young entertainers and must go. Alden looked displeased, but then roused himself, took out my first book of poems and read aloud one that he liked, 'Orange Lodge Parade'. It was a warm and splendid gesture. I got up to leave, and he threw his arms around me and said, 'Go with God, David.' I didn't manage a wonderful response, but I escaped. The next day John Metcalf told me how lucky I was.

At the end of the short conference I flew out of Fredericton, the plane rising over the tamaracks turned pumpkin-orange, something I'd never seen before, and I returned to Kingston where, between these literary jaunts, I was teaching full time, looking after my children, and keeping company with Catherine. We were both of us careless about the way we got involved, no thought of what would come of it, and as things turned out, Nancy returned from a disastrous trip to Vancouver, no longer in love and with no place to go, just at the time that Catherine's fiancé returned. And that was that, more or less, though Catherine was to turn up in my life again when I was working at the CBC four years later, her marriage on the point of breaking up.

Nancy and I were together for a few months – the book has poems about hockey, about Audubon and his birds, about libraries, about Heathcliff, about a new lover (her name was Margaret, and she introduced me to the songs of James Taylor). Then Nancy and I decided to split up again, permanently as I thought.

In the meantime I had met Dickie.

A man is sitting across the kitchen table from me. He is drunk and angry, and he is stabbing the tines of a carving fork into the wood of the kitchen table.

'Will you write the book?' he's saying. 'Will you write the book?'

It's the spring of 1971, and already I know too much about prisons. Nancy has been directing a play inside Collins Bay, a play written by one of the inmates, and while this was going on, just down the street from us, a riot began inside the old Kingston Penitentiary. It lasted for several days, and by the end a number of child molesters and other unpopular inmates had been killed.

The man on the other side of the table from me is named Richard Armer. Dickie. He's one of the actors in the play, and he wants me to help him write a book about his life. Is he crying now? Perhaps, he cried easily. Dickie Armer: deep-set shining eyes, hunched shoulders, quick feet, thick dark hair, good features probably, though often a little crazed with booze or dope. He can be cunning as a sewer rat, and yet there's warmth, the warmth of the hurt and needful.

Oh, he was a number, that Dickie. I spent much of the summer of 1971 working with him on his book. We'd sit with a tape recorder and I'd ask questions and he'd tell stories. Before the end of the summer, he'd broken parole and gone off to the United States, and I was left with a pile of tapes. I got them transcribed, and then I put chapters together, sometimes word by word in the early sections. Other parts, when he got in the full swing of an anecdote, had less editing, but to make a book out of it, I interleaved chapters about my relationship with him and how the book had happened. Dickie was convinced that if he told the truth about his criminal past, it could get him in trouble, so I changed his name and called the new manuscript *A Book about Billie*.

When I look back now at my own narrative of the time I spent with him, I'm struck by a certain innocence, but I think the innocence wasn't stupid. If I was more or less prepared to accept Dickie at face value, I was also determined not to accept responsibility for him. He'd contrive to stay with us for a few days and borrow money, but before long I'd force him out and some of the money got repaid. By the end of the summer, I'd wake in the morning and find him sleeping in a car parked outside the house. For Dickie dependency was a survival tactic.

Later, when I followed the career of Richard Nixon, I understood something about him because I'd seen Dickie Armer from close up. They were both men who came to believe their own lies, and having come to believe them, felt deeply about them, could weep heartfelt tears over them. This wasn't hypocrisy, I think, but a kind of emotional lability, a state of mind in which the inner hungers simply overwhelmed any objective sense of the outside world. In many ways, Dickie was a child, but with an adult's unscrupulousness.

It was a battle to keep from becoming embroiled in his world. I once found myself driving two women, junkie friends of his, around downtown Toronto while they tried to score, first some dope and then a needle. When I caught on, I was annoyed and got myself out of it, but this was all part of the desperate improvisation of that world, his world. You used whoever was at hand to get to the next stop.

It wasn't all bad. His affection for me, while it was exploitative, was real, I think. He liked me because I took him seriously. There were sunny summer days when we talked and laughed and drank beer, though drinking with him was a tricky thing. Before long, everything about him would change, his face, the shape of his body, the look in his eyes, the pattern of speech. It's probably the characteristic of a certain kind of alcoholism. Once drunk, he became angry, more manipulative, incoherent and endlessly boring.

After he'd run away to the States, then come back and given himself up, done all his time and got out free and clear to settle down with a nice young woman he'd picked up somewhere in his travels, he would still occasionally arrive at the door, drunk, in a state where his intense emotion was expressed in vague wandering incomprehensible sentences. Once he arrived when only my two daughters were at home, and Maggie, as the older, was stuck with him for a couple of hours. She was maybe thirteen or fourteen at the time, and she said later she thought he might have made some kind of pass at her, but he was so incoherent that she couldn't tell. Once, sitting mumbling in our kitchen, he went too far and called me a liar. I got up from my chair, dumped him on the floor and was about to break the wooden chair over him when sanity intruded, and I put down the chair, grabbed him, dragged him down the hall and threw him out the door.

Once outside, he made so much noise, that – my anger relieved by throwing him out – I somehow let him back in again. There was always an element of farce with Dickie, and sometimes he knew it.

The most painful thing to read, now, if I look back at what I wrote about that summer I spent with him, is the narrative of how, toward the end, when he was getting more lost and desperate, using whatever drugs came to hand, he would say to me, 'Why can't I live like you?' There might be answers to that, but they weren't of any use.

The end of his life, a few years later, was perfectly in character. He was living in London, Ontario, with a woman and her young son. I suspect that mostly she paid their way, but Dickie, for all his weaknesses, was good with kids, and he was devoted to this one. They came to visit us once. He had won some money in the lottery, taken a course in becoming a heavy equipment operator, was living his usual feckless, dependent, sometimes cheerful life.

We got a phone call one day from the woman he'd been living with. She'd received a call from Calgary. Dickie had gone there to check things out and look for work – the woman and her son were to follow. The phone call was from the emergency department of a hospital. He'd arrived there, apparently having a heart attack, told them her first name and a phone number. He had no identification or money. He said he was staying at the Holiday Inn. (He wasn't.) And then he died, and not being his wife, she had trouble even claiming his body.

Dickie had exploded into my life in the summer of 1971, with his fantasies of joining the revolution, though there was no revolution to join, with his belief that somehow I could write a book that would make his life a story, make sense of it, give him revenge, meaning, justification. Now he was gone, though that was hard to believe, that he wouldn't suddenly arrive at the door, smiling gleefully or full of drunken rage.

The last lines of the poem I wrote for him after I heard about his death in those muddled circumstances in an alien place:

Alone in a strange city you were still a child,
stupid with fear, brilliant with maudlin cunning.
The hole inside you grew until you were gone.
Nobody knows the name for the piece that was missing.

By the fall of 1971, I was living alone in an apartment in a small stone house on Wellington Street, between the university and the waterfront.

This is where Judy appears in my life.

Sometime over the previous year I had begun to notice, here and there in the streets of Kingston, in the halls of the university, a silent young woman of a haunting beauty. She had thick dark blond hair with a metallic sheen, and it was cut round her face so that she looked, someone said, like Joan of Arc. She had precise features, sculpted lips, strong cheekbones, clear blue eyes and pale freckled skin, luminous. From the first time I saw her, I thought this was one of the most beautiful women I'd ever seen. She wore jeans and in the winter what could have been her younger brother's cast-off winter overcoat, and in her manner there was a mixture of an inwardness that might have belonged to a saint and a certain rakish, tomboy air. I met her once at a party which she was attending with a former student of mine, spoke a few words to her, got little by way of response. She haunted me. Once during the summer I turned up at Grad House, an old Victorian mansion where there was a booze-up every Friday night, and we sat on the front steps and talked for a few minutes, and then she went off on a motorcycle with someone's husband. Finally on a Friday night during the fall, when I turned up at Grad House in a wide-brimmed black hat – something between cowboy and puritan preacher – I was able to catch her interest. We went out taking pictures one Sunday and I did a pig imitation and slipped into a river, and that did the trick, and we tumbled into each other's arms.

And my hand against your hand,
the surface of my world touching
the surface of yours makes
all rivers, the falling into all rivers
even what is lost in the depth
of the music of river and light, enough.
And we throw our hats into the water.

Judy was a graduate student who had finished her course work for a master's degree and was working in a high-class gift store while trying to get started on a thesis. (The thesis never got written.) Originally from Prince Edward Island, where she had adoring grandparents, she'd lived for years in Montreal where the family had followed her alcoholic father as he proceeded with his self-destruction and her mother held the family together by working as a nurse. So she had two lives, as a pampered and beloved grandchild and as the secretive, angry and impoverished daughter of an alcoholic. She had been brought up a Baptist and had an intensely religious, if no longer orthodox, view of the world. She believed that the Old Testament gave a pretty convincing account of what life was: arbitrary, challenging and holy. Together the two of us were passionate, combative, adventurous, thoughtful, all those at once, and as the months went on, we spent all our time together.

We made a trip to Ottawa, where I was being interviewed about *The Day Before Tomorrow*, just published. Later on we went to Toronto where we slept on the floor of the house near High Park where Don Bailey and Anne Walshaw were living with a gang of friends. I'd been invited to appear with a group of writers in front of the Ontario Royal Commission on publishing. Ryerson Press, one of the earliest Canadian publishers and one of those most committed to producing work by Canadian writers, had been sold to one of the American giants, McGraw-Hill. This was a period when there was a new energy in Canadian writing, and in the middle of it our publishers were being bought up. It was widely felt that something must be done. Writers must act. The group of us met up the night before the hearing to arrange things so that we would not appear raffish and disorganized – what writers were reputed to be. 'It should be the best free show in town,' William French wrote in his column in the *Globe and Mail* – Canadian writers were a laugh. The next day as we appeared in front of the commission, each of us well-prepared to say our piece, Hugh Garner turned up, unrehearsed, unregenerate, talking too much, interrupting, unable to remember whether Margaret Atwood was herself or Gwendolyn McEwen. This made a hash of things – weird people, those writers – but still we got to make a few suggestions. Farley Mowat, typically, got the (small) headlines by denouncing the Canada Council. I got quoted in the *Globe* report to the effect that writing should be 'an entirely public act'. (Coming on that phrase years later I recognize one of my obsessions of that time.) Muddled as the meeting may have been, the conversations before and after the public session planted the seeds that led to the founding of the Writers' Union of Canada.

Kingston was a crazed kind of place in those days, marriages breaking down, a world in which everyone knew everyone else, and everyone had slept with someone who'd slept with someone who used to love the person you were talking to in a bar or at a party. It was as intricate and crazed as Shakespeare's woodland in *A Midsummer Night's Dream*. 'The lunatic, the lover and the poet,/ are of imagination all compact,' Theseus says, and Kingston was, yes, lunatic, a place of prisons and mental hospitals, and also an imagined place of poets, and almost everyone there was stumbling about in a darkness of erotic cross-purposes.

It's late at night, and Judy and I are in Vic's apartment, along with him and his girlfriend, Margaret, a pretty blonde with an English accent and a strange hoarse voice who was one of my students the year before. Judy and I live together in a basement apartment. For now. We've met the others in the bar at the Plaza Hotel, which is a gathering place for a few neighbourhood people, and some university teachers and students – Tom is often there, sometimes scribbling a few lines of poetry on a coaster or a napkin – and a few rounders. (*Rounder* – the opposite of a square john.) The world of the university and the world of the prison are more and more connected. Victor and his partner run an after-hours club called the Razor's Edge, and both of them are involved with young women who are at the university. More men are out on parole or day parole or temporary absences to attend classes at Queen's. Even those who don't study at Queen's are often part of the same social world. (A few years later a former student who worked with me at the CBC recalled a girl she knew who'd been going out with someone from the prison, his insistence on sodomizing her: a taste he'd developed in the joint presumably.) Even with all their craziness, the brighter guys from the prison have a kind of dash and energy that must be attractive to women who are surrounded by academics. Respectable wives take up with them. How can someone who's writing a thesis on Walter Pater compete with a bank robber?

Vic was never part of the discussion group I ran in the prison, but I met him a few times in the early days, read one or two things he'd written, and on the basis of that wrote a letter to the parole board saying that he had some brains. Convinced that the letter helped him make parole, he has a sense of loyalty and gratitude. (An excessive loyalty felt by men inside for anyone they thought had helped them wasn't uncommon. Now and then the loyalty got expressed in bizarre ways.) Vic has good, even gentlemanly, manners. He's not a drunk or a dope fiend or the kind to be dependent, so it's comfortable enough to be at his place. When Judy's out of the room, he says to me quietly, 'She's beautiful.' And I agree, of course.

Then it's a month or two later, at the Plaza again, and Judy and I see him across the room, and he waves and sends us drinks. Grasshoppers, the only time I've ever drunk one. And another night we're all sitting at the same table, and when I disappear to the toilet, he tells Judy how much he likes me. That's nice, but why say so?

I'll find out.

One day, not long after that, I passed through the English department office and picked up one of those little pink slips with a telephone message. To phone Margaret, Vic's girlfriend, and it was urgent, the message said. I knew what must be going on before I made the call. The Razor's Edge had gone out of business, and there had been a story in the local paper about a bank robbery in Toronto. One of the robbers had been shot and killed by the police after his partner had driven off without him. The dead man was from Kingston, an ex-con named Tommy Warburton, who was on parole. I'd met him once.

The meaning of that scene in the bar was clear now. In case it all went bad, Vic was saying goodbye. Part of him knew that he couldn't do it any more, that he'd lost his nerve – he'd told me that – but he owed money, and robbing a bank to pay it back was his idea of an honourable way out.

I called Margaret and she came down to my office. Victor had disappeared, and the men from the Toronto holdup squad were interviewing her. She didn't know what to do, what to say or not say; she hadn't broken any laws. Some of the police questions were very odd. They wanted to know if Vic had wigs and costumes or if he took her out in the country for target practice. In an office just down the hall from me was an English professor who'd once practised law, so I got hold of him, and he talked to Margaret about her situation, what the police could and couldn't demand of her. All she could do was go to classes and get on with her life.

Victor, always the gentleman, mailed her some twenty-dollar bills from the bank job.

Seventeen

Judy and I have been out for dinner and a movie. We often do that on Friday night, and now we're driving through the snowy landscape of Prince Edward Island back to our big frame house in the country. The movie we're seen, *The Secret Lives of Dentists*, is about marriage and children and being in love with someone else, and though we often talk about films we've seen on the way home, this time we don't. For me at least it was too painfully familiar, too much like the chaos I went through thirty years before. Recently Judy was rebinding her diaries from the period, her account of the time when we were together but lacked the *sang-froid* to rearrange everything. Or I did. I never achieved the kind of cool, detached approach to the world that might have enabled us to build a life together. I lacked the right kind of courage. I was deeply involved in the lives of my children – who, in dealing with Judy, were polite, distant, detached. They had a life and had no interest in a new one. If Judy and I had been placid, easygoing people, able to handle things calmly, sensibly, we wouldn't have been so passionately linked, but even after we were apart, separated by long distances, we continued writing, and now we live together in the countryside of Prince Edward Island, both still opinionated, impulsive, but by now inclined to avoid the topics – politics mostly – that might lead to harsh words and dishes being thrown. We both shout at the dog, who, in the saintly way of dogs, is momentarily humbled and then amnesiac and back underfoot hoping for something edible. My children are parents by now, hers have all left home, and we sit by the fire, read each other's new poems, avoid the newspapers. I recall much more than I care to write. Judy has taken up studying the stars, and when we get home from the movie, she will pick up the binoculars and go out in the cold to observe them. Light from the past, glittering for us now. I learned, many years ago, that if the night is dark enough, you can see by starlight.

Eighteen

Judy and I were together and apart. There are letters, poems. 'Women and pain,' Don Bailey used to intone in those days after he'd had a few drinks. I spent some time staying with friends, then travelled from Toronto to the West Coast with Don and Anne in a car and a tent trailer. Just before we left, Don and I spent a day at the Ontario Arts Council where the two of us, along with Robert Fulford, judged a Prison Arts writing contest. Afterward, Don and I went out for a beer and ended up at David Lewis Stein's house, where he arrived from celebrating his receipt of a Southam Fellowship, which gave him a year off from the *Toronto Star* to study city planning. I was crazy in those days, and it was a very boozy evening, and the next thing I knew was waking up in daylight to find myself lying on a wide wooden platform and covered with a heavy carpet. There was a window nearby and when I looked out I saw a farm field rising toward what appeared to be the end of the world. I finally worked out that I must be in the farmhouse where Don and Anne were living, in the country somewhere northeast of Toronto. Once on my feet I began to clean up the nearby kitchen, a way of putting order in the world, and in the process, I picked up an empty tin can from a shelf over the sink, looked inside into a pool of oil from which a half-drowned rat stared up at me. That, I thought, is what T. S. Eliot would call the 'objective correlative' for the way I feel. I took the can outside and dumped it. I didn't check on the rat.

A day or so later we began to drive toward the west. This was early June, and we passed through the rock of Muskoka, the green of birch trees, spruce, maple, the green of grass, and behind it the cottages, and beyond that, perhaps, the wilderness. Past North Bay, we were reaching places I'd never been. When we reached Cochrane we parked the car and took the train to Moosonee. The early morning train was filled with an odd mixture of passengers, tourists, a few fishermen and prospectors, many native people returning to their homes.

A few miles north of Cochrane, the man in the seat next to me started a conversation. He was a stocky, middle-aged man, Ojibway, I think, who had been reading a book called *Talks on the Prayer Life* for the first few miles of the journey, reading in silence and looking a little forbidding, but he proved to be cheerful and gregarious and full of intriguing information.

At one time in his life, he had been a guide near Parry Sound, but for the past few years he had been an evangelical minister with a church on Manitoulin Island. On this trip he was going to Moose Factory to be the speaker at the ordination of a new native minister there.

He told me some interesting things about the problem of language in his ministry.

'English is a good trade language,' he said.

The ambiguity of English words provides an area for manoeuvre that the native languages don't have. He told me of reading a passage from the Bible in English and asking if his hearer believed that.

Yes, the man said, he believed that.

When the same passage was read in Ojibway and the man asked in Ojibway if he believed it, he replied that no, he certainly didn't believe *that.*

It had turned very cold by the time we reached Moosonee, and we shared tents with strangers in a park across the river. In the morning I lay in my sleeping bag, fully dressed, while the cold came up out of the ground into my bones, and I listened to the sound of dogs barking from across the river.

We drove and camped, days of cold, and then a stop in Thunder Bay, where Don immersed himself in whiskey – throughout his life, there were these spells when he dived into a bottle for a few days, seeking some kind of oblivion. Anne and I got him into the car, and we set off westward. In the evening, the tent trailer set up in a park, Don slept while Anne and I went off to a bar where a bunch of local guys, mostly First Nations, were sitting around a table playing a guitar and singing. After a while they gave me the guitar and I sang James Taylor's song about fire and rain – my party piece in those days. I couldn't play guitar worth a damn, but I sang well enough that nobody noticed. I'm not sure the local guys appreciated it, but Anne did.

I'd never seen the prairies before, but I loved all that space, particularly loved the absolute flatness of southern Manitoba. After visiting in Winnipeg with Don's friend Tim Sale – a clergyman, later to be a Manitoba cabinet minister – we set off again. A day or so later: we'd driven a long way after an early morning car breakdown, and where we were by evening, the road pointed directly into the setting sun, and as the sun went down, it burned hotter and hotter. I was driving. The road was terrible, torn up for repair, full of potholes, loose gravel, heaps of dirt that narrowed it to one impossible lane. The car slid around on the oiled gravel as the sun shone directly down the road into my eyes, blinding me and turning the earth into vague colourless shapes. Don and Anne watched out the windows to keep us out of the ditch.

In all of this I missed the turn for the provincial park where we planned to spend the night. I drove on, waiting for the sun to go down, but it dawdled at the edge of the sky. It was close to the solstice, and the sun seemed to glide sideways rather than falling. Desperate to get off the road I turned off the highway into a prairie town. Dusty main street, Orthodox church, false fronts on the shops, the prairie town in Sinclair Ross's *As For Me and My House,* but this was thirty years later when the force of the town's life was gone. The stores were boarded up. The main street was empty. The slanting light of sunset made everything strange. We looked for a place to put the trailer, drove around the block. More empty buildings. Weeds. A tiny shack with smoke coming out of a stove pipe. Two old women, the only people visible, watched us around the corners of their houses. One had a garden, covered against the possibility of frost. I drove back to the highway, and the town vanished. It wasn't to be found on the road map we were using. We drove on a few miles and found that we had changed time zones, lost an hour of time. It must have been in that lost hour between two stretches of the burning highway that we'd discovered that empty town.

Then there was a place somewhere on the prairie where we stopped for gas and food and found a restaurant and beverage room being run by boys and girls. Obviously in charge was a pretty young woman about eighteen. She and her brothers and sisters had sent their parents away for a few days' holiday. With perfect assurance, calm and personable, this girl was managing the whole place.

We drove through more prairie, almost out of gas among the rolling hills of southern Alberta. Then the almost excessive picturesqueness of the mountains. At thirty-four years old, I was seeing this part of the country for the first time. All through it I was making notes, writing poems. The series of poems, called 'When There Is Here' appeared in *The Book of the Hours* in 1979. The notes would lead to an essay which was published in *Saturday Night.*

In Vancouver the tent trailer ended up parked in the driveway outside Jim Garrard's house in Port Moody. We visited with Jane Rule and Helen Sonthoff in their home at the top of a hill in English Bay – a story of Jane's was to appear in the second Oberon collection coming out in a few weeks. Don's first connection with Jane was a prison writing contest that she had judged, but he and Anne had met Jane and Helen on a previous trip to Vancouver.

While I was there I went ahead with a plan I'd suggested to Michael Macklem. He and his wife, Anne, would be arriving in the fall on their annual bookselling odyssey, and I talked to their Vancouver writers and organized an Oberon reading at the public library with a party the next night at Jane Rule's house. Jane and Helen were very generous about offering their house and even managed to secure food and drink at a very reasonable price. Once I had all this set up, I got on the train and travelled back to Ontario. Saving money, I didn't get a berth, slept in my seat for the four days that it took to get there, talked to strangers in the bar car. I shared sandwiches with a kid who claimed that his grandmother had been at the battle of Batoche.

Nineteen

Tom and I are on our way to the West Indies. It is International Book Year, and someone has given the League of Canadian Poets money to send two poets to Jamaica and Barbados to meet with writers there, to give poetry readings. This is 1972, before OPEC altered the world economy, and there is money floating around. The League had sponsored previous tours by members, and I'd heard rumours about how the travelling poets ended up at each other's throats. My suspicion (more or less confirmed by Douglas Lochhead) was that they were desperate for two people who'd get along, and since Tom and I were friends, managed to live in the same city, had edited a book together, they thought we were a safe choice. They were right. Tom had taken up Transcendental Meditation, so I was left on my own in airports while he sat with his eyes closed, meditating, and that kept him transcendentally placid and gave us a break from each other if we needed it.

It was November when we flew to Jamaica. Our host there was Edward Baugh, a poet and academic critic of some reputation. Whoever had booked our rooms had put us in New Kingston, which in those days was a tidy enclave that centred on some Canadian banks, not a very appealing place, and with not much sense of what the country was like beyond it. The impression we got from those working in the hotel was of resentment and anger. We read poetry at the university, were taken to the faculty club, where I ran into Owen Jefferson, an economist who as a student had lived near me in Taylor House at the University College residence. We were given lunch in a house among tropic greenery somewhere outside town by a British academic who had with him a young Jamaican who seemed some mixture of houseboy, friend and, possibly, lover. Before we left Jamaica I rented a car and drove (Tom had never learned to drive) from Kingston, past Spanish Town and then to the north coast. In the early stages of that trip the car passed mile after mile of shantytowns, houses built of scrap, crowded together on flat ground, the poverty that fuelled the anger. I couldn't stop reminding myself that the ancestors of all these people had been brought here by force in slave ships. Then we turned north, passed red earth, a bauxite mine, to reach another enclave, the tourist resorts on the beaches of the North Coast around Ocho Rios. We were late in finding lunch, and wandering around a strange town in the intense heat, sunlight burning on my bare head, I came on a plaque reporting that Christopher Columbus had spent a winter here after being shipwrecked, recovering from illness. One of his lieutenants paddled in a flat-bottomed boat across the open sea to the island of Hispaniola to get help. Dizzy with heat and hunger, I imagined Columbus in his sick delirium, trapped, waiting for rescue.

We picked up a hitchhiker, a genial man who worked on the beach at one of the resorts, and sitting in the back, he guided us through the wooded hills to the place he lived, and then pointed out the way to Kingston. It was beginning to grow dark, but we got the car back to the rental agency, and the next day flew to Barbados.

Another connection to my university days: Bruce St John, who was our host in Barbados, had been a voice student at the University of Toronto, and he and I had attended a course in music history together. Barbados did not appear to be imprisoned in anger in the way Jamaica was. We had rooms at the university's faculty club, and Bruce St John set a young poet from St Lucia, Robert Prince, to guiding us about. He took us to a beach down the hill from the university where we swam in the warm, bright water of the Caribbean. In the evening we went to a little arts centre in Bridgetown, and everyone read poetry. Bruce sang some traditional Bajan street cries and gave a wonderful performance of a poem written in the persona of an old woman talking to her son.

Paradise, it seemed, until I woke that night and knew there was someone in my room – I'd left the balcony door open. I sat up, spoke, and he was gone, my trousers and wallet with him. The next day I borrowed some money from Tom, and in tattered shorts I made my way into Bridgetown where I bought a pair of jeans. I couldn't greatly begrudge the thief the money he'd got. After all, I was in Paradise, and the rules are different there. Soon enough we had to fly home.

Apart from the pleasure of a voyage into the sun, the trip inspired an ambitious long poem. In school, when I was ten or eleven years old, I had been fascinated by the stories of the explorers. We heard, no doubt, only the heroic outline, but the historic tales were magical to me. Just as my childhood interest in fish and wild birds led, not to the career in forestry management I'd imagined, but to poems about them, so my fascination with the explorers, the long voyages, the fountain of youth, the gold, was not the interest of a historian but of a poet. Now I had been to the islands the early Spanish explorers had settled.

I had recently finished a poem – originally planned to be a novel – based on the medieval narrative of the voyage of St Brendan. By now I was back living with my family, and Judy had new men in her life, but we tended to run into each other – more or less accidentally – and we wrote to each other. I'd told her about the Brendan poem. Meeting her one evening in the halls of a building at Queen's, I talked about the trip I'd just taken, about Columbus shipwrecked in Jamaica and half mad. 'You should write a book called "Voyages",' she said. The suggestion was the germ that led to *Atlantic Crossings*, a book-length poem about the European invasion of North America.

I began to do some reading about the slave ships, the 'triangular trade', as it was called, from Europe to Africa for slaves, across the Atlantic to North America to sell them, then home to England with a cargo of sugar. The trip across the Atlantic was called the Middle Passage, and that became the title of my long narrative, one of four sections that made up the final book. After the painful events of the previous years, I was in a heightened, even febrile, emotional state, and the contacts with the prison had made me aware of the violence and mischief possible in the world, its rage and hardness and depravity. All this went into the slave ship narrative. The surface of the poem is deliberately beautiful, its central character so sunk in moral paralysis that everything is beyond his reach, therefore distant, lovely, no matter how corrupt. A study of *acedia* perhaps. When Michael read it, he said he was looking for some development in the narrator. 'This is a state,' I wrote to him in reply, 'where you don't learn, don't open, don't move.'

Before long I had two sections of the poem completed, 'Voyage with Brendan' and 'The Middle Passage'. Over the next weeks I struggled to find the other pieces of a four-part whole. It had to be four parts, like a classic symphony or string quartet, balanced but kinetic. I had the sense that the Norse voyages would be part of it, and for a while I thought that the third section would be called 'The Last Journal of Robinson Crusoe'. I sketched out an account of the Norse voyages to Vinland, and planned for a trip to Newfoundland in the spring.

We owned a large station wagon in those gas-burning days, eight cylinders and with a lot of space in the back, and in May, after finishing the term and marking exams, I set off on my own to see Eastern Canada and reach the Viking site at L'Anse aux Meadows. Each night I found someplace to park and unrolled my sleeping bag in the back of the wagon. I cooked on a Coleman stove. The leaves were coming out in Kingston and Montreal, but as I drove round the Gaspé, there was still snow in the woods. The south shore of the peninsula was a bleak, desperately impoverished area, or so it appeared to me driving through, and the road was torn up in every town, for new sewers, I think. The car took quite a pounding. I drove through New Brunswick, took a turn through PEI, looking for places Judy had told me about, and then up through Cape Breton to get the Newfoundland ferry at North Sydney. It was an overnight trip, and I shared a cabin with three other men. In the morning there was a little bustle as one of them slipped out of the cabin with the woman he'd brought down from the bar with him sometime after the rest of us were asleep.

Ashore in Newfoundland, I began to drive north. I remember a road sign: WINDS ARE STRONG IN THIS AREA. IF YOU ARE HAVING DIFFICULTY CONTROLLING YOUR VEHICLE, GO BACK. The only road sign I've ever come across that told you to give up. I'd been travelling alone for several days at this point, and I was determined to attain the Viking site that night. It's a very long drive, through the powerful, bare landscape of western Newfoundland, and somewhere past Corner Brook, I turned from the Trans-Canada onto a road which was then unpaved, covered with gravel. Within a few miles the car's muffler, much abused by the roads of the Gaspé, fell off. I found a gas station where a good-natured man wired it up for me so it didn't drag, but he couldn't fix it. On the gravel road, I couldn't go fast enough to outrun the noise, and the roar of the engine was driving me crazy. So I stopped and parked, somewhere near Trout Harbour. I found a store, in the front room of a little house, and bought something to eat from a tiny smiling man who was playing a record of Stompin' Tom singing 'The Man in the Moon Is a Newfie'.

The next day was Sunday. The only way I could get the muffler repaired was to go back to Corner Brook, and once I'd done that, waited for a day for a garage to open, had the car fixed, I didn't have the gumption to start north again. So I turned toward home. After all, I reflected, it was what the Vikings appear to have done. I could use that in the poem.

It was only after I finished a draft of 'The Vinland Saga', as I called the last section, that I decided what the third section must be – a scherzo, something quick, bizarre, almost comic – and I was drawn back to the first moments of inspiration, Columbus shipwrecked, a little out of his mind, and the megalomaniac, self-pitying, slightly addled figure provided the voice I needed.

From a letter written at the time: 'the men who conquered North America denied everything but the will to self-assertion. They denied or destroyed something of themselves [in] destroying what they conquered. Yet it could be explained as self-assertion, self-creation. That's the limit of that kind of doctrine. It recognizes nothing but the will.'

I found contemporary illustrations for each of the poems – the most striking a diagram of the deck of a slave ship, hundreds of bodies chained side by side, discovered in one of Wilberforce's books attacking the slave trade – and Michael Macklem put the whole thing together as a very attractive book which appeared about a year later. It was reviewed, from coast to coast, nearly always by poets. Later it was produced for radio by the CBC. After finishing it I more or less stopped writing poetry. For the time being at least. I'd said what I could.

By now I had begun to read manuscripts for Oberon, and Michael proposed that I should take responsibility for their poetry list. I was certainly willing, and I was responsible for the publication of Joseph Sherman's first book-length collection, *Chaim the Slaughterer* and *The Earth Book*, the powerful third section to Tom's quartet of books based on the four elements. I found covers for both books, a Graham Coughtry painting in the Agnes Etherington Art Gallery for Tom's book, and an original woodcut by Margaret Capper – who worked in the Queen's design office – for Joe's.

Around this time, one of my colleagues, Kerry McSweeney, told me that McGill-Queen's Press had turned down the John Glassco translation of St-Denys-Garneau, so I contacted Glassco and arranged for Oberon to do it. At lunch with George Johnston during a conference that was held in Kingston (he explained to me how to pick and cook bulrushes), I learned about his translations of Norse sagas, and when I suggested to Michael that Oberon might offer to publish them, he agreed and asked to me write to George. This led to the publication of his translations of *The Faroe Islanders' Saga* and *The Greenlanders' Saga*. One of the fascinating things about these versions of the Old Norse texts was that George Johnston translated what was there, not what a modern reader might think ought to be there. When the tense changed from past to present, the translation reproduced it exactly, catching the sense of urgency in the storytelling.

Later that year I received a long fiction manuscript that Michael wanted me to assess. The author was someone I'd never heard of. I remember the sunny day when I settled down in the front room at Baiden Street to read it. This is good, I thought, this is very good. 'There were moments,' I wrote to Michael, 'when its intensity and truth actually reminded me of Faulkner and Lawrence, but it still has its own time, place, rhythm.' The manuscript was the first novel by David Adams Richards, to be published as *The Coming of Winter*. Michael suggested at some point that he thought it might be too long, and I wrote back, 'I don't know if I agree that it's too long. It seems to me solid as a rock in a way that few novels are.' I went even further. 'My intuition is that Richards might be the beginnings of a *great* (and I mean that) writer.' David and Michael were both crotchety men, and difficulties arose over the editing of the book, Kent Thompson somehow involved in the dispute. When I heard about it, I just repeated myself – However difficult it is, do this book. (A footnote to the story: Oberon did David Richards' first five books, but only when he moved to a commercial publisher, seeking greater sales, did he win the Governor General's Award. Enough to make a suspicious man like Michael even more distrustful.)

It was a fine time to be involved in Canadian writing and publishing. More good things were being written, and publishers were keen to take them on. The Kingston *Whig-Standard* hired me to do a weekly book column for a while – I even reviewed *Jonathan Livingston Seagull* for them. There had been a lot of talk about the need for more and better reviews, and *Books in Canada* came into being, and I began to do some reviewing there. In the spring of 1974, Doug Marshall, who was managing editor, assigned me Margaret Laurence's big new book, *The Diviners*. I remember writing the review in a room in the Windsor Arms, in Toronto overnight because the next morning I had an appointment at the CBC with John Hirsch.

Twenty

Long John Silver: that was what I began to call him, later on. The reasons for it were not related to my vague memories of *Treasure Island,* but to the sense of not so much tallness as length, the endless arms that swung a little with his quick walk, the long legs, their extension often exaggerated by pants that were too short, the fact that he hovered over you as he spoke. Then there was something in the personality that was too large: too much energy, too much impatience, too much hungry need, too much, too much, and with it a fierce piratical greed. Everyone was drawn in to be part of his dramatic moment.

I worked for John Hirsch, for two years, from the spring of 1974 to the spring of 1976, in the television drama department of the CBC. My memories of those two years remain vivid and detailed. I had never met Hirsch before I was summoned to his office on the fifth floor of an office building at Bay and College and more or less offered a job. He wanted someone to deal with writers, and he'd talked to Dennis Lee and Robert Weaver and come up with my name. John was well known for his theatrical work, founding Manitoba Theatre Centre, directing at the Stratford Festival and in New York. He had recently been brought in to be the saviour of English language television drama, and he was in the process of hiring a number of sub-saviours. I was to be one of these. It was only later on that I learned how he got my name and how I ended up in that corner office, with its poster of a gaudy cartoon vulture saying, 'One of these days I'm going to kill something!'

I spent quite a bit of time in that corner office over two years, but the image is always the same, Hirsch folding and unfolding the long arms and legs, nodding, gesticulating, gobbling mints and occasionally belching quietly. His digestion must have been a ruin. The head was small, at the top of a long neck, just one more aspect of the inordinate length. He was balding. A black beard with a few grey hairs interspersed rounded the shape of the face. The eyes were a little protuberant, dark and intent. And the voice: still a slight accent, and a rhythm of speech that seemed to belong to a highly sophisticated rabbi, with very accurate consonants and a slight crooning, a lilt. I had listened to George Jonas, another immigrant from Hungary, but his accent was entirely different. John's voice was always soft, careful, when I heard it, even when he was being most unreasonable, and he almost always was. I heard stories about shouting matches, but while I knew him as a supremely difficult man, he didn't, in my presence, come across in a raised voice.

There was a story he told about appearing in a small part in some New York production, as a janitor. The play began with his entrance, and every night the audience laughed. This wasn't what was wanted, and he was replaced. It was easy, seeing him stride down the office hallways to understand what the audience found so risible. He wasn't funny looking, and he moved gracefully, but there was something uncontainable, something outré, as if he might have been a new breed of darkly poetic giraffe, or an importunate and improbable stork. And, sometimes out of embarrassment at having nothing to say – he was not a master of small talk – he would pull faces.

We never had any personal relationship, and I seldom saw him outside the office. Once we met at a theatre, when there were tickets for a few people from the drama department; there was, of course, too much of him to fill a theatre seat, especially when he didn't like what was happening on stage. Arms and legs began to go astray, the torso bent and stretched and suffered. Another time, Sutton Place had a reception for those who made use of the place to book outside guests. Hirsch was there, and I went along with someone else from the department. There were door prizes and gambling games, and John had won a bottle of wine, but to get it he had to stay for another half hour or hour, and he didn't want to. Since I looked like hanging in for a bit, I got elected to pick up his bottle of wine and deliver it to his office the next day. He certainly was not going to abandon it altogether. This was a man who knew a place on Queen Street where you could get groceries in damaged tins and packages at a discount and who told others about it, being helpful. In the course of the reception, as he picked over the plates of food, he explained how he had survived his poor days in Winnipeg by going to weddings and filling his pockets with food which would keep him going for days afterward. He loved telling these stories about how – tough, wily and resilient – he had managed to get where he was, though they were always stories about Winnipeg or New York or maybe Stratford. The other story, his survival in Auschwitz, the only one of his family to come through, was not part of the routine. Perhaps he discussed it with his intimates, over the years, but it was not included in the show.

And it was a show, a fabulous narrative that began with a little boy dancing for Nijinsky and reached his embattled present within the CBC, where he was trying to teach us all what drama was about. I didn't actually hear him tell the Nijinsky story, but he wrote about it in a memoir published in James Reaney's little magazine, *Alphabet*, how the mad old man and his wife came to visit John's family in Hungary, and John was told to dance and did. Of course it would have to begin like that. And New York, all the wonderful vulgarity and excitement. The producer's wife who would sit beside him at rehearsals giving him sandwiches and artistic advice. Splendour and struggle and comedy. All of us, it was suggested, were small and tame and repressed, and we must become larger and brighter and more aggressive and funnier.

Every now and then, in the first few months, he would have a meeting of the department, usually at someone else's urging I suspect, to explain and harass and encourage. The one I remember most vividly was in an ugly windowless room, everyone sitting in ugly standard issue chairs, Hirsch delivering one of his set-pieces about how he alone could do nothing, solve nothing. We must do it. Publicity. Well, he got his name in the papers. We should go out and get our names in the papers. It was up to us to generate our own hype. The endless arm took a great sweep through the air and came toward us, the middle finger rising and falling to emphasize his words.

'Ladies and gentlemen,' the soft, insistent voice said, the rabbi teaching, 'we are in a whorehouse here. And people are getting fucked. And you cannot just sit and listen to the blind piano player.'

What a performance it was, the whole thing. Fix it, do it, make it wonderful. Don't be afraid of conflict and collision, but be new, be splendid, be serious.

He was impossible almost on principle. A producer who had worked with him in New York as a designer told me how he would demand more and more lights for a stage production until finally someone would tell him there was no more wattage available. His reply was simple. 'If you can't do it, get me someone who can.' A four-year-old given to tantrums but with a mind of startling speed and brilliance, he was convinced, I often found myself thinking, that he could set in a straight line three points on the earth's surface. The curvature of the planet meant nothing if he refused to acknowledge it.

Two things to keep straight. The performance wasn't just theatre: he was a man of some real spiritual power. And he was monstrous: it wasn't just a joke when, after I'd been there a year or so and a number of people were leaving, I called them ships leaving a sinking rat. He would promise the world and then blame the one to whom the promise was made if delivery didn't take place. When someone was to be let go, he would hide out to avoid having to pass on the bad news.

One of his devilish skills was always to put his interlocutor in the weak position in any discussion. I'm not sure even yet how it was done, but as soon as there was a hint of disagreement, you found you were defending yourself, explaining the inexplicable, but as soon as you did, it was clear that you were making excuses for the inexcusable. And the figure of Hirsch would move off down the hall, leaving you to ponder your sins. His favourite sentences all began, 'You must.'

Early on, I'd got the habit of dropping into his office first thing in the morning, before the level of hysteria had risen and the door had closed for his day's appointments. Caught like this, he was capable of surprising simplicity and directness. I was there was one day after a large public affair – it may have been the ACTRA Awards – and when the subject came up, he said he found these things difficult. He never knew what to say to people. He appeared to be telling me this simply because it was true, but of course that too had the effect of putting you off balance. You expected another act from the big show and you got a human being, and perhaps you were patient for a few days more.

As the months went by, I became convinced that he needed hysteria and disaster, and if the place had been too quiet for a while, he would look for someone who could become the day's or week's victim. Things had to be changing, had to be in motion. At one point I was more or less ordered to fire a story editor – it didn't matter which one – because that part of the department had become almost stable. He would arrive in a dark cloud of grievance with a script in his hand, something that one producer or another was planning to shoot, and the word would come down that he was displeased. It wouldn't do.

I had my most intense run-in with him in just such a situation. I was the story editor of the police series called *Sidestreet*. It had begun in one of John's confused and visionary frenzies, then in the middle of the second show everyone working on it was fired. Three of us working in the department saw the series fall into our laps, and for our first couple of shows, John was pleased, but then the morning arrived when John was not pleased. He didn't like the script we were planning to shoot and he would not allow it to be done. A meeting was scheduled in the office of John Ross, the executive producer. John Ross, Brian Walker and I gathered for the meeting. Hirsch arrived and stated his case against the script. The others were a little inclined to mollify him, to keep the peace, but I wasn't convinced that the script was inferior to others he'd liked, and I fought back. By this time I'd been working there for a while, and I didn't feel like backing down. After all, he said we had to fight these things out. There was always a lot of dramaturgical talk in the air, about the purpose and structure of scripts, and I had learned from it, and from John himself, as he intoned the words, 'What is this about? Why is it interesting?' So when he turned to me and said, 'Tell me what this script is about in three sentences,' I was able to do it without missing a beat. I was proud of myself, but it didn't get me anywhere.

A compromise was reached. A new writer was brought in to fix the script, and it went ahead. Perhaps the anecdote reveals nothing but my bull-headedness colliding with his. By the time I left the CBC after two years, the others working on the series tried to keep the two of us apart, at least when scripts were to be discussed, and when, after I left, a producer wanted to hire me for a script-doctoring job, John said to her, 'David and I have a problem,' and insisted that he and I talk before I was hired. We did, though I hardly remember the meeting. I assume I agreed to be agreeable, since I got the job.

In those days, of course, he was under a great deal of pressure from the complex bureaucracy above, and he was also under pressure from a certain thoughtless conventionalism around him, those who assumed you made television by doing what Hollywood did. In many ways it was (and perhaps still is) very unclear just what Canadian television drama should be doing, and the struggle to define this and find an audience was a thankless one. In the first year that I worked for him, we got along because our unspoken assumptions about aesthetic, political, spiritual values were close enough that I understood more or less what he was after. But patience and compromise were never a part of his armoury. I came to believe that he understood the idea of building, but the part of it that he truly loved was demolition, clearing the ground. He was a brilliant wrecker, and a gadfly of genius.

His charm was real and substantial, but it gradually wore thin. Yet he was an authentic visionary. He hated clichés but he understood that popular drama had to be simple, sometimes formulaic. He had a vision of an exciting, populist Canadian drama, and sometimes he achieved it. I remember some kind of reception or meeting in a hotel room which ended up with John discussing, with substantial insight, the nature of spiritual discipline. He cared about these things as very few around him did.

There were perhaps a couple of dozen people at work in television drama in those years, racing in and out of the offices on the fifth floor of the Continental Can building. Just beyond John's corner office when I first arrived there, was the office of his assistant, Barbara Potter. She had earlier worked with him when he did some directing at the CBC, and he wanted someone he liked and trusted nearby. It was Barbara who called me to make the first appointment with John, and she helped me find an apartment for the first summer, a place on Belmont left empty by a touring actor. I stayed there for a month or two and then found myself a smaller but brighter place, a bachelor apartment on Macpherson Avenue.

Within a year Barbara was gone, angry and disappointed. Whatever she had expected from John hadn't come to be. The new world he was trying to build had a high price, and no doubt she paid part of it. Other empty offices on the floor had names on the door of producers, once powerful figures, who now came and went with no clear role in the new dispensation. Ron Weyman had been influential; now it was unclear whether he had any future in the department. David Peddie, who had bought stories of mine for adaptation, was working on a couple of shows based on stories by Alice Munro, but he too faced uncertainty. George Jonas – who had produced my little film – no longer had an office, and would pass by looking lost and disconsolate. A couple of years later, he remade himself in radio with the *Scales of Justice* series, which then went on to TV and became a kind of industry for the merchandising of Eddie Greenspan. Now he's a columnist for the Asper newspapers, a certain witty malice to the pieces I've seen.

Starting out at the CBC I had one great piece of luck: between the time that I had agreed to take the job and the day I set to work – while I was finishing up the manuscript that became *The Glass Knight* – I was walking along a Kingston street near the university and met a former student, Patricia Fitzpatrick. She had been enrolled in a senior seminar I taught a year earlier. She was very smart, lively, energetic, but although she got good marks, it was always clear that her intelligence wasn't an academic one. When I met her on the street that day, she explained that she had been studying journalism at Carleton for a year, was just finishing up and looking for a job. I suggested that she get in touch with me once I started at the CBC. She did, and it worked out splendidly for both of us. The only way I could get her hired was at a very low salary as a stenographer, but she took the offer and became my secretary, assistant, flak-catcher, whatever was needed. I trusted her, and she was loyal to me. I handed problems to her and just said, 'Fix it, Pat,' and she did. There were always a lot of scripts wandering around the department, unsolicited submissions, or samples of work, or things handed to John Hirsch, and she worked out a system for keeping track of them and getting them read by someone or sending them to the National Script Department, which was run by Gloria Cohen, widow of the infamous drama critic Nathan Cohen. As a public corporation the CBC felt responsible for reading and responding to every script that came in the mail, no matter where it came from, but the few scripts that actually went into production were generally commissioned to fit a particular slot and were usually from writers with some experience. So the National Script Department was invented so that every script sent in was given a careful reading by someone, and the writer received a response. I'm not sure anything that came in that way ever achieved production – there were too many scripts already, too few places for them.

Pat got the problem of wandering scripts under some control, so nothing was lost or ignored. She was a brilliant fixer, and gradually, over the months, she began to do more script reading, some script editing. Not long after I left the CBC she made a sideways shift to the Public Relations Department, and from there she moved on Young People's Theatre and then to a position in public relations at Sun Life. We often had lunch when I was in Toronto, and suddenly, after the move to Sun Life, she was wearing very stylish, obviously expensive clothes. She was flying all over North America as part of her job. Then I heard, from a friend of her mother who lived in Kingston, the bad news that Pat had breast cancer, and not much later that she was dying. I wrote to her, trying to make clear my affection and gratitude. Then she was gone.

During those years at the CBC I commuted on a weekly basis, leaving Kingston on the early train Monday morning, so that I was the office by about ten, and leaving at five Friday afternoon to return home. While I was in Toronto, I did nothing much besides work. I would arrive in the office between seven and eight, which gave me an hour or so free to read, think, organize, before the crowds began to gather. I was starting from nothing. I had some theatrical experience, I'd had one television script produced, I'd edited poetry and stories, but I suddenly had a job with undefined responsibilities, and all kinds of difficult personalities to deal with. Back in Kingston after the first week, I climbed on the bathroom scales and found that I'd lost seven pounds.

What I tried to do first was to get people to tell me things. My job, Literary Manager, was invented by John Hirsch, on the basis of a position found in some theatres, but theatres generally produced one show at a time, on a single stage. In every corner of the fifth floor, groups of people were planning productions and of many kinds, some going into studio immediately, some only hypothetical. I went from office to office, asking questions, getting to know who was who, learning about the endless problems.

In one corner two producers were putting together a kind of soap opera/family epic, to be written by George Robertson, who had invented the Quentin Durgens series, stories about a small town member of parliament, played by Gordon Pinsent. In another corner Perry Rosemond was starting work on *King of Kensington,* assembling a staff of writers, building a show around the charm and comic talent of Al Waxman. John Hirsch was determined to give this show enough time and space to grow, to allow for the development of sample scripts, of a pilot program, a budget to write off initial attempts so that the series wasn't hatched and instantly put on the air to fail. His determination produced a show that actually had a significant run, a homely and home-grown product – as much fun as going to lunch, as I sometimes did, along College Street at The Bagel. (I once went there for lunch with Catherine when she turned up at my office, and as we were paying, Lily, the tiny old woman who was at the cash, stared up at her and said, 'Dollink, how did you get to be so beautiful?' Only at The Bagel.)

On the other side of the building, Ralph Thomas and Stephen Patrick, who had come to the CBC from documentary and journalism, were taking the first steps toward the series which would be called *For The Record,* films that were to be based on the headlines and what was behind the headlines, but to be produced with some style and stride. They started out working with journalists and went on to hire some of the best directors around, Peter Pearson, Robin Spry, Allan King, Donald Brittain, and Claude Jutra among them.

In my first few days, someone passed on to me a most valuable document, the drama department's monthly script inventory. It was the one piece of paper I always kept in my desk, It recorded what scripts had been commissioned, who had commissioned them, and what stage each one had reached. Traditionally in film and television, scripts were developed in stages, with a lot of consultation with producers. In the Hollywood studios writers had always been considered expendable or interchangeable. Film is expensive to make, and a nervous producer might go through any number of writers looking for a script that would guarantee success. In Canada the contract under which these anxious negotiations took place was the one established between the CBC and ACTRA, a union which had begun by representing performers, but then developed a writers' branch. (This later broke away and became the Writers' Guild of Canada.)

At the time I was working for the CBC, the contract stipulated that writers would not to asked to work on spec, and that all contracts would go through three stages, outline, first draft and second draft, with some provision for a final polish. Many kinds of scripts were being developed, by new and old producers. Before Hirsch came there had been a kind of interregnum in the drama department when nobody was wholly in charge, and even when there was an effective head, there had always been varied groups of producers trying to get their shows on the air. Some TV dramas were shot on film and others on videotape, and the two techniques were handled by different sets of producers and, of course, different sets of technicians, though most of the crews were on the CBC staff. Every budget was broken up into notional expenses for CBC staff and facilities, and the cash paid to those outside the corporation. Above the line and below the line, I think they were called. The Drama Department didn't pay out cash for a CBC studio and a video cameraman, but obviously some CBC department did. And everything cost a lot and needed a very high level of organization.

Compare the making of a radio drama. A few actors did a read-through, then went into a studio and taped the show in three or four hours, sometimes with actors playing more than one part, the whole thing supervised by a producer and perhaps one staff technician. The tape was edited by the producer, music added, often from available tapes, and the show went on the air. I don't have exact figures in front of me, but a television drama cost something like ten times the amount needed for a radio drama of the same length. Also television was a medium that was noticed, loved, attacked, while radio drama went on quietly reaching its small devoted audience.

The result of all this was that television producers were at least ten times as crazy as radio producers. I was working in a madhouse. Scripts were commissioned and held ready, just in case someone announced there was an empty slot and an aspiring producer or one who was on the edge of oblivion would be able to run up the hall crying, 'Look, here's a great script that can go into production tomorrow,' thus saving the department from disaster and becoming the latest local hero. Many scripts were developed and at some stage abandoned, written off. There was a specific budget for write-offs, and necessarily. It was cheaper to write off a script than to get into a mess during production.

The script inventory was the map to this chaos, particularly important when a new regime and an old regime were still operating. It allowed me to go to a producer and say, What is this script called *The Horsemen?* And to find that it was a ninety-minute crime story by an experienced scriptwriter, so that when I talked to the writer – I talked to as many as possible – I knew that he had done this script and would be hoping to see it go into production. So the script inventory was the one piece of paper in my desk. Everything else was in my head.

There were a few script readers and story editors already at work on the fifth floor when I arrived. The senior story editor, and one of the two with a staff appointment – the rest were on contract – was Alice Sinclair, Lister Sinclair's former wife. She had been more or less in charge until I came, and I tried to tread very carefully, not to give offence and create bad feeling. In the event Alice and I got along very well. We liked each other, and she was getting close to retirement, and I think had no interest in power or joy in battle. Small and brisk, with a deep voice and a no nonsense manner, she was intelligent, well-educated, funny, and she had a life outside the CBC. She commuted every day from her place in the country near King City, where she was a dog breeder, an expert on Doberman pinschers and Rhodesian ridgebacks. Tiny woman, enormous dogs. There were photos of her dogs on her office wall, and she could while away an idle moment over lunch with the books of bloodlines which she kept on her office shelves. In those days Lister Sinclair was a CBC vice-president, and once when he was in town, Alice took me off to meet with him after work – a kind attempt to give me a connection near the top. We had a drink and a pleasant, inconsequential chat.

The other story editor on staff was Doris Gauntlett, who spent all her time working on George Robertson's series, and I simply left her to get on with it. Everyone else was on contract, and in the months before I arrived, there had been many short-term contracts issued – sometimes only for a month or so, people who worked at home reading and sending in reports. It soon became obvious that this was a useless expense, since a written report cut no ice with anyone who was actually going to put a show into production. A story editor could only work directly with the producer who was going to mount the show, so I stopped renewing all those contracts – sad for those who'd been doing the work, but they'd been no closer than the fringes of a real job. There were two young women working in the office on slightly longer contracts, and I assigned both to work directly with two more senior story editors for the run of their contracts. Then I promoted one and didn't renew the other. The one I promoted, Anne Frank, went on to a long career in script development and production for the CBC and then in various outside production houses. (Everyone was taken aback momentarily on meeting Anne – the name of course. I once introduced her to the irrepressible Larry Zolf, who, not missing a beat, said, 'Read your book. Loved it.')

The senior story editors were Jim Osborne and Richard Benner. Jim, quiet and sound and sensible, went to work for the journalistic series. Dick Benner was an American, who had come to CBC by way of the University of Calgary, where he had taught drama. He was quick, lively and irreverent. If he'd ever been in the closet he'd long ago left it, and the sensibility of the gay liberation movement was behind a lot of what he did – including a little half-hour film I later commissioned from him about a young man's first homosexual experience, *Friday Night Adventure* it was called. When I arrived he had begun working with Julius Roffman – another Hirsch recruit, with some Hollywood connection I think – on a series of contemporary stories. Matt Cohen was commissioned to do a script for them, one that was produced a few months later. I'd early on brought Hirsch the idea of adapting John Metcalf's comic novel, *Going Down Slow*, about the misadventures of a schoolteacher who is both idealistic and wildly reckless, and the rights to that were purchased. Barry

Pearson (who like John Metcalf had been a teacher, and who had been one of the scriptwriters for the successful Peter Pearson film, *Paperback Hero*) set to work on the script. John Metcalf was brought from Montreal – in keeping with Hirsch's desire to have real writers around the place – to consult on the work. After a few hours of consulting, John stopped into my office to say that while he was grateful for the money this was bringing in, he found the process of adaptation a little ... was *coarse* perhaps the word? John, in spite of his occasional ferocity on paper, is a gentle person with refined standards, and Barry Pearson, endlessly cheerful and ebullient, looking for punchy story lines, made him deeply uncomfortable. The show was directed by Peter Carter, who was at his naughtiest – no longer drinking he had endless energy to burn up being difficult – and the film was sexy enough that the nervous CBC executives hid it at some impossible hour of the night, after 11 p.m., I think, when Helen Shaver's bare breasts wouldn't be noticed by certain members of Parliament.

The 1974 edition of the Oberon *New Canadian Stories,* which I'd edited with Joan Harcourt before coming to the CBC, was about to appear, and I told Dick Benner that it contained a brilliantly realized story about women in a mental hospital, *Ada,* it was called, a first publication by Margaret Gibson Gilboord. (She soon dropped the last name.) I managed to get hold of proofs and Dick bought the rights to the story, which was adapted by Dick himself after a couple of failed attempts by others, and was directed by Claude Jutra.

Margaret Gibson and Claude Jutra: this may be the place to write about Nicholson's. It was the restaurant on the ground floor of the Continental Can building, moderately bright toward the front where there were windows, but dark as a subterranean cavern further back. TV Drama wasn't the only CBC television department in the building. Public Affairs, Children's Broadcasting, Arts and Science were all there on other floors, and Nicholson's was, inevitably, our local. An unremarkable restaurant at best, Greek in spite of the name, always busy at lunchtime. I spent a lot of hours there. I hate working lunches, but I had them at Nicholson's, and it was where you went for a drink after work, sitting in the dim corners near the back door that led in from the lobby, perhaps waiting for a crew to arrive to watch the rushes, the unedited footage they'd shot the day before. By early evening it was more bar than restaurant, sometimes quiet enough, but a lot of creative people passed through – I remember a not very coherent conversation with CBC News' star broadcaster, Norman Depoe. You could see odd things there. One evening, glancing across the cavernous space I watched Peter Reilly, a CBC News reporter, drinking alone at a table in the middle of the room. He spoke to no one, just stared down at his drink until, seized by some wild distress, he put his head back and howled out loud.

When Claude Jutra came to Toronto to direct *Ada*, he was introduced to Margaret Gibson, and the two of them hit it off, and she got the habit of coming to Nicholson's to meet up with him after he had finished shooting, when he returned to see the footage from the previous day. Margaret would arrive for their date in an off-the shoulder red gown, bare arms, face made up, long blonde hair brushed out – all this in Nicholson's, that plain little downtown beanery – and in her party get-up she would sit quietly in a small booth until Jutra arrived.

(Interestingly the only person ever banned from Nicholson's was the perfectly proper Alice Sinclair. Once after I'd left the CBC I proposed lunch there, and Alice said no, it couldn't be Nicholson's, she was banned. I stared at her. Finally asked why. She had, it appears, been overheard criticizing the food. They would tolerate any amount of drunken misbehaviour, but not that.)

The collaboration between Margaret Gibson and Dick Benner continued after the filming of her first story by the CBC. Another story of hers, 'Making It', was to appear in the Oberon annual the next year. It was based on the friendship between an eccentric, pregnant young woman and a gay man who works nights as a female impersonator. Talking to Margaret, Dick discovered that the drag queen was based on Craig Russell – by then working in New York and starting to become well-known – who had been a close friend of Margaret's when they were in high school. Dick put the whole thing together as the movie *Outrageous*, which was released in 1977. He wrote the screen play, directed, and the film was produced by William Marshall and Hank van der Kolk (the two of them had just founded the Toronto Film Festival). It had some real success, and when I looked for it recently on the internet, I found a few references: one called it 'seminal' (of all things), and the other said it was 'a cult classic'. I suspect that Dick would have been delighted by both descriptions. I lost track of Dick Benner after that film – we'd both left the CBC – though I can find references to a number of writing and directing jobs he did. Years later I went with a friend to see the Toronto AIDS memorial and found his name there, along with that of John Hirsch.

When I arrived at the CBC, in that summer of 1974, the drama department was producing a series called *The Collaborators,* a crime series it was, based on the connection between the police and a forensic science lab: ahead of its time. Perhaps it had its roots in *Wojeck,* the earlier dramatic series about a crusading coroner with John Vernon. (*Wojeck* was derived from the career of Morton Shulman, as the current *Da Vinci's Inquest* was derived from the career of Larry Campbell.) I'd watched *The Collaborators* on the air a few times over the previous year, and it had, at least at times, some of the better qualities of Canadian TV shows.

At the time I began to work for John Hirsch, he was due to make a decision about whether *The Collaborators* would be continued or cancelled and replaced. Obviously a police show drew audiences, and John was enough of a populist to believe that his shows must find audiences, must try to work within the accepted conventions. He was, after all, having Perry Rosemond develop a sitcom. But it was clear he didn't really like *The Collaborators.* Still, it was there. He was indecisive. I was told to look at the scripts, find out what was going on. I did my best. The show's producer was René Bonnière, a French (not Québécois) film director. The associate producer was Brian Walker, who had emigrated from England, done this and that, including running a bar in Yorkville, then begun at the CBC as a prop man, putting the Friendly Giant's little chairs in place, then worked his way up until he was first assistant director, the main organizer of all the day to day shooting schedule, on a variety of films, including *Jalna,* where, he once told me, he got to start the First World War, cueing planes, soldiers, guns, whatever else was involved in the mock battle. *The Collaborators'* story editor was Don Ginsberg, who was by profession a film editor.

I went to at least one script meeting for the show. You must find out what's happening, Hirsch would say. What are they up to? So I went to the script session. Carol Bolt was the writer. She had adapted the *Olivia's Scrapbook* story a couple of years before – badly, and she knew it. René Bonnière had directed that show, so while I was an outside intruder at the script conference, I had some connection with these people. René was a pleasant and very charming man, but I found he was extraordinarily vague about what he wanted, where he thought the story should go. He was vague and Carol was defensive. The only person on the team who struck me as having a clear head and a quick analytical mind was Brian Walker. Hirsch continued to be indecisive. Don Ginsberg's contract was coming to an end, and no one would tell him if it would be renewed. Hirsch was avoiding him.

Finally I think it was John Kennedy, the department business manager, who told Ginsberg his contract wasn't being renewed. Kennedy was a smart CBC manager, a former unit manager who had worked his way up and increasingly had a good deal of power in the department. He affected to have no particular artistic or intellectual interests (though he later became head of the department), but John Hirsch trusted him. Kennedy knew how to handle the CBC bureaucracy. I talked to Hirsch first thing in the morning before his door was closed, and to John Kennedy last thing in the afternoon after his door was open. These informal conversations were the only things that kept me abreast of what was going on. If I'd waited for formal notification of anything I would have been lost.

It finally became clear that *The Collaborators* was going to be cancelled, and in its place was to come something new. Hired to create this something new were Chalmers Adams, as executive producer, Geoffrey Gilbert, brought from England to be story editor, and John Saxton, to work with Gilbert on developing the scripts. John Saxton was my suggestion, someone whose reputation I'd known from theatre and who had showed me sample scripts which indicated he was interested in the construction of crime shows. I knew nothing of the others, have no idea to this day how Hirsch found Geoffrey Gilbert and brought him to Canada. Obviously he had some significant background in English television.

It is a strange world, television. It was, of course, a Canadian, Sydney Newman, who more or less created television drama for the BBC, but now we were bringing British experts to help create television drama for Canadians. As so often, we were between two worlds. Hirsch saw great shows, relevant, inventive, from the BBC and said we should be able to do that. Other people at the CBC saw the successful shows that came from the United States and regarded them as the standard to be met. Add to that confusion the fact that television is a collaborative medium, and every show had dozens of people working on it, and the skill and opinions of every one had some effect on the final outcome. There is always a lot of gossip about films as to who was responsible for the success or failure. A simple example: *The Rowdyman,* a film made in Newfoundland with Gordon Pinsent, who'd written the original story, as the star, was generally accepted as a successful movie. It was directed by Peter Carter –

chalk one up for PC. But there were those who would tell you that when that film was being made Peter – who was on the wagon by the time I ever met him – was at the low point of his alcoholism, so sick he had to choke down a large slug of brandy to stop the shakes and begin the day's work, barely functioning. Who held it all together? Perhaps Gordon Pinsent. Is that true? Approximately, no doubt, but maybe Peter drunk and sick could still do what was required. Maybe the film cutter made it work. With a medium as fully collaborative as film, it's hard to say.

The people assigned to create a new police series went out and talked to the Toronto police, and came up with an idea for a series about community policing – the officers who were assigned to anticipate problems, work on the streets, get to know people within the city's various communities. The series was to be called *Sidestreet*. Hirsch wanted a show which wasn't just gunplay and punch-ups, a series that could deal with social problems, and the new conception promised that. Geoffrey Gilbert and John Saxton interviewed a bunch of writers, contracted some, and began to work with them in locations outside the CBC offices, so what the rest of us heard about what was going on was mostly gossip. Shooting dates were already lined up, and in a place as big as the CBC, you miss a shooting date at your peril.

The impression given to the rest of the department by those developing the series was that Geoffrey Gilbert, the English pro, was going to teach the rude colonials how to do things right. Gilbert was not a winning man, short, plump, red-faced; the sight of him with John Saxton, who was very tall and slender and handsome, was a comic one. These things have an effect, and Geoffrey Gilbert had a superior manner that got people's backs up. Chalmers Adams wasn't experienced enough to know how dangerous this was, that he should compensate for it. He too went about being forceful and condescending. One of the writers commissioned was Don Bailey. It made sense. By now he had published two books, and he certainly knew something about crime and the police. Getting on for the production date, the new team handed Hirsch their golden scripts. I was one of those who read them. John called me in and asked me what I thought. Which was the best of them? In a way it seemed like a trick question: he knew perfectly well that Don was a friend of mine, that I might be biased, but I said what I thought, that Don's was the best of the lot. He agreed with that, without hesitation, but overall he wasn't impressed.

Somewhere in the middle of all this I discovered that Saxton and Gilbert had cancelled Don's script. They didn't like it and said he shouldn't go on to another draft. On my own I told him to go on with it anyway. I'd see that he got paid. Then the script they had planned to shoot first, when timed by the script assistant and then by Brian Walker, with all his practical shooting experience, was said to be too short. The waters were rising. The new group had set out to be arrogantly independent, but they were working within a large department where the bad feeling they'd generated was coming back to haunt them. They had to find a different script to shoot, and Don Bailey's – on Hirsch's orders, I suspect – was it. It was years later Don told me that they called him in from Peterborough on Christmas Day to work with them on revisions.

The first show was produced. More or less. John Wright, the director, was new to the CBC, and not very experienced in general, and the shooting wasn't quite completed in the days available. Soon a second script had to be done – a story by Michael Mercer, a playwright from BC, the one that had originally been planned as the first to go into production – but longer by now I assume. And then the contracts of all the three principals came up for renewal, and none was renewed. The series had a pile of uncompleted scripts, Sean McCann and Stephen Markle contracted to play the leads, production dates, and no one in charge.

Three of us inherited the show, John Ross, who had a private production company, as executive producer, Brian Walker as producer, and I was story editor. I'm not sure if anyone ever asked me if I wanted the job or told me to do it. It just became clear that it was mine. Fortunately John Ross was eminently sane, pleasant and calm, and Brian and I got along, became, in fact, quite close friends. A shooting date was imminent, a script on hand by Mort Forer about a Métis woman and her family and their housing problems. It appeared to be the only possible script to shoot, and the three of us got together with Dick Gilbert, who had been hired to direct. There was always a question about how many changes a director could ask for in a script – none if the producer was tough – but we were in a mess. Dick Gilbert wanted a great many script revisions. I listened, made notes, took the script home to my apartment, and when I came back the next morning I said I couldn't promise that revisions so substantial could be done in time. A script is a house of cards, I said, and you want to take out one card too many. It will collapse. Everyone looked glum. This was Friday and we went off for a weekend of worry.

For some reason I wasn't in the office on Monday, an official holiday or some family matter. When I got in Tuesday morning Brian was smiling. All was well.

Go back two or three steps, to the period when Geoffrey Gilbert and John Saxton were teaching writers how to write. One day I looked up from my desk and Tony Sheer was standing in my office doorway. Tony was an experienced film writer, had done quite a bit of work for Ron Weyman. I'd spent some time talking to him when I was trying to meet everyone. Like Don Bailey, Tony had decided to leave behind a life of crime when he got out of prison a few years before. He knew that I'd done some teaching in the prisons, and that gave us something to chat about, Tony speaking in his odd, precise, almost pedantic manner, a little British, a little Jewish, a mixture of Damon Runyon and Laurence Olivier, I always thought. Before he started to write he'd done some acting. I remember Peter Madden's name came up, the man whose play Nancy had directed inside Collins Bay. Tony knew him, of course.

'Even before his last bit,' Tony said – no, enunciated – 'Peter had already seen,' the voice grew ever more precise, forming italics, '*the error of his ways.*'

I knew the *Sidestreet* team had commissioned Tony to write for them, after some of the other scripts fell by the wayside. Now here he was, blond hair, shark's grin, big shoulders hunched, in my doorway. The soft, punctilious, familiar voice spoke.

'Do I have to work with these clowns?' he said. Stared at me with that slightly ominous look.

'No, Tony,' I said, 'you don't. Come in and close the door.'

So, telling no one, I worked through the outline with Tony, and off he went to complete a first draft, and it was that first draft that arrived the Monday I was away. He gave it to Brian Walker, who gave it to John Ross and John Hirsch. It would be the next script shot. Production planning had already begun. The story was about slum landlords and their tenants, and Tony, a very smart cookie, had walked the fine line between cop show suspense and serious drama. He even had a stunt, a house burnt down, a figure running out covered with flames. John Hirsch loved the show when it was put together, and the three of us in charge were able to feel secure for a week or so. But we had to keep coming up with scripts. The Mort Forer piece now had time available for revisions, though not much time. I had a large hand in the final version. One night I went home with the script and a bottle of whisky and produced a new version by morning. That splendid actress Monique Mercure came from Montreal to play the Métis woman, and she gave the show the energy it needed.

Always scrambling, we got the scripts together, and they were shot. The final problem to be solved was the incomplete footage of the first Don Bailey script. In the meantime Don had written another script which had been produced, but every time Brian ran the first show through the Steenbeck he cut a little more of it. We ended up with just over thirty minutes of edited footage – we needed fifty-two minutes. The story was about a thief just out of jail and his dealings with two detectives, based loosely on two real Toronto detectives – the famous heavy squad – whose names I'd been told in the prison, along with tales of some of the more colourful of their activities. (Lest this be taken as mere prison mythology, I heard the same things years later from a retired Toronto police detective.) One of the detectives had been played by Al Waxman at his most menacing, and, bad luck for us, his fattest. In the meantime he had lost a huge amount of weight in order to do *King of Kensington*. Also, the show was shot in winter, and that was an important point in the plot. It was now early summer, leaves on the trees.

Working out a way to complete it became my problem. I tried to hire Wilton Shiller, a writer living in Toronto who had some reputation as a Hollywood hack. He turned down the job. I showed the footage to various people in the department, Pat Fitzpatrick, Barry Pearson, and with a lot of help I worked out a story line: Waxman was killed, offscreen, and we outlined a series of indoor scenes that worked as a conclusion to what was already in the can. Then Don Bailey came in from Peterborough, and one night, working in the empty offices with me and a production secretary who did the final typing, he wrote the lines. The new material was shot by Don Haldane, an old pro who'd done a couple of other shows, and we had fifty-two minutes ready to go on the air. Peter Madden told me later it was his favourite show.

While a significant amount of my time was being spent on *Sidestreet*, and I passed a lot of evenings in Nicholson's with Brian, before or after the rushes, I still had to keep track of what was happening in other parts of the department, though some of these were increasingly well-organized. John Hirsch had early on decided he wanted to bring in the brightest young directors on the Toronto theatre scene and train them to do TV, and I met with Martin Kinch, Paul Thompson, Ken Gass, Steven Katz and others. George Bloomfield, who'd done a lot of studio directing in the past few years, was supervising the production of a number of half-hour shows on videotape. The intention was to produce a separate series on film, but for a long time no one was put in charge of that, and I commissioned a certain number of scripts, so that something would be available. I commissioned material from film-makers like Martin Lavut and David Cronenberg, both of whom went on to direct their own scripts. A few other scripts were developed and kept in inventory, and later on Gerry Mayer – nephew of the famous Louis B., and a Canadian by birth – took over as producer for the series.

Allan King, best known as a documentary film-maker, the man who made the revolutionary *Warrendale,* had worked out a complicated development contract for a production of *Who Has Seen the Wind,* to be adapted from W.O. Mitchell's popular novel, produced in segments on television and assembled as a feature film. The adaptation was being written by Allan's wife, Patricia Watson, and at some point the script was passed on to me for comment. I remember reading it on the Monday morning train to Toronto, but most of the script editing on this project was done by Alice Sinclair. She and I both thought it would be a good idea for the CBC to adapt a number of respected Canadian novels, and Alice did detailed summaries and editorial reports on a few of the most obvious, but we were never able to get any of these large projects anywhere near production. That fine director Eric Till wanted to produce a Margaret Laurence novel – I think it was *The Stone Angel* – but that project too remained in limbo. Years later someone managed to make *The Diviners.* And while Allan King did make *Who Has Seen the Wind* as a feature, the television version was never produced. There were roadblocks in the way of almost any large scale project – money, organization, a lack of daring at many levels of the corporation.

The part of the television drama department where there was the greatest continuity was Robert Allen's corner of the world. Bob Allen had won everyone's respect as the producer of *Festival,* the series that made ninety-minute dramas in studio, classics or adaptations, though not much Canadian material. I think Hirsch had earlier directed for *Festival,* and that was where Eric Till's brilliant version of Katherine Anne Porter's novella, *Pale Horse, Pale Rider* appeared. Bob Allen was polite, cheerful, and a survivor. Not too long after I arrived he found in the files a copy of my play, *The Hanging of William O'Donnell,* pulled it out and began to circulate it to readers. I wasn't best pleased to have this flawed work from several years earlier appearing, but at some point I'd sent it in, so it was on my own head. I was new, a threat, and I think Bob Allen was using the script, subtly, as a weapon of defence.

Grahame Woods, the one-time cameraman who had become the most successful of CBC scriptwriters, wrote, for Bob Allen – or perhaps it was for Beverly Roberts but it was in was in Bob's hands when I saw it – a dramatization of the trial of Henry Morgentaler, the Quebec trial at which the jury, more or less in defiance of the prosecution and the judge, refused to find him guilty. That trial led eventually to the legalization of abortion in Canada. Trials are always dramatically effective material, and Grahame Woods had written an excellent and careful piece of work. I was one of those who argued very strongly that it should be produced. Bob Allen was nervous about the controversial material, but since the script was an accurate presentation of what had happened in court, it was effectively a news report and at that level couldn't be faulted. I can't remember all the arguments against it. That it was already over, stale news. Various others. Essentially, I think, those who came from a CBC background, Bob Allen, John Kennedy, had been trained to avoid controversy. I argued the other side as forcefully as I could, as did Beverly Roberts, but the script was set aside, and the drama department lost an opportunity to be up-to-date and exciting.

One of John Hirsch's projects was to bring more serious writers in to work side by side with those who were primarily scriptwriters. I did some of this, and so did others in the department. In the first few months Matt Cohen, Marian Engel, Gwendolyn MacEwen, Rudy Wiebe and Alden Nowlan were approached and a number of them discussed or began scripts. (This wasn't a wholly new idea: Fletcher Markle and George Jonas had made similar attempts a couple of years before.) While travelling in the Maritimes I commissioned a half-hour film from Tom Gallant, a writer and singer from PEI, and later Bill Gough from Newfoundland wrote one. Both of these were produced, and Bill Gough ended up doing a lot more writing and becoming a drama producer.

Lists of names, but my days were like that, lists of names of writers, directors, producers who passed by to talk about one thing or another, one after another, and somehow I managed to keep it all straight. Things were always a little frantic. I remember one day saying to Peter Carter as he passed by, 'I have the revision of that scene for you.' 'Shot it this morning,' he said and kept going. Very late one afternoon I was walking back toward my office along a deserted aisle of cubicles, and from somewhere ahead I heard a familiar, sumptuously theatrical voice. Turned a corner, and there in an open space was Tiff Findley, on his knees, his arms raised to heaven, acting out a scene he was planning for some producer. I don't know whether he sold the producer on his idea, but he was certainly doing his damnedest.

John Hirsch wanted Canadian writers introduced to those doing the best work elsewhere. I arranged for two English playwrights and television writers, John Hopkins and Alan Plater, to come to Toronto and spend a couple of days meeting with writers new to television. Found myself at the airport international arrivals gate holding a sign that said ALAN PLATER, and introducing myself to the man who came toward me.

This was in the days before bombing threats and security guards, and anyone could walk into the building. Strangers arrived at my office door wanting to write scripts, and some of them did. A pretty young woman with a lovely Irish accent turned up, Fiona McHugh. She'd done some work for TVO and was interested in working for us. We had a long and intense conversation. We were both fans of Eric Till's *Pale Horse, Pale Rider*. In fact Fiona, when she was thinking of leaving Ireland, had chosen to move to Canada because of that beautiful film, which had been shown on Irish TV. She was very interested in a woman painter called Christiane Pflug. German by origin, she had lived and worked in Toronto, had a significant success, and then committed suicide, not many years before. John Hirsch had talked about wanting to produce experimental works, mixing documentary and drama, so Fiona began to work on a script about Pflug. It was a fascinating idea, but I never quite succeeded in selling it to a producer. Fiona was one of those who attended one of the workshops with the English playwrights, John Hopkins, I think, and later on she was involved in the earliest stages of planning for *The Great Detective*.

Another day my door was darkened by the shadow of a huge stranger. Larry Gaynor, he said he was. Well over six feet, broad as well as tall, he filled the doorway. Graeme Gibson and Peggy Atwood, he announced, had told him he should come and see me. He had known Graeme, it turned out, when they were at military college together. So we talked. Larry had an endless fund of gab, a lot of it stories from his years spent in England, where it appeared he had hung out with the great comedian Spike Milligan, and known, among other raffish and bohemian types, Christine Keeler, the party girl/prostitute who helped to bring down a Tory government when it was discovered that she had been sleeping with both the British Minister of Defence and the Russian military attaché. Larry was endlessly amusing, a voice to match his size. I'm not sure how he convinced me he could write, but he ended up doing a half-hour script called *Fight Night*, about a man who is humiliated by some toughs in a bar and wants to go back for revenge. The script turned out well and was produced, and it was some time later that he told me he'd stolen the idea from a BBC script written by the husband of one of his English girlfriends. Later on he too worked on *The Great Detective*.

During the writing of his first script he appeared one day, filling the doorway as usual, proudly displaying a cast that covered his wrist and forearm.

'My falcon landed too hard,' he said.

On another occasion I walked in the back door of Nicholson's and saw a strange group in one of the booths. Robert Sherrin, a new producer in those days – still at the CBC and now producing *Opening Night* – was being jovially beset by Larry and an equally large military school dropout and scriptwriter, John Ancevich. Bob was smiling politely and appeared to be looking for a way out.

My first year at the CBC ended at about the same time as the shooting for *Sidestreet*, and my life grew a little calmer. I went for walks in the evening, now and then visited with Peter Harcourt, who was teaching film at York and living just down the street. Or I walked over to an apartment near Casa Loma to visit Henry Shapiro, who was on sabbatical in Toronto, where his children were living. *Atlantic Crossings* was in print, and *The Glass Knight* was on its way to publication, revisions, proofs passing by somehow, and one night, I went out for a long walk, and at the corner of Avenue Road and Davenport I had the idea that it might be the first of a four-novel series, using the same four-part musical shape as the long poem, writing about various aspects of life in Kingston. Somehow I knew, that night, more or less what each part would be like – though the last of them wasn't written until five or six years later. Except for occasional bits of script revision, I hadn't written a word for months, but I began to set my alarm for an early hour, drag myself from bed, and do a little work before I left for the office. What I began to write was a story that became the first half of *A Sound Like Laughter,* a very funny story, it seemed to me – though not to everyone – in which all the characters got what they wanted, though mostly by misadventure.

It was some weeks before John Hirsch and his bosses decided whether *Sidestreet* should be renewed. I went back to my other jobs, and since Hirsch wanted to do a series about immigrants to Canada, Brian and I began developing some scripts for such a series. At least one of them was later produced. Finally the decision was made that *Sidestreet* would return, but in the meantime the shape was changed. The original series had used Sean McCann and Stephen Markle as the leads. Sean McCann is a fine film actor, who has worked successfully at a wide range of parts over the years – I saw him recently in the musical *Chicago* – but he is not the classic leading man, not handsome, not dashing, though he communicates a very human warmth. Casting him as the series lead was daring, but there were second thoughts. Stephen Markle was a good-looking young man, but in the first year we increasingly avoided giving him important scenes, as he came across to most of us as insincere and unconvincing. So in the second year Sean was kept on, but only as a senior officer making occasional appearances, and the two new leads were Donnelly Rhodes and Jonathan Welsh.

Donnelly was archetypally handsome, an actor born in Winnipeg, a member of the first crop of students at the National Theatre School, who had spent years in Hollywood, doing all kinds of films, and had most recently played one of the male leads in the popular soap opera, *The Young and the Restless.* He was a relaxed and convincing figure in front of the camera, and Jonathan was a very solid actor who could play whatever lines were given to him. So with a bit more warning this time we set out to create another series of shows. If the series had begun using two former criminals, Don Bailey and Tony Sheer, it continued using two former policemen, Ted Wood and Peter Yurksaitis. Both of them had pounded the beat in Toronto in their earlier lives. Ted Wood in those days had just published a sensitive book of short stories and was an agreeable and modest writer. Later on he began publish a series of crime novels about a tough cop, and on the one occasion when I met him, he appeared to have taken on a new persona – the tough, no-nonsense guy – to go with his new books. John Hunter (later to write *The Grey Fox* and a number of other films) and Barry Pearson also wrote scripts that year, and we were able to explore some difficult areas, a cop who can't keep his personal and professional lives separate (at the end of the show Donnelly arrested his friend and colleague, powerfully played by John Colicos), a teenage boy who is planning to shoot his family. For that show, which had its roots in a real event, I had Barry Pearson reading R. D. Laing, and I think we managed to portray the troubled boy, the family that lives by evasion, without any too-easy psychological explanations. That show was, I think, also the only occasion in two years when one of our cops fired a gun. At the end of the show, Donnelly is forced to shoot the armed and obviously dangerous boy, and afterward he turns away, and the show ends with the camera close on his face. He has tears in his eyes.

By the time the second series of *Sidestreet* shows was completed, I had decided to leave the CBC. I'd been on leave of absence from Queen's, and I had to fish or cut bait. It was pretty clear the entertainment industry was not where I wanted to spend my whole life. I had done little writing, and that was what I most wanted to do. Interesting, though, that when I took a few days off to attend a poetry event at Dalhousie I'd been invited to – to read with Joe Rosenblatt, Louis Dudek, Robert Creeley from the U.S., Jon Stallworthy from England – I came back talking grumpily about egos masquerading as souls. (One definition of the poet.) In television drama ego was ego, and there was a certain healthy brutality to the whole thing. In the second year of *Sidestreet* Brian hired a second story editor, another one from England (though he'd arrived in Canada on his own, and for the second time), and while Gerry Davis was a pleasant man, nice to talk to and work with – we initially split the scripts and each worked on different ones – there was a kind of built-in if polite competition, and before long I had final responsibility for most of the scripts. I had been right more often and more quickly.

The last and most successful of John Hirsch's English imports was Peter Wildeblood. A tall, elegant man in late middle age, Peter had been arrested many years before, tried and imprisoned for being a homosexual – not for any particular homosexual act, far less an assault – but because his correspondence was seized and gave evidence that he had been involved in a sexual relationship with another man. He served his time, and when he got out, instead of slinking away, changing his name and sneaking off to one of the colonies, Peter bravely wrote and published an account of his life and trial, called *Against the Law*. The book was immensely influential, as among the first to give a straightforward account of a homosexual life without defensiveness or any hint of shame.

Peter once told me that the *Sunday Times* had listed his book as one of the most important of the last fifty years, right beside *The Catcher in the Rye*. Not long afterward, and perhaps partly because of that book, the Wolfenden Commission was created, and after its report, the English law was changed.

Of the various English imports, Peter was the one who stayed longest with CBC TV drama. He was both very smart and very charming. In my second year at the CBC, I began to collaborate with him and others on preparations for what was to become *The Great Detective*. More than one person had noticed the book of that title – an account of Ontario's first professional police detective and some of his cases, written and published early in the century – and had suggested the idea of a TV adaptation. Hirsch assigned Peter to create a series, which is of course a much different thing from having a bright idea. Alice Sinclair worked with Peter as story editor, and Fiona McHugh did background research and created a kind of outline of the life of a fictional detective. Writers began to work on scripts – Fred Euringer was one, Margaret Atwood another. She had already written a CBC script based on the story that later became *Alias Grace* and was presumably at home in the nineteenth-century ethos. There was, however, a long hiatus between these early preparations and the actual production of the first shows. By the time production began, I had long since left the CBC, and I was hired to write a script that was produced as *The Case of the Suspicious Soprano*, about a company of travelling performers and a murderer stalking a Victorian theatre.

I enjoyed the speed and energy and melodrama of the time I spent at the CBC. I fought and argued, foolishly no doubt, with John Hirsch, but adventures in the crazyhouse weren't designed for a lifetime commitment. I announced that I'd leave when my contract ran out. That summer I'd settle back in Kingston. I arranged with Queen's that in the fall I would only teach part time, on half salary. I figured I could make up the difference doing free-lance work. For two years I had taken on all the problems that came to me and solved a lot of them. I was strong enough to survive.

No doubt I was changed by the years in TV drama. I was immersed in the problems of inventing and revising plots for hours of every day. When I sat down at six in the morning to work on my new piece of fiction it tied itself into wondrous narrative knots. I had seen with fascination how completely artificial film was, how open to manipulation, even before the days of computer-generated images. Why don't we put the second act first? a film editor said to Brian and me one day when we arrived to watch the first rough assembly of a show. Donnelly had a great story about his early days in Hollywood. He was playing an Indian in some kind of western, and he was instructed to make a certain move and turn and look back. He was asking questions about why or how, and finally the director put a hand on his arm, pointed to the camera, and said, 'Don't worry, chief. Magic box fix everything.'

It was all wonderful, in its way, but I was ready to move on. So at the beginning of the summer of 1976, I left the CBC. Anne Frank invited me and the other story editors round to dinner, and John Hirsch sent me a little note of thanks – we weren't on the best of terms, but I had worked hard to achieve what he wanted – and then it was Kingston and summer, and I had bought a crudely built, unbeautiful house near the village of Ompah in the woods north of Highway 7, a hundred acres of bush with it, and that was part of another new life.

The people I worked with most closely in that intense spell of time are mostly gone now, Pat Fitzpatrick prematurely, Alice Sinclair some years after her retirement, by then a great authority on her beloved Rhodesian ridgebacks, Dick Benner and John Hirsch of AIDS. From the *Canadian Screenwriter* I learned a year or so back that Tony Sheer had died suddenly. Don Bailey's fatal heart attack took him last summer. Brian Walker had his some years ago.

Brian and I worked together constantly for months on end, cobbling together shows at the last possible minute, analyzing, repairing, laughing, drinking too much. Far too many nights spent at a table in Nicholson's, where I drank beer and skipped rounds while he ordered one double rye after another, his body – burly, with a huge gut – seeming almost to inflate as the evening went on, so that he appeared to sail along just above the floor. Now and then he would invite me home with him where his wife Clare, who worked in the casting department, would make dinner. Clare was always polite, but I don't think she was especially pleased at my arrival – she didn't exactly mind, but she would have preferred to be alone with him – however, she was devoted to 'Bears', as she called him, and accepted his comings and goings. On weekends, work left behind, they had a different kind of life. Brian was an avid and well-informed gardener and Saturday found him at work in the yard.

Brian and I kept in touch after I left. I did one script for *Sidestreet*, now with Stanley Colbert – an American import this time, though he'd been in Canada for a while – as executive producer and story editor. Stanley revised my script in a way I didn't much like, but I took the money and ran. Brian stayed at the CBC for a while, but then he and Clare decided they were going to quit their jobs, sell the house where they lived and another nearby they also owned, and spend their lives travelling through Europe in a trailer. And they did it. Brian quit earlier than Clare, and it took a while to sell the properties, so with time on his hands, he went on the wagon, quit smoking and started riding his bicycle for hours a day. The next time I stopped off to see him, I didn't recognize the man who met me. He had lost all his fat, as much as a hundred pounds, I would guess, and this small, muscular man, his face no longer a fiery red, was a stranger.

So they disappeared to Europe and I heard nothing but third-or-fourth-hand reports for a couple of years or more. Then one day the phone rang. 'It's Brian,' a voice said when I answered. They were back. They'd had a fairly serious traffic accident with the trailer and had decided to return to Canada. We began to meet up now and then when I was in Toronto. Brian was working for Nelvana, which made animated films and children's television, their offices near the Toronto waterfront. Brian was smoking, drinking, had put on all the weight he'd previously lost. By now there was no likelihood that we would ever work together again. We were just friends.

He and Clare were separated, he told me one afternoon. He'd been involved with some other woman. It wasn't serious, he said, and Clare should have ignored it. He was living alone in a apartment somewhere on King Street. I think he gave me the new number. By now it was the late eighties. There seemed to be a chance that he and Clare would get back together.

In September of 1989, Nancy and I spent two or three weeks in France, the latter part of it renting Matt Cohen's wonderful little house in Provence, near Carpentras. A fig tree grew in the small yard, herbs growing wild by the sides of the road. We had rented a car in Avignon, and we would arrive at the local *caves* to buy wine at the same time as the growers were delivering the grapes which would be crushed to make the next year's batch. We drove to Orange to see the Roman amphitheatre, into the foothills of the Alps. A whole world of delicate sensuality and ancient history. Sometime after I was back, I was talking to Don Bailey on the phone.

'Did you hear about Brian?' he said.

'No,' I said, without a second thought. 'What's he been doing?'

'He's dead.'

A heart attack in his little apartment on King Street. Dead is dead, of course, but I thought it a sad and lonely way to go.

Months later I heard more of the story from Don Ferguson of the Royal Canadian Air Farce, when they were doing a Kingston show. Chatting at dinner afterward I discovered that Don's wife was Clare's close friend. The night of the heart attack Brian had been on the phone to Clare. They were often in touch, maybe getting back together, and that night they were supposed to be going out to dinner. He called to say he wasn't feeling well, and they'd have to cancel, and while he was on the phone, he felt worse and asked her to send an ambulance. They didn't make it in time. I felt better for hearing that story, knowing that he'd had some human contact at the end, was waiting for rescue.

There's nothing to be done about the past. You tell some stories, don't tell others. Like the letters you don't write. In the dark of night it comes back in intense images, lovely or sad, unaccountable, something that might give the shine to a poem someday. John Hirsch changed my life. I've never met another human being who existed on such a large scale, what they call a sacred monster, I suppose. I remember one day long after I'd left the CBC when I was standing on a Toronto street corner. A small car went by, and I noticed the driver, who was altogether too tall for the little machine, looking as if limbs might begin to hang out in all directions, and he was waving wildly at me as he lurched through traffic. It was John. That was the last time I saw him.

Twenty-one

I watch the action on the TV screen, the mysterious visual effect played out in front of my eyes: we observe everything on the cathode ray tube these days. In this case it's my own heart, seen in an image created by ultrasound, expanding and contracting, valves opening and closing. The Heartbeat Show. Another attempt to figure out why I have palpitations. Earlier on I did a stress test, pleased to find that it showed no sign of coronary artery disease, so in these stormy days of winter I shovel the snow without apprehension.

At our house in the country, we have only a small black and white television, and we watch mainly the early evening news on the CBC. Now and then I turn on *Da Vinci's Inquest,* a curious link to the past, Donnelly Rhodes once again playing a cop for the CBC. The rhythms of police shows are a little different now, more continuity from show to show, a series that is also a serial, more plot lines in each episode, a little different flow to the dialogue, and a freedom to use four-letter words that would have upset John Kennedy – who seemed in my CBC days to represent the old proprieties as well as the demands of the budget. (I hear that John, like much of the CBC it seems, has retired to the West Coast.) The first time I turned on the show, it opened with an astonishing tracking shot, in which Nicholas Campbell, as Da Vinci, moved through and out of a long alley, playing scenes with a variety of characters, the whole thing covered by one extended, flowing shot, several minutes of it, not a single cut. Very inventive and stylish work.

The heart that displays its controlled slippery spasm on the video screen has been propelling me through time since the day I was born. Minutes remembered, minutes forgotten. One night recently, as the winter wind drifted the snow across the roads making them impassable, Judy went to the Franklin stove where a wood fire was burning and set alight all the pages of her diary from a period of life she wanted to be rid of, and the flames moved slowly around the inked lines on those pages, like a shot from an old-fashioned movie, taking a long time to reduce the dense pile of paper to ash.

The ultrasound technician sets up lines on the screen to record the size of the chambers of my beating heart, then gets me to move to a different position on the table so she can record the action from another angle. It's not possible to watch the screen now, but the Heartbeat Show goes on whether I'm observing or not. A few weeks later – after some inexplicable delay – I'll be told that what was seen on the screen and recorded shows a heart that has only slight variations from the normal. No explanation of why it begins to fibrillate, and for the time being it seems to have stopped. I'm immortal again.

Twenty-two

A rowboat rides on the surface of a deep lake with woods on all sides of it, in the distance a cottage where we rented the boat. Somewhere down in this cold clear water there are lake trout, fish which have been destroyed by pollution in most waterways of southern Ontario, and even here in this isolated shining lake the acid rain will take its toll. The four of us, Nancy and I, Maggie and Kate, have driven here down back roads from our old house at the edge of the bush near the village of Ompah where every night the panoply of stars is very bright in the blackness of the wilderness sky, the only other illumination a glimmer from the window of a house half a mile down the road. The land here is part of the Precambrian Shield, largely useless for farming, and in the darkness you remember that there is nothing but woods and barrens between this house and the North Pole.

Maggie is very thin now, is vegetarian, avoiding all refined sugars, an early experiment with hunger, later to become anorexia, which she will survive, though at times it seems a near thing. (Years later as we walked down a street in Toronto, Maggie thin as a whisper, moving slowly, like one grown very old and depleted, I said to her, 'Maggie, I'm afraid you're going to die.' 'No,' she said, 'I'm not going to die,' and somehow she saved herself.) In these her sugarless days, she goes into the woods and her body is safe from the mosquitoes, but the rest of us can't venture into the trees or down to the beaver pond until late summer when the dry weather kills them off. It's not a great place for summer holidays, the plain old house, but we stay here now and then. Over the next few years I will come alone, often in the fall when the bugs are gone, when it's possible to walk through the forest on the old logging roads, to cut up for firewood trees felled by the ambitious beavers.

The land near Ompah was always very beautiful in the autumn, and the house a good place to work, writing on a little portable typewriter – no phone, no mail, no company. Once I came on Thanksgiving weekend, with Maggie and Kate and Bev Stewart's daughters, Hollie and Julie. It was dark as we drove up Highway 38 in the evening, and as we got beyond

Sharbot Lake, we noticed there was snow at the side of the road. When we reached the house the electricity was off. Nothing to do but go to bed. In the morning, we found the power was back, the sun shining. In the woods lay a few inches of new snow, and all the red and yellow leaves hanging over the snow were at their most vivid, the reflected sunlight making them even brighter, a little epiphany of freak weather.

Often I would arrive alone, as late as November when the leaves were all fallen, and the ground was covered with them, the woods all rich browns and grey, the bones of the landscape visible. On these chill nights I sat by the fire and then slept wrapped in a sleeping bag on a couch near the stove.

> The words have vanished with the listeners.
> The Holy Spirit, master of metaphors,
> is only wind over the high country.

> The abandoned world offers its wild particulars,
> leaves in the air, a single leaf on water.

> The jay cries One, One, One,
> and love resolves itself into beauty.

> The rain falls like rain.

The shape of my life was very different after I left the CBC. Nancy had been alone with the children five days a week for the previous two years, and once I was back, it seemed my turn, so I took over quite a bit of the cooking, was usually available to drive the children here and there, for this and that. It was an Olympic year, 1976, and the games were being held in Montreal, with the sailing Olympics held in Kingston. It is part of the Olympic mandate to put on cultural events in conjunction with the athletic ones, and Nancy had been hired to run the cultural happenings in Kingston. A retired military man was the figurehead, but she did most of the programming and nearly all the day-to-day organization, with the help of a local committee and volunteers – I got volunteered to write a historical pageant as framework for performances by all the city's ethnic communities. Nancy worked very long hours all through this. The climax of the Olympic celebrations was a weekend of events outside

Kingston's City Hall, ending with an open-air concert, the street closed to traffic, the night full of the beat of music, swaying bodies.

By now Kate had been doing gymnastics for several years. We would travel with her to Ottawa for regional competitions once or twice every winter. At the Montreal Olympics her hero, the new Russian star Olga Korbut was to appear. We bought tickets and drove up to watch a day of competition. In those days Olympic gymnasts were grown women, and I have photographs from that meet of the world's best, Ludmilla Tourishcheva, who had a mature and solid body, but the tiny slender Olga Korbut was able to throw a certain number of more daring and dramatic moves – all of them commonplace to competitors by now – and increasingly gymnasts, like the Romanian Nadia Comaneci, were unmatured girls, whose low body mass allowed astonishing feats. Kate was never as quick and daring as some of the other gymnasts in her club – in fact she nearly quit the sport after seeing *The Other Side of the Mountain,* a movie about a paralyzed skier, and suddenly realizing that what she was doing was dangerous – but she was a graceful and solid competitor who didn't blow up under pressure as so many did, and she eventually made it as far as the provincial finals.

Half-salary, which was what I was getting from Queen's, was a start on making a living, and Nancy now had a regular income, but I soon began the hustle of freelance work. Peddling my ass up and down Yonge Street. Doug Marshall, the editor of *Books in Canada,* decided that he wanted a column on first novels and gave me the job. W.H. Smith, the booksellers, agreed to subsidize an award for the best first novel of the year, the finalists being selected from those I reviewed most favourably, and in the first year the award was given to Michael Ondaatje for *Coming Through Slaughter,* still perhaps one of his most controlled and perfect pieces of fiction. The other finalists that year were Carol Shields and Mary Soderstrom.

I liked reviewing books, and for the next twenty years or so I reviewed regularly, for *Books in Canada,* the Hamilton *Spectator,* the *Toronto Star, Saturday Night,* the Kingston *Whig-Standard,* and later the *Gazette* in Montreal. It was an enjoyable discipline, and it got me free books and helped to pay for the groceries. I was never a demolition expert. There is a comment by Dr Johnson – I have it at second hand and have never been able to locate the source – that it is the business of a book critic to give an account of his delight. To make a fetish of one's high standards may be only another kind of vanity. It is currently fashionable to believe that we need more harsh reviews, but that is only one more bit of modish cant. Resentment, disguised as critical judgment, is much in vogue and very ugly. I learned, as far back as the CBC days, that you can only properly edit something which, in its essence, you like – you note the places where your response is cold or hesitant or confused and try to understand why. Probably the same is true of criticism. There is no significance in damning what you don't understand. Too much of what purports to be thoughtful reviewing is preoccupied not with art but with reputation – a making and adjusting of lists, along with a certain pleased revenge on those who can be slagged because they have succeeded – the tactics of F. R. Leavis run to seed.

Though a book review is a piece of journalism, its first duty to be lively and interesting, it is also the attempt to come to terms with something new, what aspires to be original, and to describe and place a new thing requires care and a certain amount of self-knowledge or self-analysis, a struggle to discover and examine your biases and limitations, a recognition of what pleases you most easily, what is against the grain of your own sensibility. Without this kind of rumination, a review is nothing more than an outpouring of self-satisfaction. Genuine critical opinion is an accidental byproduct of committed reading. Certainly anyone who has read and written and edited for many years should have developed some instinct for what is alive and vigorous in a piece of writing, but the wish to have opinions, the desire to appear clever or show off your easy sophistication can easily take over. I know I took pride in gratuitous wisecracks that no longer seem so smart. On the other hand the reviewer risks fawning over the emperor's new clothes, especially in considering work that presents itself as novel and experimental. In many ways a review, even more than a piece of imaginative writing (which may rise above itself by some mysterious process in the imagination), is a reflection of the mind that produced it.

On the whole I reviewed books to their strengths, though I don't believe I failed to see and analyze weakness. Books I couldn't enjoy I tried to avoid. There was a period when Lew Gloin at the *Star* sent me all their poetry books, in boxes, and allowed me to review whatever I pleased. He was paying me well, so I went on with this as long as I could, but after a few months, the tedium of it wore me down. Far too much of the poetry was rhythmically flat, merely anecdotal, not poetry at all, really.

One of the books that came to hand from those cardboard boxes was a new collection by Irving Layton. I had reviewed a couple of Layton books in the sixties. At the time I wrote about an increasing bitterness and vitriol in the poems, especially by comparison with the buoyant and inspired poems that had made his reputation. His new poems were less like Nietszche and more like Juvenal, I said, and this acrid quality increased in the poems written during the 1967 Arab-Israeli war. I'd met Irving once or twice in that period (though I never knew him well, as Tom Marshall did), and talking about reviews he once made a sensible comment I've never forgotten. He didn't care what reviewers wrote, he said, so long as they quoted the poetry. That gave the reader some chance to make up his own mind.

When I returned to reviewing Layton in the eighties, I found myself thinking again about the I.A. Richards definition of tone, and about the implicit reader of Layton's poetry, and as I reflected on this, I observed that Layton's sense of his reader was sometimes formal, sometimes merely rhetorical, sometimes theatrical, a little as if he had no precise intuition of anyone there. Here was a powerful voice, a voice that needed to speak, but was on a difficult footing with those who listened in. For all his reputation as a poetic wild man, Layton in person was, in my experience, rather gracious, characterized by old-fashioned good manners, and there were poems that had a quality of grace and formality. In the more hortatory poems there was a hint of 'the orator shouting in an empty stadium'. This wasn't meant to sum up Layton's poetry, nor to denigrate it, but I think still it may help to suggest why wonderful poems appear side by side with silly squibs – that there is no sense of an audience that could tell the difference or might care about it. Or maybe it's an product of Layton's insistence that he had to shatter the decorum of poetic propriety in order to find his own manner and create poems of some scope.

It's a deep and complicated thing, the relationship of the poet and the imagined audience. In a memoir by the Russian writer Nina Berberova I discovered an interesting passage. (She is writing about Gorky.) 'A writer speaks out not to bring forth *in others* a corresponding emotion, but to free himself. The poet who is in need of an audience does not feel alive without it. He exists only in inter-relations with his audience, through the recognition of those who identify with him, and in this case he does not even sense the lack of freedom in which he lives.' Some of Layton's angriest and most pugnacious poems suggest a poet too tediously concerned with his possible audience, boasting to it or reviling it, while many of the finest of the poems rise to a level of classic impersonality.

Layton once began a poem with the line, 'Whatever else, poetry is freedom.' Perhaps in the best case that meant freedom from the audience as well. Al Purdy has an astute remark in his autobiography, *Reaching for the Beaufort Sea*. He's writing about the period in the 1950s when he first met and admired Layton in Montreal. 'Irving seemed to hypnotize himself with his own voice, feeding on echoes of his own opinions. But warm, with a feeling for other people.' Those contradictory things are reflected in the odd mixtures and obliquities of tone in the poems.

I last met Irving many years after I'd written that *Toronto Star* review, when I was living in Montreal – 1993, I think it was – at the awards ceremony for the QSPELL literary awards. The poetry award had just been renamed the A. M. Klein Award, and Irving was there to speak about Klein. He still looked remarkably bright and fit for a man over eighty. After the ceremony I went over to him and said hello, not sure whether he'd remember me, but he did, and while we were chatting an attractive young woman, short and sturdy like Irving himself, came up to where we stood.

'David,' he said in that bright, precise tenor voice, 'let me introduce you to my wife, Anna.' We nodded or shook hands.

'Isn't she beautiful?' he said.

'Oh, Irving,' I heard myself saying, 'aren't they all.'

There was a long silence, and he murmured something polite and said they must have me round to dinner sometime. In the circumstance I didn't think that very likely.

Looking back on that moment and on the words that came out of my mouth – all unthinking – I believe what I said came from the thought, not just of Irving's multitude of wives, but of all the lovely women who had dazzled and captured the imagination of poets, me included. In *The Rain Falls Like Rain* I had published a poem about the 'much-bemused poet', offering a comic view of the dilemma.

Isn't she beautiful? Aren't they all.

During the years when I was making a chunk of my living from book reviews the Hamilton *Spectator* was expanding its review section. I think it was Matt Cohen who put me on to the *Spec*, and one of the books they sent me for review was Leon Rooke's *Fat Woman*. It delighted me, of course, though earlier, in the years when I was doing the Oberon anthologies, I had looked at Leon's stories and rejected them. When I went back to the Oberon series I began to publish him frequently and with pleasure. I have now and then debated with John Metcalf, always a Rooke fan, whether Leon suddenly found his way and began to write with a new energy and focus around the time of *Fat Woman* – as I have always thought – or whether it was only that I belatedly learned to understand him – John's position.

I was once on an Ontario Arts Council jury with Gary Michael Dault, and in some context I said of a writer that I'd written one of my best reviews of his book. Dault was astonished and scornful that I should speak of a book review as a serious piece of writing, but I am unable to distinguish one kind of writing from another. I didn't always live up to my own standards, but I think a book review should be as well-constructed and as keenly written as any other essay, and to be any good, it requires as much thought.

Though I usually avoided books by writers I knew, I made an exception for Alice Munro. Alice never wrote badly, so my job as a reviewer was simply to suggest what she was up to in her latest explorations. I still like the phrase I used when reviewing *Open Secrets:* 'This is gossip informed by genius.' That was quoted, as I knew it would be, on the jacket of her next book, though it was attributed only to the Montreal *Gazette.* I also reviewed two or three Timothy Findley novels, happily enough, since I admired them. I once got a letter from Tiff about my review of *Not Wanted on the Voyage,* praising it as itself a creative act. 'You made discoveries,' he said, and that seemed true. Any serious review should make discoveries. However, as later books appeared I began to feel that he was writing past his best, and I phrased a couple of reviews very carefully, attempting to be critical and respectful at the same time, and then I began to avoid the books. I'd said most of what I had to say, (though one of his best books, *The Piano Man's Daughter,* came out after I'd stopped reviewing him).

Not being an academic I have usually waited until I had a public forum of some kind to do any critical writing. It was only in 1999, when I needed to give a talk at the New Brunswick Writers' Workshop that I finally wrote an essay on Hugh MacLennan which I had planned for years. It was my sense that MacLennan had become unfashionable in the years after his death, and that someone ought to take the time to write about his novels, to make an assessment of the nature and extent of their achievement. The talk I gave that summer became an essay that was published in John Metcalf's *Canadian Notes & Queries* and later in my collection, *Living Here*. MacLennan was a man rooted in history who had lived on into an unhistoric epoch, and one of those writers whose narrative, whatever its sometime weaknesses as fiction, was the embodiment of a decent and dignified mind. He deserved a serious account of his work. The public has a short memory, and we easily lose track of even substantial pieces of work. I was once told a story about Margaret Atwood being asked why, after all her success, she still did publicity tours. 'If I don't, they'll forget me,' she supposedly said. True or not, the story suggests how easily reputation comes and goes.

It was in the summer of the year 2000 that I was offered the chance to review *Near Water*, the final volume of Hugh Hood's twelve-volume series, *The New Age*, for the *Ottawa Citizen*. Hugh had recently died, and I decided that I ought to read and consider the entire twelve-volume series, and the *Citizen* agreed, though they abbreviated my review before publishing it.

As far back as 1973, Hugh Hood had spoken publicly about his projected series of novels, *The New Age/Le Nouveau Siècle*. The first of the books, *The Swing in the Garden*, appeared in 1975, and he had a plan for eleven more, the last volume to appear in what then seemed the distant and mythic year 2000. At the time of his death *Near Water* was in the press. W.J. Keith later wrote about how he had done the final editorial work on the book at Hugh's request when he was too sick to do it himself.

My own experience of *The New Age* went back to the publication of *The Swing in the Garden*, which I admired greatly. It is a book that demands to be read on its own terms, very slowly, and without undue demand for plot and event, but it is a finely articulated portrait of Toronto and childhood, full of love for every single detail of geography and nomenclature, a passionate love affair with the early life of Hood's main character, Matthew Goderich.

The second book, *A New Athens*, moves to eastern Ontario, the city that Hood calls Stoverville, to be found on his map just about where Brockville would be on ours. The opening passage follows Matthew Goderich on a walk through the countryside. Hood, in his obsessive, learned, lyric way enumerates every single plant that Matthew can find around him, a way of defining the uniqueness of this spot on earth. *A New*

Athens ends with the discovery that Matthew's mother-in-law has been, for years, more or less secretly, an inspired visionary painter, perhaps a little in the manner of Stanley Spencer, seeing eternity figured forth in the details of her own small community. What Hugh Hood himself, perhaps, wished to do – though in the middle books he seems to have got distracted from that spiritual intention.

Every two years or so, from 1975 on, a new addition to the series appeared. Oberon Press published the early books, but in 1979, there was a collision between Hugh's oddities and Michael Macklem's oddities that led to the end of their professional relationship. John Metcalf has written a good deal about Hugh Hood's eccentricities. I hardly knew the man, but I heard a revealing story about him from Ron Graham, who was working on a series of programs in which Patrick Watson interviewed writers. Ron phoned and asked Hugh to appear on the series. After ascertaining that he wouldn't have to drive over any high bridges to get to the studio, Hugh said yes. Then he phoned back to say that he'd been asking himself whether Haydn would have appeared on television and decided that the composer wouldn't have done it. Therefore Hugh wouldn't do it. Obviously a deeply serious man in his own quirky way, Hugh had planned for the third volume in his series, *Reservoir Ravine* – which made reference to the stock market crash of 1929 – to appear in the fall of 1979, on the fiftieth anniversary of the event. Michael, always a little inclined to take writers' whims with a grain of salt, didn't take Hugh's insistence on the point altogether seriously, and the book arrived from the printer in the summer. Hugh exploded and began to make what Michael regarded as abusive phone calls to the innocent people answering the Oberon phone. And that was the end of their connection with the series.

It was after the fifth book in Hood's series, *The Scenic Art*, that I, as a reader, abandoned him. The book deals with Matthew Goderich's experience in the theatre, at university and during the first year of the Stratford Festival. I found *The Scenic Art* an annoying book with a hint of smallness very different from the love for the surface of things that was Hood's greatest gift. But prompted by the news of Hood's death, and the chance to review *Near Water*, I reread the first five books and then went on to read the entire series. Looking over the twelve I was confirmed in my opinion of the power of the early books – books as accessible to the serious reader now as when they were written. But I liked *The Scenic Art* no better a second time through. The weakest parts of *The New Age* are those which involve Tony Goderich (who later runs off with Matthew's wife), and show business. None of this has any depth or resonance. Hugh had no real feeling for drama.

The middle books of the series decay from brilliance into a modest competence, though most of them have finely written chapters. However, reading the final book, it seemed to me that the series, which began so brilliantly, ended in splendour – perhaps because he left behind the plots involving show business and the world-famous and returned to seeking eternity in a grain of sand. *Near Water* takes place over a period of a day or so, the last hours in the life of Matthew Goderich.

Matthew Goderich is, as Hugh Hood was, a practising Roman Catholic. He is a believer, not much tempted by scepticism, though perhaps given to a quietist and private form of belief. (It struck me as odd that a long series of books about a Roman Catholic living through the twentieth century should never mention the second Vatican Council – compare Anthony Burgess.) *Near Water* is almost entirely a discursive book, which follows the mind of Matthew Goderich, learned, quirky, comical, slightly manic. Three chapters into the book Matthew suffers a stroke while lying on an old recliner on the dock, and the rest of the narrative recounts his attempt to move off the recliner and drag himself up to the deck above. It is a powerful, harrowing and beautiful account of a man moving toward death. One might be reminded of some of Beckett's hopeless cripples, except that Matthew is possessed of faith and hope. He moves in the company of angels. A passage from one of the earlier novels in the series is perhaps the correct gloss on all this.

'Many of the greatest painters, musicians, and writers of our time have been persons of devout and contemplative temperament. The roll of worshipful, mystically inclined artists in this century is a long one. But the theoretical critics of the present time deny their cousins the artists their true function. Theoretical analysis of the power and the action of the arts is often perverse, even untruthful. This has helped to persuade many lesser artists to surrender all claim to special wisdom.' Hugh Hood did not surrender that claim. *Near Water* is the narrative, erudite yet lighthearted, of a man moving closer to the Divine Presence. I'm not sure that the conventional story of Canadian literature has a place in it for any such eccentric and visionary achievement, but the book is there in print, and may be rediscovered.

Back in the 1970s when all Canadian writers were feeling their oats, Hugh Hood set out to create a masterwork in many volumes. In my view, that great project didn't succeed, but the early books are brilliant, and at the end, in the face of incapacitating illness, he made something like a masterpiece. These days fashion has turned another way, toward the year's prize-winners, toward the books that have made it abroad, and I have a sad suspicion that my little review in the Ottawa *Citizen* was the only account of the whole series to be written. But one can imagine Hugh, if his faith bore him out, at rest in – let's say the middle reaches of Purgatory – smiling at it all.

Not all the reviews I wrote over the years were literary. Review books sometimes offered the chance to learn about other things. I made discoveries of other sorts. I remember my pleasure and fascination in reading Richard Dawkins' *The Blind Watchmaker,* a book in which he sets out to show – *pace* Hugh Hood – that the rich and beautiful forms we observe in living organisms don't justify teleology, the assumption of a divine creator with a complicated plan. Given the scale of the universe and its age, life in all its complexity could perfectly easily have happened by chance.

Happenstance, coincidence, miracle: those we love we might easily never have met. A book review by the physicist Freeman Dyson tells me about Littlewood's Law of Miracles, which defines a miracle as something with a one-in-a-million chance of happening, then shows that we experience about a million events a month, so that we are likely to experience one miracle a month. (See Carol Shields' wonderful stories in her book, *Various Miracles.*) How many miracles I must have neglected to note and record, though of my hundreds of poems, a good number are accounts of moments of blessedness.

Twenty-three

In 1976, back from the CBC, settled once more in the old stone house in Portsmouth Village, I had established what was to become my regular pattern of life for the next years, frequent trips to Toronto looking for work, intervals in Kingston spent writing in the big room at the back of the house which we'd added when doing renovations a few years before, an upright piano on one wall, a couch that pulled out to make a bed for visitors on another. I sat in front of a wide pine table, staring out the window into the garden and across the neighbour's yard. I had arranged my timetable so that I taught my course on the fiction of the nineteenth century in a single weekly seminar three hours long. The other days were free for looking for work or doing it. One of the people I began to work for was John Douglas, recently arrived in the radio drama department at CBC. I had met John, as I've said, when I was working for Straw Hat Players. In November of 1976 Quebec elected the first Parti Québécois government. In the previous years I'd watched with fascination the growth of separatism. I'd read Pierre Vallières, Hubert Aquin, set *The Glass Knight* during the weeks of the October crisis and the book – which had just appeared in print – attempted to reflect the times. John Douglas commissioned a play in which I once again used the unsettled state of Quebec politics as part of a story. This one attempted to take seriously the common metaphor of a political marriage, a divorce. It was called *You Can't Hear What I'm Saying,* and it told the story of a woman who is overwhelmed with discontent in a marriage that seems, superficially at least, untroubled. In the background, the political events of the day were overheard – a lot of material straight out of the news, the recorded sound of real happenings – the connection of the two elements implicit but not spelled out. The title stated the story's theme, the near-impossibility of the political dialogue that was going on.

The script was ready to go into production when John Douglas, who couldn't have been much over forty, had a heart attack, so Bill Howell, a poet who had also recently arrived in the department, took over and did the actual production. John came back, and we worked on one or two other scripts, but then he decided to step away from production, become a freelance and write, and another figure from Straw Hat Players came to radio drama. Bill Davis and I had been good friends, and he had encouraged and directed *Katy Cruel* back in our university days. We soon started on a script called *Moving In*, a half-hour comedy about two young lovers who have decided to share an apartment. Their moving day – all their varied possessions loaded on a rented truck – is as crazed and stressful as these things always are, and it nearly ends the relationship. But they survive.

So I was hustling and writing and teaching. Once a week I met a group of bright senior students at Queen's – including, in my first year back, a young woman who was one of the brightest students I ever knew, a wonderful mind; she graduated and vanished, as students do. Under the rubric of nineteenth-century fiction I was free to teach whatever I pleased, and increasingly I concentrated on a few great novelists, two or three books by Jane Austen, at least two by Dickens, a couple each by George Eliot and Thomas Hardy, the best of good company. I was reading first novels and turning out a column once a month, and during the period that I was working with John Douglas, and then with Bill, I also wrote an episode of *Sidestreet* for Brian Walker and Stanley Colbert – it was called 'Revenge'. I did some script doctoring on a story about the 1837 rebellion and also on a TV adaptation of a play by Lister Sinclair, and a little later wrote an episode of *The Great Detective* for Peter Wildeblood and Alice Sinclair. And I was editing a book.

I had attended, in the autumn of 1976, some sessions of a weekend seminar on the work of Margaret Laurence. At one of those sessions I argued with John Moss – who was now teaching at Queen's – about the quality of Canadian literary criticism. Soon enough I had decided to put together a collection of critical essays, which I hoped would be richer than journalism but with a wider scope than academic criticism. Michael Macklem, always ready to co-operate with a bright idea, agreed to publish it. The book included an essay on the films of Allan King by Peter Harcourt, one called 'The Literature of Quebec in Revolution' by Kathy Mezei, a former Queen's graduate student now teaching at Simon Fraser, a feminist piece on Alice Munro by Bronwen Wallace, an essay on theatre, long discussions of James Reaney and Margaret Laurence. The whole thing, which took its title from the George Woodcock essay on Laurence, was called *The Human Elements*, and my introduction said, 'This book begins with the assumption that Canada now has a mature literary culture.' I had learned from John Hirsch to be confident and assertive. The book was a lively and varied collection, and I believe it sold well. Not long after it came out I began to work on another book of essays, but this time essays not on art in itself but on the complex interplay between art and the world of money and politics. The book was called *Love and Money: The Politics of Culture*. The contributors ranged from Frank Milligan, a career civil servant and former associate director of the Canada Council, to John Metcalf, who contributed a piece of high-spirited satire from the novel that was to be published as *General Ludd*. It included an essay from Michael Macklem called 'Seed Money' in which he argued that Canadian literary books are almost certain to lose money, and that the idea that publishers can be taught to be more businesslike and thus make a profit on them was a foolish one. That was a provocative argument, but it was coming from a small Canadian publisher who had reached a peak of success – good books, inventive design – and Michael knew what he was talking about. There were other essays on television, censorship, one on the low quality of music criticism and a deterioration of CBC music broadcasting. My introduction was an analysis of some of the issues involved in the attitudes toward highbrow and popular art. *Love and Money* did well. Michael Macklem used to like to recount how the limousines would arrive from various government departments to pick up copies of the book for bureaucrats who were too busy to walk to the store.

All through this period I was writing fiction, first a novel called *Jennifer*, and then a second section of *A Sound Like Laughter* in which everything that happens in the first part unwinds and is rewoven in different form. *Jennifer* was to be the second movement of the four Kingston novels, and was a firmly middle-of-the road book, about a woman alone with her children and about the question of responsibility. Middlebrow? Well, yes. Who is responsible, the story asked, for those who aren't responsible for themselves? Jennifer works in a mental hospital, teaching a form of symbolic communication to those who can't speak. (I had learned about the Bliss symbols while doing research for Westminster Films – Don Haldane's company – research that was meant to lead to a documentary, but that film never got made. Still, everything gets saved and used somewhere.) From the prison days I knew about the pain and impossibility of institutions. Of hope for the hopeless. We lived only a block from the gate of a major mental health facility, so I was always aware of the lost lives behind the walls of those neat buildings on their long green lawns. Little groups of retarded adults arrived at our door every Hallowe'en. The troubled young man who comes to Jennifer's door early in the novel was someone I might have known; however, all the specific details of this embodiment were invented.

The book placed itself in the centre of the daily life of the middle classes – though at one of those moments when suddenly everything in life goes wrong – and that's probably the reason it sold, in its various editions, better than any other novel of mine. More than one reviewer said it was like a soap opera but better written, more truthful. An odd memory: my daughter Kate, fifteen at the time it was published, used to pick it up and reread it when she wanted a book that offered comfort and reassurance.

In ways much of my life was as simple and straightforward as Jennifer's. For all the apparent flurry and bustle of the list of projects I was involved in, most of my days were spent at my writing table or cooking dinner or reading books or perhaps watching television with my kids. That's what writers do: they sit and write, and when they're not writing they think. I had also by now begun to sing regularly in a choir at an Anglican church near the university; it was directed by my friend Bill Barnes and had enough good singers, some of them Queen's students, to make music of a decent quality. This was the beginning of a return to singing that made music more and more central to my life for the next twenty years.

By the time *Jennifer* was published, Nancy had taken a job as the manager of the Grand Theatre, a nineteenth-century building that had been renovated as Kingston's civic auditorium, and that position – the job she was born for in many ways – was the focus of her life twenty-four hours a day for the next fifteen years. She turned the placid, feeble institution, dark many nights of the year, into a place where there was always something happening, saw it through two renovations, the construction of a second small performing space, opened a café in a courtyard off a back lane, began a children's series, a jazz series, a summer theatre, produced an inventive version of *The Nutcracker* with the Belleville ballet school and soloists brought in from the National Ballet. Everyone in the city knew her by name. I was on her list of volunteers for this and that, and our old friend Christiaan became the bartender. On busy nights I would work as a second bartender, and the two of us took great pride in the number of drinks we could pour during a fifteen-minute intermission.

Most of the poets who had been part of Kingston life had left, but Bronwen Wallace had returned after a few years in Windsor, Ontario, no less political, no less committed, but married, with a son, and immensely more relaxed and amused. I often remember her story about arriving back in Toronto by airplane after a visit to the West Coast that was part of an attempt to sort out her emotional life. Her little son Jeremy was with her, and as the plane was coming in to land, he said in a voice loud enough to be heard all down the rows, 'OK, Bron, are you going to live with Chris, or with my dad, Ron?' When *Jennifer* was still in manuscript, I asked Bronwen to read it for me and offer suggestions. In those days, working with her partner Chris Whynot, she was making films as well as writing her poetry. I regularly wrote letters of support for her grant applications.

Oberon Press published her first book – a volume shared with Mary di Michele – in 1980, and two more after that. I remember she came to me late in that decade, when she had an offer from McClelland and Stewart and wondered about the morality of accepting it, since Oberon had been the publisher to make her reputation. I could only say that I thought she had to seize the opportunity that had been offered. It was the idealism of the small presses, much of the time, that brought books by new writers into being, but if the writer hoped to find a large audience, maybe even to make a living, chances are that would happen with a house that had a bigger budget for promotion, a bigger sales staff.

By now Bron was a figure in Kingston life. She wrote a newspaper column and made frequent appearances with Peter Gzowski on *Morningside*. In those days, to be a regular with Gzowski was to be one of the immortals. I met up with her on the street, at parties. I remember running into her and Chris on Princess Street, and she threw her arm around my shoulders, which was what I needed most on that particular day. Once I was bartending at the Grand on my birthday, and Bronwen appeared with Patrick Lane and Lorna Crozier to invite me to meet them and Tom for a drink when I finished. Her feminist convictions had led her to spend part of her time working at Interval House, a women's shelter, and the horror of what she'd seen there turned up in the poems, and yet the book she was working on was called *The Stubborn Particulars of Grace*. Her poems, which I'd once described as being like good conversation, were growing larger in scope, more fully poetic. She had begun to work on a book of stories to be called *People You'd Trust Your Life To.*

Then it was 1989 and I was on the stage of the Grand Theatre, the eight hundred seats full. Bronwen was dead and I was one of the two hosts (it seems the wrong word, but what other is there?) at her memorial service – which went on far too long because so many people wanted to express their affection and sense of loss. In her last weeks, Bronwen had been involved in the planning for the event and sent a message asking me to do this. In those days she was being cared for by shifts of friends as hour by hour she lost out to a cancer first discovered in the cells of the cheek. I would run into Chris Whynot at the city swimming pool and get the latest bulletins on how things were going.

Sometimes it seemed that in her last days Bron, dying so prematurely, was becoming, to her friends and guardians, a kind of feminist saint and martyr, and the fervour of those who were committed to seeing her through was not always discriminating. A close friend felt shut out – she wasn't part of the team. After Bron's death someone organized a showing called 'The Films of Bronwen Wallace', without so much as contacting Chris Whynot, who had collaborated on every one of those films and had, I believe, led her toward film in the first place. Bronwen greatly deserved loyalty and care, but zealous enthusiasm is always a dangerous thing.

And Tom, along with Bronwen, was always part of my life in Kingston – though he spent a sabbatical year in a Toronto apartment and kept it on for a year or so afterward as a *pied-à-terre* – I sometimes stayed there if it was empty. Other times I rented a hotel room, or stayed with Brian Arnott, a theatre consultant that Nancy had hired for the Olympics, or with Don and Anne when they moved back – in each case discovering new areas of Toronto. Tom was beginning to write fiction. He had invented a witty and rueful academic poet named Harold Brunt and created a delightful story about the adventures of Harold and his difficult wife, Rosemary. When he showed it to me, the new comic narrative was interspersed with a lot of material from an ill-fated earlier novel, less interesting in itself and which weighed down the narrative. I came up with a suggestion that allowed him to keep the idea of an earlier serious narrative written by Harold but reduced it to a minimum and gave it a more dramatic form. 'Why did I kill Angela?' the first chapter begins, and off we go. Tom was grateful for the bright idea, and dedicated the book to me. He was to return the editorial favour when I wrote *The Only Son* a few years later; he remarked that he found one section boring, and I cut eighty pages.

Not long before *Rosemary Goal* came out in 1978 a young couple who had been working in a bookstore in Ottawa had moved to Kingston and opened a bookstore called Printed Passage. In future years the store kept expanding and moving to new locations until it was swallowed by Indigo. In their first store Wayne Oakley and Barbara Allen were keen to have things happen, to create excitement, and I proposed a joint launching for Tom's book and for John Metcalf's book of two novellas called *Girl in Gingham*, which had also just arrived from Oberon. John lived not far outside Kingston near the hamlet of Delta. Wayne and Barbara were keen, and it was a high-spirited and boozy occasion.

It was around this time that I was asked to judge a student writing contest at Queen's. The poems were presented anonymously. One of them stood out as notably better than the others, and I gave it the prize. Might never have known who had written it but Tom, who kept track of things, told me that the winning poem was by a young man named Steven Heighton whose work interested him. It was through Tom that I first met Steven some time after that. Like Tom he graduated from Queen's, went away – in his case to Japan and various other parts of the orient – then returned to Kingston to write. In 1989 and 1992 I used two of his short stories, inventive pieces with their roots in his Japanese period, in the Oberon best short story series. Steve was by then the editor of *Quarry*, able to handle the increasingly difficult Bob Hilderly when few others could, and he was central to the Kingston writing scene. More and more new people were arriving in town, Diane Schoemperlen, Merilyn Simonds, Wayne Grady. Douglas (as he still was then) Fetherling took a job at the *Whig-Standard* and wrote a history of the paper.

Steve Heighton was always a good friend to Tom, who was very fond of him. In 1991 when I suddenly couldn't find Tom – we had planned to meet up at a Writers' Union meeting, but he didn't turn up and no one had seen him – Steve was one of the people I phoned. Steve and his wife Mary went round to Tom's house – I'd driven past, noticed mail piled up in the box – trying doors and peering in windows, while I, on a whim, phoned one of the hospitals and found him there. He'd had a heart attack and told no one. Tom, always made uneasy by affection, was quite irritable with Steven and me because we'd found him and told others about it, though I suspect he was secretly pleased that someone had cared enough to go looking. He later, with typical indirectness, made a kind of roundabout apology for his initial irritability.

After *Jennifer* appeared in the fall of 1979 I got a letter from an editor named Diane Lutynec (soon to marry and become Diane Young) who was working for Stoddart Publishing. She liked *Jennifer* and wondered if I had anything they might look at. In fact I did. By now I had written the second half of *A Sound Like Laughter,* and Michael Macklem at Oberon had seen it and turned it down. The comedy of the book was perhaps a little harsh. ('Whistling in the graveyard' was Michael's phrase: the other thing I remember him saying about the book is, 'You cannot tell a lie.' Meaning the story was too painfully true to be funny, I suppose.) I shipped the manuscript to Stoddart and got on with finishing *The King's Evil,* the very odd book I'd started a few months before, an account of a half-mad, obsessive, embittered radio producer on leave of absence from the CBC, who becomes immersed in a bizarre world of historical fantasy. Well, that's one way to put it. The book includes material about art forgery, ciphered messages, an escaped slave in Virginia, a transvestite English aristocrat and what else not. I think of it as a book I might reread some day, but not quite yet. Like the earlier play, *The Hanging of William O'Donnell,* it was story that insisted on bursting the bounds of my previous work – for better or for worse. Writing in *Maclean's,* John Bemrose said it was my best novel, and even the more negative reviews treated it with a certain wary respect, as if it could bite.

While Oberon was moving toward the publication of *The King's Evil,* Stoddart accepted *A Sound Like Laughter.* And at just about this point in my life I gave up my job at Queen's. In the spring of 1980, as planning began for the next academic year, it became clear that I would have to alter my timetable – teaching the same number of hours, but over two days a week, not one. Also the course was to be split with a brilliant young teacher – once my student – and there was a hint that her section might be more popular. This had never happened to me before, and it made me think twice. Maybe the best of my teaching was finished. I'd always said that I would someday quit doing what I'd begun from economic necessity – and I thought perhaps it was now time to call my own bluff. My two years at the CBC had taught me that I could survive outside the university. I went home one day and announced to my family that I was considering quitting. Nancy and Maggie both instantly said that I should do it. Kate was a little more worried that we might all go hungry, but by now Nancy was working full-time at the Grand Theatre, Maggie was in university, and Kate was in high school. If I was ever going to walk away from the university, this was the time. I told George Whalley, once again department head, that I was leaving, took my share of the pension plan – $14,000 dollars it was – put it in a savings account, and began life as a freelance writer. (Twice during the next decade, Queen's called me at the last minute to ask if I would teach a single course for a year – for the derisory sums that sessional lecturers are given. I said yes and it went into the pot with the rest of my freelance earnings.) Quitting a tenured position to earn my living by writing was one of the braver things I've done, and I always found it annoying that even ten years later it was widely believed that I still taught at Queen's.

It was in my generation, and perhaps the one just before, that the universities – expanding to accommodate the students born in the period of rising birth rate after the Second War – became a home to a majority of young writers. (Less true now perhaps, though creative writing departments have expanded.) It's possible that the growth of the universities made possible the increase in volume of Canadian writing by offering a safe shelter to those who wanted to create poetry and novels, but I had always felt some mistrust of the comfortable academic environment. At my best I had been a good teacher, but as Claudette had pointed out to me, I didn't really want to teach. I wanted to learn, and going back to even the greatest works of art, year after year, had the potential for stagnation. Better to be on the run than risk becoming stale.

The academic world I was abandoning was seen at its worst in a University of Ottawa conference on Morley Callaghan to which I foolishly accepted an invitation in the spring of 1980. A few weeks before the event, I got a call from David Staines, who was organizing the conference, asking me to be on the closing panel. I think he'd got the idea from Kerry McSweeney at Queen's, who, censorious himself, liked to encourage my sharp tongue. I said no to David Staines' request. What I told him was that I didn't much like most of Callaghan's work, but I saw no point in publicly attacking a writer who had worked hard and was now an old man. Staines persisted. The other members of the final panel would be Leon Edel and Alfred Kazin.

Vanity is a terrible thing: I thought I would like to be on a panel with those two big names and I said yes. Well, I was punished for my vainglory. David Staines had misled me, of course, and the final panel did not contain either of the great names, though I believe Leon Edel passed through the conference at some point. In fact the only amusing thing about the whole event was the trip there. I had spent the previous day in the damp cellar of the house near Ompah, trying without success to prime the pump. I had been much splashed with water and mud and had no way to clean myself up. When I tried to start the car to drive to Ottawa, I found the battery was dead, so I had to push the car down the steep driveway, jump in, put it in gear and let the clutch out abruptly to turn over the engine and get a spark. The same thing when I dropped off garbage to the local dump – fortunately at the top of a slope. By the time I arrived at the Chateau Laurier I was muddy, sweaty, in general a mess, but like the character in a commercial for American Express that was showing at the time, I got into the shower, changed my clothes, and emerged looking quite respectable.

The papers delivered at the conference were, for the most part, strikingly tedious, and worse, never came to grips with Callaghan in any serious way. I tried to sit still. Time came for the final panel. I had expected a spontaneous discussion based on what we'd heard and what we'd thought of it. No such thing. The panel chair read from his notes a summary of all the tedious papers we'd already suffered through. Another panel member read a flat little disquisition about Callaghan's short stories. By now my anger was ready to boil over. Rage, I've found over the years, makes me articulate, and when my turn came I spoke at some length, without notes, suggested that the papers we'd heard, while describing this or that element in Callaghan's writing, didn't confront the fact that the books just didn't work. I used the analogy of a chair, which could be described in great detail without revealing that if you sat in it, it would collapse beneath your weight. I had recently read a very early Callaghan novella, *An Autumn Penitent* – one of the more convincing pieces I'd come across – and I argued that its comparative success was due to the fact that it was about a psychopath, and that Callaghan's rather inert style suited that subject as no other. It seemed to be the reason the earliest books had achieved an international reputation. 'One could legitimately say that the central characters in all these books are psychopaths, that what Callaghan is doing is providing a delicate and fascinating dramatization of the psychopathology of lower-middle-class life,' I said.

(I know all this because the sessions was recorded and later published.) Then, I argued, Callaghan had been led astray by Maxwell Perkins and Jacques Maritain. 'From World War II on, Callaghan's fiction is,' I decreed, 'negligible.' And so on – not bad for a spontaneous outburst delivered without notes, but I had of course fallen into the trap prepared for me. I was playing the fool for them, the literary clown, a performance delightfully outrageous. That was my place in the academic world, and I was wise to get out of it.

In front of me as I write this is a little pile of file cards, each with a date at the top, and a list of projects. The first of them is dated March 1980, and I assume that I wrote the list because I had just decided to quit my job and I knew I had to keep turning out new work if I was to survive. At the top of the list is a title that no longer means anything to me. I would guess that it was a television script that was never produced, and some-how the details, producer, story editor, history, have entirely vanished from my memory: very strange. The second title on the list is *Party Girl*. This was a radio play that I was working on for Bill Davis, about a young woman who has come to the big city and wants to lead a raffish, adventurous life. I was often uncomfortable with the rather static and theatrical form that too often characterized radio drama, and over the years I found ways of playing around with it. In *Party Girl*, the entire show is made up of what is captured by a small tape recorder that the central character has bought. She uses it as a diary, and sometimes tapes what's happening in her life. This made the rhythm of the script edgy and irregular. Scenes never reached their conventional climax, and the listener was constantly pitched rapidly forward into new events. (Fifteen years later I played with a similar kind of rhythm in a novel, *The Time of Her Life*. Readers noticed there was something odd about it, but only Peter Harcourt put his finger on exactly what it was – he likened its rhythm to the films of Jean Pierre Lefebvre.)

By the time *Party Girl* was ready for production, Bill had been fired by the new head of radio drama, Susan Rubes, and the script was produced by Yuri Rasovsky, who came from National Public Radio in the U.S. We discussed casting, and I suggested, as I had to Bill, that the lead was perfect for Chapelle Jaffe. I had seen her work on television and on stage, and she had a wonderful ability to create memorable working class characters. Rasovsky, in the way of directors, wanted to be very clever ('I want to cast against type'), and he used Chapelle as the best friend, and for the lead he used Mary Pirie. I was present at some of the taping, and I thought that she was acting up a storm in a way that was transparently false. Still did when I heard the show cut together, but she won the ACTRA award for Best Actress for that performance.

Also noted on my March 1989 list is a manuscript by Anita Mayer. The manuscript was about Anita's experience in the Second World War, as a Dutch Jew hidden by a gentile family, found, sent to Auschwitz and to a work camp where she survived, though all the rest of her family was lost. An Anne Frank who came through it, and in fact Anita had met Anne Frank in Auschwitz. My first connection to Anita was by way of Claudette. Anita lived in Prescott, but after I read the manuscript I met up with her at a hospital in Kingston where her husband was being given cancer treatment. The way she told her story was well-thought-out, honest, but she wasn't an experienced writer, and the book needed a lot of work. I sent a sample to Oberon, and it was agreed that I would do the very extensive editing. What I always said – accurately – was that all the words were Anita's, but all the punctuation, including paragraph breaks, was mine. The book was published as *One Who Came Back,* and is still in print, partly because Anita, believing it to be a story that must continue to be told, has kept on making school visits, giving talks, getting the book into people's hands. I had grown up haunted by the stories of the camps, and it pleased me to have helped keep one of the stories alive.

Next on the list is a title: The Home Children. A year or so before I had written, on commission, a poem which was to be set to music and performed by schoolchildren as part of the local observation of the International Year of the Child. It was Jim Coles, music consultant to the local school board, who asked me to do it, and the music was written by Clifford Crawley, a composer who taught at Queen's. I attended the occasion in a local arena when the piece was performed by a vast gang of schoolchildren. Couldn't make out a word of the lyrics, but I used the slightly Blakean little poem in a book. Not long after the performance I saw Jim Coles at a concert. He came up to me at intermission, smiling, and said he'd had an idea for something bigger, an opera. I would write the book, Cliff the music, and somehow it would use a gang of kids and be produced in co-operation with the school board.

'I don't really like opera,' I said.

'Well, think about it,' he said, as people do in that situation.

Within a week I had an idea. There had been at least two books published about the home children, poor kids who were sent out from England by philanthropists, including the famous Dr Barnardo, to work on farms in Canada, the idea being that they would have a healthier life than was possible in the slums of England. Since children were central to the story, it made the perfect subject for an opera to be done with the schools. So in 1980 I was writing the libretto for what became *Barnardo Boy*. It was produced two years later.

Also on that old file card is the second volume of critical essays which I was now editing: *The Human Elements 2*. Then the list contains a couple of things that were abortive, and finally a note that makes clear that I was thinking about a summer narrative, to be the last of the set of four Kingston novels. I'd known, for several years, that I wanted to write a summer book, all sensuousness and sensuality, but it had lain dormant. I think what propelled it into being was the thought of bringing back the character of Elizabeth from *The Glass Knight*, by now a poet, who, after a lesbian affair in England, has chosen to be celibate. Her rejection of the life of the senses gave the story the right dramatic edge.

On the next card, dated four months later, several of the same projects appear, are completed, crossed off. More ideas that would never be realized. At the bottom of the list it says Spy Novel, with a question mark after it. I had an idea, and at some point wrote a page or two, but I was also working on revisions of *The King's Evil*, and starting to write the novel that would become *It Is Always Summer*.

What happened to that spy novel is a typical story of free-lance life, mine anyway. I had the beginning of a plot, an idea to be developed, but the day came, later in the year, when I needed to make some money. In the fall I went to Toronto saying to myself that I mustn't come back without a job. Bill Davis was gone from radio drama, and I knew none of the producers except Bill Howell, and he and I could never work together. I walked into the office of Paul Mills, who had just been hired to produce one-hour radio plays, introduced myself and suggested that I had some experience and would like to work for him. He asked if I had any ideas, and I recited the plot that was intended to be a spy novel. He looked interested and asked if I could I give him something on paper. I was staying with Don Bailey out on Logan Avenue, and that night I appropriated Don's typewriter and produced a proposal of a page and a half. The next morning I was in Paul Mills' office with the proposal, and he bought it. It became a radio play called *Old Wars*. Urjo Kareda, who had been an arts journalist at the *Globe* and later ran Tarragon Theatre, had been hired as a story editor, and he worked with me on the script. It was produced and broadcast at least twice, and was the beginning of a very happy working relationship with Paul Mills that went on for the next two or three years until he too vanished, to be part of the committee planning the new CBC headquarters. Nearly ten years later, in 1989, *Old Wars,* expanded and turned into prose fiction, was published as a novel by Viking Penguin. The *New York Times* called it 'moody, suspenseful, and very well-written'.

Twenty-four

A rainy Saturday in late winter and I am sitting behind a folding table. On the table a few books for sale. One of the regional arts councils called to say they were sponsoring a display at which local artists could sell their wares, and would I like to come? Not what I much wanted to do, but since my neighbours had the goodness to ask, I thought I should turn up. This is where I live my life now. Then the event got postponed for one week because of a blizzard, then another on account of more stormy weather, and Hugh MacDonald, who was to share the table so we could keep each other amused, is in Nova Scotia. Around me sit men and women with hooked rugs, needlework, baked goods, a man caning a chair, a musician selling his discs, and a few painters.

The man hooking rugs is explaining how he gets his material from second-hand clothing stores, women's old wool coats that are cut into thin strips and hooked through the canvas to form a geometrical design or a map of the island. In the same way, I suppose, I rip apart old material from my life and turn it into new stories, The man caning chairs explains that you can calculate the price of his work by counting the holes around the edge of the seat: its costs seventy-five cents a hole. His cane is soaking in a little tin of water beside his chair.

The handsome woman who's selling baked goods picks up one of my books and reads a poem to herself. She's recently come to the Island and plans to open a practice in alternative healing. The Island woman whose skillful watercolours are displayed on the table next to mine gets to telling me about an occasion when she found herself introducing two recent arrivals to each other, both women divorced but well off, both very 'upper-Canadian' – which means something between stylish and snob-bish, or maybe both together. She tells me how one of them introduced her to a man said to be an illegitimate son of Edward VIII. I remember a similar story used to be told about Edward VII breeding bastards on his royal tour. It's an archetypal story, and it hardly matters which Prince of Wales bounced the local beauty.

On a rainy day after two postponements, there's not much of an audience, maybe a half dozen people pass through the large room, but just after noon musicians arrive and perform, Celtic fiddle tunes with guitar and piano, a tall, dark girl of maybe eighteen tossing off jigs on the fiddle while beating time with her feet, which are clad in comic pink socks with pigs on the toes. A couple of painters buy copies of my books, and in mid-afternoon I pack up the rest and set off to drive home in the rain, along the labyrinth of small country roads, past fields still covered with snow, woodlots of dark spruce. The roads I follow are familiar, but if I turned off the known route, I would be lost, though the criss-crossed old roads of the Island create a web in which you can eventually find your way – just keep driving and sooner or later you'll notice a sign or something that looks familiar. Many of the old farm buildings I pass are becoming derelict. The life of small self-sufficient farms, though it lasted longer here than in some parts of Canada, is gone now. Farm fields are bigger, the work more industrialized, dependent on heavy machinery and modern chemicals. There is land empty, for sale cheap. This is a place where people have come to escape city life. Potters, artists, musicians are hidden away on these country roads.

Twenty-five

In 1982 Clifford Crawley's opera on my libretto was in production, and I was onstage as Dr Barnardo. The story concerns an elderly man who is roughed up by a group of kids, then helped by a young woman who goes with him back to his apartment, where he begins to tell his tale, how he became an orphan, was picked up by Dr Barnado out of the night streets of London and sent to Canada. Throughout the tale, crossfades blend the story of the present with past events. At times it is quite operatic – the aria of the dying mother, two brothers parting in war, Dr Barnardo's favourite rhetorical set piece. At moments the old man and his child self overlap, especially in his performance at a school concert of those impassioned lines of Victorian rhetoric, Ernest Henley's poem, 'Invictus'.

The show was produced as a collaboration, by Jim Coles for the Kingston Board of Education, Steve Smith as manager of the Kingston Symphony, and Nancy as manager of the Grand Theatre. It was directed by a local teacher, Gord Love, and conducted by Jim Coles. The old man, the figure who had to carry the weight of the show, was played by the wonderful Jan Rubes, Czech originally but Canadian for many years, now reaching the end of his long career as an operatic bass, and about to begin a new career as a film actor, most notably as an Amish patriarch in *Witness*, with Harrison Ford. Jan had the experience and force of personality to hold the show together, and he was very generous in his coaching of other performers. Me among them. I had no thought of appearing in the show, but as auditions went on, local singers fell into place for most of the roles, but Dr Barnardo, which Cliff had written for a bass, had no one. So I auditioned, and the part was mine. I had some experience on stage, and my voice was suitable.

It was a stretch, but I had both Nancy and Jan Rubes coaching me. Nancy once handed me a walking stick and said, 'Your hands look awkward, carry this.' When I was rehearsing my big scene, one of Barnardo's famous stories, sung in counterpoint to the hymn of the children embarking, Jan said, 'When you're singing about the trip to Canada, Canada is out there,' pointing to someplace above the audience. In the last

The author performing in *Barnardo Boy*.

scene of the opera, various figures from the old man's past appear on stage, intoning bits of their music. What was coming from the orchestra was a generalized haze of sound, with just enough tonality that I learned to pick a G natural out of it. It was all an adventure, and by the time the show went on my performance was acceptable. As a measure of *Barnado Boy*'s success, I recall the school matinee. This was a full-length two-act performance, all singing, no spoken dialogue, and eight hundred and thirty schoolkids sat quietly in their seats for all of it. Polite children no doubt, but they gave every evidence of having followed and enjoyed the show. Evenings, we filled the house, and afterward men and women who had been Barnardo children were invited to the reception, where they would talk about their experiences, what they remembered of their years in England and forced emigration.

Busy as I was in the next years of my life, writing book after book, journalism and radio and television to make a living, I also became more and more immersed in music. The Kingston Symphony had a new conductor, Brian Jackson, and he took over a local chamber choir, the Pro Arte Singers. I auditioned, and he accepted me. I had, after all, a wonderful instrument, the thing that was a part of me, but I quickly learned that my belief that I could read music was ill-founded, and my assumption that I was singing the right pitches sometimes questionable. Though Brian didn't really like rehearsing – he was very quick and it was tedious to him – he was a brilliant choir trainer and teacher, terrifying to sing for, even though he was usually cheerful and funny. He had a sharp ear and a sharp wit, and I sang scared, but I learned to work at home, to test intervals with the piano, and I worked on voice production, took a tip passed on by Jan Rubes. A year or so later I arranged for a few lessons from Patricia Rideout, who came from Toronto to teach voice at Queen's. Singing more music, and more difficult music, my reading improved. A couple of years later Brian chose me to do the solos in the Beethoven *Mass in C,* and later on, in *Messiah.* I remember moments of great pleasure: a rehearsal of the William Byrd five-part mass, the singers seated in a semi-circle, arranged randomly, not in sections. Brian beat a few bars, then sat down in the group and sang tenor, and we went through the mass like that, unconducted, just listening and singing.

Brian and his partner Denys Mailhot became friends, as did Steve Smith, the symphony manager, whose office was across the hall from Nancy's at the Grand. I sometimes worked for Steve as a symphony stagehand. I spent far more time with musicians than writers. When Brian left Pro Arte, he was replaced by Tom Baker, who travelled from his place in the country north of Toronto for rehearsals and performances. (One of the other competitors for the job was the cathedral music director, John Gallienne, later jailed for his sexual abuse of choirboys – no connection with not getting the Pro Arte job one would say, but there was a quality about his audition sessions with the choir that suggested an emotional emptiness.) Tom Baker often stayed with us when he was in Kingston, one more musical companion, and of course there were all the singers I was working with.

The accident that placed a good instrument in my throat led me on, and over those years I sang Christus in the *St Matthew Passion*, solos in works by Handel and Beethoven and Mozart, sometimes in terror, hovering on the edge of humiliation, but sometimes with a sense of the music coming to be in and through my body. I got the chance to do these things because Kingston is a small city; there weren't all that many soloists to choose from. As a writer I worked alone, arranging and rearranging words, and music became the thing I did with other people. I worked with most of the local conductors and orchestra musicians. The most vivid moments of all this music were the dress rehearsals, with their race to get everything done within the union time limits. Stand up, sing, make way for someone else. The audience was the other singers and the instrumentalists. It was intimate and fraught and splendid. At a dress rehearsal for a performance of the Mozart *Requiem,* I learned that the double bass playing five or six feet away, doubling our notes, was a seventeenth-century Amati instrument once played by the eccentric virtuoso Dragonetti. Its resonance joined with ours to fill the spaces of the old cathedral, the past and present linked. There was an unnatural excitement in it all, and such joy within the body as the sound of the voice hummed in the flesh and bones. At the very least I came to understand that a singer is the slave of the instrument in a way that's true for no other musician. Language can offer only an approximation, metaphors. Precise intonation is felt before it is heard. Singing this great music is a bodily act of love, and though singers are not quite as much at the mercy of aging as dancers and athletes, they are still much at its mercy.

When I moved to Montreal in 1992 I'd been advised to try to sing for Patrick Wedd, and I pestered him until he gave me an audition for his church choir. I was accepted, and that choir was the climactic musical experience of my life. The Church of St John the Evangelist was Anglican, and very high, and there was enough money that the church had a paid organist and five paid soloists, all of them wonderful young singers, mostly products of the music program at McGill. A number of the twenty or so other choristers were or had been musicians of some sort, so the calibre of their work was high. The church services were largely sung, plainchant, mass, introit, anthem, and apart from the Sunday service, there was evensong once a month, and a great many of the traditional church festivals were also celebrated. The choir sang at all of these, which meant a great many hours of singing in the high gallery at the back of the beautiful brick church.

It's an early evening in November, with the last bit of light a metallic green behind the westerly stained glass windows. I am one of a group of six men in the choir gallery high above the long nave, and after singing the plainsong mass for the dead, we are gathered in a rough circle to sing the Russian Contakion. ('Dust thou art and unto dust thou shalt return.') Three of the men are professional musicians, the first tenor, the conductor (who is singing second tenor), and one of the basses. I am the other bass, and there are two baritones. It is the end of a very long service for the feast of All Souls. Nearly a full half hour has been passed in reading the names of the dead. Almost at the end, we sing the rich four-part harmonies of the Russian anthem. As the service has gone on, the sky has moved from afternoon to night.

Singing like that was an experience that was both close and intense and yet impersonal. For three and a half years I sang beside Normand Richard, the cantor and bass soloist. Much of the time we were the entire second bass section. You listen to each other's breathing, especially in the kind of sustained music where you must breathe at different times. Normand and I enjoyed singing together, and we were friendly, but at a personal level we were merely amicable acquaintances, yet once the music started there was a kind of intimacy.

A couple of months after I left Montreal, a number of the singers I'd worked with turned up on PEI with a professional choir. Afterward I was chatting with them.

'We miss you,' Normand said, then paused, looked momentarily awkward, plunged on, 'and personally too of course.'

I was perfectly delighted that he put it that way.

Twenty-six

The days when I was appearing in *Barnardo Boy*, starting to sing for Brian Jackson, were also the most active period of my writing life. In 1982 I published, *It Is Always Summer*. I had finished writing it before Stoddart brought out *A Sound Like Laughter*, and when they saw the new manuscript, they were enthusiastic and decided they'd like to reverse the order of the two books and do the summer novel first. Stoddart's books were released in the United States by Beaufort Books, and *It Is Always Summer* was the first of my novels to appear in the U.S. That same year Oberon brought out *The Rain Falls Like Rain*, a collection of new and selected poems. I was writing radio plays for Paul Mills and George Jonas, articles for *Quest* magazine, then edited by Michael Enright, though I worked mostly with the managing editor Lynn Cunningham. This was the period when I was writing *The Only Son*, a novel that came into my head one autumn day as I was driving back to Kingston after spending a few days at the old house in the woods. The previous night I had eaten dinner in a little restaurant in the village of Ompah. While I waited for my food to come I wandered about the empty room studying the old photographs on the wall and discovered that at some time in the past someone had operated – of all things – a shoelace factory here. A shoelace factory: that was both comic and intriguing, and the next day as I drove home along the country roads I began to tell myself a story, the old life represented by that shoelace factory oddly linking itself to what I'd recently been told by a stranger I met on a restaurant terrace in Toronto one Sunday afternoon, what he said about his family background, how he was the son of servants in a rich household, but in fact – or so he believed – the son of the man who employed them. During my days working in the grocery store in Niagara I had delivered groceries to the summer houses of millionaires; I had stood in the back kitchens of the rich. All the way to Kingston, the events played out in my head.

Three very different novels in that period were so strongly impelled by imaginative necessity that they fairly leapt into being when I sat down to write – *It Is Always Summer*, *The Only Son*, and *The Bishop*. They are very different books, but all of them possessed me, the sensuality of the summer novel, the intricate social relations and emotional danger of *The Only Son*, and the lyricism of *The Bishop*. Diversity of reaction: two comments about *The Only Son* are worth quoting. 'The first quarter of David Helwig's new novel is by itself a little masterpiece ... I think Helwig throws his masterpiece away in [the] concluding half.' That's George Galt in *Books in Canada*. Leo Simpson, writing in the Hamilton *Spectator* said the exact opposite. 'You start reading this novel and by page fifty you find yourself grumbling ... *The Only Son* has the shape of a bomb, opening with a long quiet fuse that leads to a mind-stunning bang.' Two intelligent, serious reviewers, both treating the novel with respect, but with opposing ideas of what it achieves. You can only write, obviously, to please yourself, and the eventual consequences play themselves out among complicated people in a complicated world. What you think you're writing and what is perceived aren't always congruent.

Another small example: around this time I was in the *Morningside* studio for an interview with Peter Gzowski about one of my books, and as I was leaving I told the producer that I had a bright idea for him. I wanted to do a series about little-known characters from Canadian history – but I intended to make them all up. He was intrigued, and I produced a set of five, a week's worth, ranging from an inventor of musical instruments – things called the cold piano, the water organ, and the bag-clarinet – to a seventeenth-century explorer who believed that the Inuit were speaking a dialect of ancient Greek, and Mackenzie King's veterinarian, whose favourite treatment was castration. So I polished them up and we went into studio. The interviews were scripted, of course, and Peter was not keen. 'I don't do stuff like that,' he said. 'Don Harron does stuff like that.' (Harron had previously been host of the show.)

As we went through the series I got better at making the material sound as if I was recounting it spontaneously, and the five were taped and went on the air. I remember Nancy saying to me at the time, 'You can't tell lies on the CBC,' and I was later told by Richard Handler, who had been one of the show's producers, that there was a lot of internal dissension about the little hoax – if hoax is the word; the tales ventured very close to absurdity and I'd always assumed that the audience would catch on, if not to the first, at least to the second or third. After all I had a Dutch explorer sitting out on the ice reading the *Odyssey* to the Inuit – was anyone going to take that seriously? Some did. Very few people, of course, hear a radio program every day. They catch bits of it, at work, riding in the car, so there was no cumulative effect. I got a typed note on nice letterhead from a man who worked in some downtown Toronto office asking for more information about the explorer. When I wrote back and said he didn't exist, I got a one-word answer. *Touché,* he wrote. Months later, when I was reading in Ottawa, a woman in the audience came up to me to tell me how much she'd laughed at the series. She could still quote her favourite line, about the vet – 'They said he'd walk ten miles in a blizzard to cut a rooster.' Those who knew they were a hoax thought they were funny – which was what I'd intended – but a certain number of people took them literally and weren't amused. Comedy, irony, take place in the undefined mental space between the mind of the writer and that of the audience.

No matter how carefully you shape the elements of a piece of writing, it begins to have a life of its own, and there may be surprises about how it's received. Scripts pan out in their production, or don't. I think of two radio plays I wrote about that time for Paul Mills, one about some characters interested in parapsychology and another about art theft and forgery. The first was a competent script, did everything it could with the story, had one of my favourite comic characters, a dog named Swedenborg, who – this being radio – is never seen or heard, only talked about; still, the script stopped at a level of competence. The script about art forgery had, I thought, some greater depth, though it was sixty minutes long and perhaps needed ninety minutes. In the event, the production of the parapsychology story got on the air every possibility that was in the script, a fine performance by Patricia Collins and a brilliant one by Hugh Webster – frightening to observe in studio: he was playing an asthmatic, and one thought he might die in front of the mike. (Oddly, though one of the country's finest and most experienced professional actors, he was late for rehearsal – caught in traffic somewhere – and arrived without his reading glasses – had to run off to another studio and borrow a pair from Peter Gzowski.) The art theft script, on the other hand, somehow never came into focus in the production. One of the characters was played by Austin Willis, who was getting along in years. He had one very extended and very intense scene, a monologue, in effect, which he delivered splendidly in the final rehearsal, the mike unfortunately not turned on. When he tried to do it again, it became clear that he was exhausted, the performance weaker, his hand shaking enough that the rustle of paper was audible. One way and another what seemed to me a more exciting script got on air as merely competent, the competent script as something more.

In those days, it was still possible to drop in on editors and producers, at the CBC in particular. That was how I'd begun to work with Paul Mills in the first place. A few years later, after the growth of terrorism, bomb threats, the doors were locked, as they are still. I can't imagine how freelance writers operate now. How do they meet producers, get or sell ideas? It was in the spring of 1982 that I popped in to see Peter Wildeblood at the CBC, in an office next to the one I'd sat in six years before. He had read a novel of mine, and was trying to convince me that I was really a fiction writer. I was in search of work that paid.

'What I'm looking for,' he said as I was leaving, 'is a story about the woman in the half-ton with a sixpack.'

I think he'd observed some such woman at the liquor store, or perhaps he'd only imagined her. I mulled over what he'd said as I sat on the train to Kingston, and almost as soon as I was home I sent him a note. What you want, I said, is a story about harness racing. Not many days later I was back in his office discussing it. I knew a certain amount about harness racing from Nancy's father's involvement, first owning horses, later a track. Peter was about to go to Los Angeles for a week or so, but before he left he commissioned me to write something called a development outline for a three-part series. I did a bit of research at the harness track in Kingston and set to work. The fastest way to produce that much story, I decided, was to ignore script form and simply write it as fiction, mostly dialogue with enough narrative to set up the important locations and events. In just over a week I turned out ninety pages, two and a half episodes in detail, the rest a brief summary made after I reached the point of exhaustion.

Peter came back from Los Angeles full of Hollywood anecdotes: he had attended a party at a house that once belonged to Lana Turner, where he was shown the brass plaque screwed into the floor to mark the spot where Johnny Stompanato bled to death after Lana Turner's daughter stabbed him. We discussed my outline, and we started out to produce, at some speed, three scripts for shooting dates that were imminent. My ninety pages set up the characters and most of the action, and from there on we worked more or less collaboratively. I wrote the first episode while Peter wrote the second, and we both wrote parts of the third. There was enough interplay in the discussion and revision that when the show was being shot while I watched from the control room, I said to Peter about a line I liked, 'Did you write that or did I?' Neither of us had any idea.

The three episodes were directed by John Trent, who was the owner of a thoroughbred and knew something about racing. It seemed a good augury when Trent and I separately said to Peter that he must cast Sneezy Waters, who had recently expanded his career by doing his show, *Hank Williams, the Show He Never Gave*. I'd seen him at the Horseshoe Tavern. The lead for the three shows was the appealing and capable Florence Patterson. The footage was cut together, and it made a convincing series. Then suddenly John Trent was dead, killed in a traffic accident, a head-on collision with – of all things – a drunken policeman. And Peter told me that John Kennedy, who was now head of drama, wanted an introductory episode because, so far as I could understand it, the first one was too dark and sad and Flo Patterson didn't get to wear nice clothes. I thought this was one of the dumbest suggestions I had ever heard. Of course the first episode was dark – things are bad for Marge, the widowed track owner and for the kid she catches breaking in to steal something, but we can sense that there is some link between the two, and things look up in the second episode, so that by episode three we have a happy ending. They win the big race, a fairy-tale ending. This was popular drama, as I understood it, and I grew up on the movies. It's possible the three episodes should have been made into one three-hour special, but they didn't need a prologue. At first Peter insisted that he would have no truck with Kennedy's suggestion, but somehow the pressure increased, John Trent was not around to defend his show, and Peter ended up writing a new episode, in which Marge's husband mooches around dying of cancer, and the dramatic surprise of the original first episode – what the hell is wrong with this bad-tempered woman? – is lost.

In spite of this, *Backstretch,* as the series was called, won the CBC's Anik Award as the year's best entertainment series and was renewed, more episodes the following season. This was great for me, since having invented the series I got a nice payment for every episode that was made, and I wrote one new episode, but on the whole the second series, what I saw of it, was intolerably dreary, and that episode was the last television I ever wrote. But the first three, the John Trent episodes, are a happy memory. And my three or four months' hard work on the series earned me a year's salary, with a little more coming in for the second season.

In the summer when *Backstretch* was being shot, I finished work on

The Only Son. Around that time Michael Macklem called me to say that John Metcalf, who had been editing the Oberon anthology, most recently with Leon Rooke, had decided to move to General Publishing and to take the book, or something very like it, with him. Michael asked if I would take over the series again. This would allow them to assert its continuity. Oberon had the genuine article; all others were imitations. Involved in the deal was the editing of the important series of stories by new writers – three per book – that John had started as *First Impressions,* which then went on to become (bizarrely) *Second Impressions* and (even more bizarrely) *Third Impressions.* I said I might be willing to do the books, but nothing on earth was going to make me call a book *Fourth Impressions.* It was, I think, Nicholas Macklem who came up with the title *Coming Attractions,* and the series continues under that title to this day. Among the writers who appeared in the early years of *Coming Attractions* were Bonnie Burnard, Rohinton Mistry and Diane Schomperlen.

If I was to take over the annuals, I needed (or at least wanted) a co-editor, and I remembered that Sandra Martin had done a review of the first five years of the series for *Tamarack Review.* I had never met her, but those who had spoke well of her, so I wrote and invited her to join me, and she accepted. Calling the annual anthology Best Stories meant someone had to look at every story in every magazine, and soon my daughter Maggie took that on. I worked with Sandra on the series for four years, and then Maggie became my official co-editor, for that and *Coming Attractions.* It was good to have someone of a different generation looking at things with me.

Twenty-seven

I dream about my parents a lot, last night again, though it's thirteen years since my father's death, eleven since my mother's. I was an only child, and at one time they were all of life to me. (We dream of those who loved us too much, those who didn't love us enough. In dreams, time vanishes, and moments of distress from years long past seize us, nothing healed.) During the years I lived in Kingston, we visited back and forth. My father picked up antique furniture in the Kingston area, pieces he'd take back to Niagara to refinish and sell. They spent time with their grandchildren, always a little disappointed, I think, that Maggie and Kate weren't closer to them, though the two girls did their best. A generational break, perhaps. My mother felt some kind of identification with Maggie and worried terribly about her as she proceeded on her own serpentine, eccentric path toward adult life – studying classics, working in a second-hand bookstore, starving herself – her first book of poetry, about the medieval witchcraft trials, accepted for publication by Turnstone Press when she was just nineteen. Maggie's departure from home had been difficult for her; in 1983 Kate left without, it seemed, a second thought, to study chemistry at the University of Toronto, beginning the years of work that would lead her to a career as a conservation scientist. I like to think of her scraping bits off famous paintings to analyze the pigments.

My parents loved to travel, and in the late summer of 1983, just as Kate was about to leave home, they set off for a couple of weeks in England with a tour group, but just after they arrived, we got a call from my mother to say my father was in a London hospital. He'd had a heart attack. Within a few minutes I'd arranged to fly over, and set off for Toronto to catch the plane.

I had arrived in England twice in the past, each time, like this one, in September sunlight, but those other occasions I'd gone to live there. This was a trip outside the continuity of time. Once the plane had landed, I met my mother at the hotel. My father's condition was not, it appeared, immediately dangerous, but they were preoccupied with money, insurance, travel arrangements, my mother's diabetes. He was in a hospital in the Fulham Road, a short cab ride away. Jet-lagged, a little disoriented, I was standing in the hospital elevator beside my mother, waiting to ride up to my father's ward when I saw him in a wheelchair in the corridor outside, his face pale, ill, worried. He had been taken for X-rays, and while he was there, the hospital porters decided to call one of those inevitable, spur-of-the-moment English strikes. Left there for an hour, cold and distraught, he finally set out to walk back to his ward till someone stopped him.

The next day I wandered through the now polyglot wilds of Kensington, running errands, looking for places my mother might walk to give her a break from hospital and hotel. Newspapers on the street were in German, Italian, French, Arabic. In the hotel restaurant, I overheard a business meeting between an American and a German about oil refinery technology; they had chosen to meet in London. The hotel was wholly international. Signs in Spanish and Japanese. The desk drawer contained the New Testament and the teaching of Buddha.

By Thursday the doctors had decided that my father could leave hospital the next Monday; they considered it safe for him to fly back to Canada ten days later. I made arrangements for a hired car to drive my parents to Dorset to stay with the only friends they had in England – exiles from the Shaw Festival. I made them new hotel and airline reservations. In the afternoon, I left my mother visiting at the hospital and took the tube out to Kew, where I had lived with Nancy and our children in 1969. Kew appeared to be little altered, a respectable Edwardian suburb. London, I realized on this trip, is, for all the traces of ancient history, largely a nineteenth-century city. The school that my children attended had become a district educational centre, used for adult arts and crafts, but Newen's, the teashop opposite Kew Gardens, was unchanged. On the way back to the station, I was walking past familiar stores and thinking that this much of London was the same when I noticed that the two neighbourhood women walking beside me were speaking German.

The patient in the hospital bed next to my father was a retired seaman with a fine clear English complexion. He moved with difficulty, even with his cane, and he was back in hospital – where he was a familiar figure – because he fell, and his home help, or so he believed, panicked and sent for an ambulance instead of simply getting him back up. When the doctor wanted to show the oddities of his gait to students and interns, he stepped out with dignity in his pale orange pyjamas, though his legs struggled to obey the commands of his brain. Bright-eyed and well-spoken, he was convinced that in the early hours of each day, the mice in his flat talked to him, and from outside the window, he heard the chanting of monks. They repeated, over and over, *benedictus, benedictus, benedictus.* When a doctor asked if it might not be the sounds of traffic, he admitted it might, but seemed no less to believe in it. *Benedictus, benedictus, benedictus.* It wasn't clear whether it disturbed him or whether he was contented to accept the blessing the monks offered.

On Saturday my mother and I made a short visit to the antique market at Portobello Road, and on Sunday I visited the V&A, where I saw two caskets, both ivory, small enough to be held in the hand, each a thousand years old. One was carved with the faces of Christ and the saints, fixed, staring eyes, a row of identical oval faces, stylized and hieratic, the only difference the conventions of each saint's representation, some bearded, some clean-shaven, Paul portrayed as balding. Nearby another ivory box of the same period, this one decorated with classical myths, Bellerophon, the rape of Europa by Zeus disguised as a bull, shining naked bodies, buttocky nymphs.

On Monday my father was released from hospital and on Tuesday, the hired car came to drive my parents to Dorset. Once they were safely on their way, I lugged one of their heavy suitcases to the airport bus for the trip to Heathrow. The boredom of airports, miles of moving sidewalks. The plane carried me through six hours of sunlit sky to Toronto, where, while I was away, Kate had started university at the college I attended nearly thirty years before.

Living is such a variety of rhythms in counterpoint, the day by day moments of observation, surprise, enlightenment, the continuities, fulfillment of intentions, the accumulation of books written over a number of years. A face seen in a crowd, the details of what once happened, new places. Now that Nancy and I had no children at home, we were free – within the limits of her demanding job – to travel, and in the next few years we went to New York City two or three times, to Cuba, to England, to Italy, where I was doing research for a book related to opera. I have vivid memories of that trip. Verona: on a spring day we sat in the garden of a small café, and just beyond the end of the garden, the Adige river tumbled and roared in full spate as it made its way down from the Alps, and then later we visited the ancient church of Sant'Anastasia and in a dim back room (the reference books say the Pellegrini Chapel, but I

238

remember closets, furniture, a sacristy) we came on Pisanello's haunting fresco of Saint George and the Princess, painted in 1437, the saint with an odd, sly, sexy face, two hanged men in the background; I later wrote a series of poems about it. On later trips we went to Paris and Provence. Nothing very exotic, but important all the same, Rome, London, Paris, the great cities.

Over those years Nancy and I lived lives that were sometimes joined, sometimes merely adjacent. We spent time apart and back together. Other women offered me pieces of their lives. Irresistible: nothing is so entrancing as learning the secrets of another existence.

All other is full of wonder:
that the desired flesh contains
the world gives birth
to the long breath of articulation.

Stories told out of school
jailbreak the shy inventor
bemused by plenitude.

A Random Gospel, a book of poems published in 1996, contains a section called 'An Old Story', which gives an account, in nineteen poems, of a love affair that began in 1983 and went on, in a jagged, complex, badly handled way for the next ten years. Judith – dark, intent, elegant – was the source of many things I wrote over those years – an obsession, an inspiration, one of my failures. Kingston being Kingston, what began with two people became a triangle, a rectangle, a many-sided polygon, all too complicated for words. I feel no great pride in how I behaved through it all, but the books are there – hers and mine – and we are both safe now, many miles and a generation apart – her child the age of my grandchildren.

Twenty-eight

The Christmas season of 1982 was a quiet time, two novels, *A Sound Like Laughter* and *The Only Son,* completed and set to be published in the next couple of years, *Backstretch* in the can but not yet broadcast. I sat around the house rereading one of Shakespeare's romantic comedies. For Christmas, Maggie had given me a book called *Catchpenny Prints,* page after page of simple images from seventeenth- and eighteenth-century broadsheets, a whole world reflected in those simple prints, educational, patriotic, whimsical. On New Year's Eve I went to a costume party at the apartment of Bron Wallace and Chris Whynot. Everyone was someone else, Virginia Woolf, a hauntingly strange and pretty wood nymph. The next day, thinking about all that, I wrote a poem. I had been writing poetry only occasionally over the previous years, but that new poem began a series derived from images in the book of prints, allusive poems, free to leap from one idea to another, full of references to history and yet also anachronistic when they wished to be, an outpouring of high spirits. It's possible that the freedom of their movement was influenced by the ghazals of John Thompson and Phyllis Webb, and in fact Phyllis Webb told me a few years later she thought they were parodies of *Water and Light,* her book of ghazals. They certainly weren't that, though the poems often had an ironic tone, a comic twist. When I had completed a dozen of them, I sent them to Michael Macklem. He said that if I'd write another twelve he'd turn them into a book. Not long after the series was finished I was in Toronto and ran into Robert Weaver in the College subway station. He said that CBC *Anthology* hadn't broadcast anything of mine for a while, and did I have any poetry? Yes, I said, and sent him the new series. In the meanwhile the first twelve had been accepted by Constance Rooke for *Malahat Review.* The Catchpenny Poems had arrived as an unexpected gift, and it seemed that everyone liked them. Next thing I knew I received a form letter from the CBC saying that my poems had been sent on to the final judges of the CBC literary awards; it took me a few minutes to realize that Bob Weaver must have decided to enter them in the contest. Not long afterward I got a call telling me that they'd won, and after they were broadcast, read for radio by Neil Dainard, Oberon published them in a book, one of the most beautiful Michael Macklem ever designed, the images from the ancient prints used in black and white and as ghostly halftones appearing behind the poems on some of the pages, the large metal type giving the whole thing an aura of antiquity. There was a kind of blessedness about the whole experience of those poems, new voices speaking them to me, all but unsought, then a sense that my delight was shared by those who read them. John Metcalf called me from Ottawa when he read the book to say how much he'd liked it.

In the summer of 1983, George Whalley, who'd been undergoing treatment for stomach cancer, died, and with all his other colleagues and former colleagues I attended his funeral at St George's, the Anglican Cathedral. It was an austere service, the bare liturgy, one or two hymns, no other music besides the organ playing before and after the service, and a wide range of men and women came to pay their respects, academics and musicians, wives and husbands who were no longer together. One of the hymns was the one that begins, '*Immortal, invisible, God only wise/In light inaccessible hid from our eyes*,' and the service, simple as it was, had some powerful resonance. George was the son of an Anglican bishop, played the church organ as a boy. Was that why I began to imagine a bishop's funeral in just such a large old stone church?

Not long after that I began the novel that became *The Bishop*. Nancy and I had recently moved to a large house on Montreal Street that we renovated with an crew of workers led by Dennis Crossfield, who was becoming something of an expert on old Kingston houses. Our mason quarried huge stones for a back staircase. The house was part of a terrace of tall limestone houses built by the military a hundred and fifty years before. The one next to us was unrenovated, and unregenerate. In one of the apartments lived Kingston's most famous prostitute, 401 Rose, so named because she sometimes worked the highway, servicing truckers. She had a T-shirt with *401 Rose* printed on the front, and when setting off for the evening in the bars, she sported white cowboy boots, a white miniskirt and a white cowboy hat. Her home life, however, was quiet and private, and she was good about lending us her phone when we were doing the renovations. In the basement beneath Rose's apartment lived a raffish pair named Marty and Gloria – bad teeth, troubled minds – who survived on disability pensions and had melodramatic scenes in the night. We would wake to hear Marty beating on the door and crying out

('I'm a man – I bleed.') because Gloria had locked him out again.

As I thought about my bishop's funeral, his earlier years came to life in my imagination, a mission in the Arctic, an unhappy marriage, London in the Second War. A creature like Marty but even more fuddled and miserable, took up residence in the basement of my imagined cathedral. By now I had been singing in an Anglican church every week for several years, and while I didn't have it in me to believe in their religion, I was willing to make the imaginative leap and inhabit a man who was a committed and serious believer. A fiction writer should, surely, be able to create the world of those whose beliefs are unlike his own. The book begins with the bishop incapacitated after a stroke and ends with his funeral, but the shape was more abstractly conceived – its freedom of form influenced in some way by the weekly series of concerts of Schubert's piano music being played in Kingston and a few other cities by the wonderful Anton Kuerti. In the first section of *The Bishop* the images were essentially comic, in the second primarily tragic; in the third part they had the soft magic of romance, and then, in a kind of epilogue, the funeral was described, and from there the book vanishes into the poetry of time passing. When I was within a page or so of the end, I knew where I was going, but on the weekend before I wrote the last words, I was looking through a book of photographs, saw one of a white horse in a churchyard, and had a glimpse of a new final image for the book. Monday morning I set to work. What I wanted to do was difficult, but I felt I could pull it off. As I started to write, alone in the house, typing on a little portable, a key began to stick. Every time I typed a 't', I had to pull the lever back by hand, and each time it broke my concentration. Finally I pulled out the paper, picked up the typewriter and threw it in the front seat of the car. Downtown at an office supply store I told them the trouble and said I needed to rent a typewriter. Instantly. I put the rental machine in the car and raced home, and what I had imagined was fortunately still there, available to me, and I wrote the lyric, mysterious ending.

Around the time I was finishing *The Bishop*, Nancy and I spent a week or so in England. I looked at all those English bookstores where my work hadn't appeared for many years, not since the arrangement between Oberon and Dennis Dobson ended, and I thought I must do something to get my books there. When I got back, I wrote to Penguin Books, the Canadian branch, sent them *The Bishop*, and asked if they might be interested in paperback rights. By now Diane Young had left Stoddart, and after her departure they had rejected *Old Wars,* which they had verbally committed themselves to publish while she was there. Now they had *The Bishop* under consideration. Cynthia Good at Penguin wrote to say that if they were interested it would be in all the rights, so I found I had made a multiple submission without quite intending it. When Stoddart wrote to offer to publish the book, I called Cynthia. She was part way through the manuscript, raced to the end and made an offer, which I accepted. Since Stoddart had felt free to change their minds about *Old Wars* after accepting it, I didn't feel too bad about giving Penguin *The Bishop,* and, at least in paperback, it did get around the world a bit more. I got a letter from New Zealand, and from Germany a begging letter from a man who sent it off, I gather, to a lot of writers, offering to leave you his estate and requiring only a page written in your own hand. I assume he made a few pfennigs by selling the handwritten pages.

It was in the year after the publication of *The Bishop* that Tom Marshall published his best and most successful novel, *Adele at the End of the Day,* the story of a rich old woman with a sexy and scandalous past who is living out her last years in a suite in what is recognizable as the old Windsor Arms Hotel in Toronto – where Tom liked to stay when he was in the city. Intercut with her history is the narrative of her bisexual son who is living alone in New York, drinking too much and inclined to give in to a somewhat melodramatic self-pity. Adele is a splendid figure, passionate, ironic, strong-minded, and her story brings together Tom's poetic fantasy with his love of gossip and his deep-seated sense of history. The interweaving of past and present, of Europe and North America, is skillfully done as the book moves from lyric comedy to a dramatic conclusion. *Adele at the End of the Day* was very well received, with a splendid review in the *New York Times,* and Tom, after some thin years when he was writing fiction but without a lot of success, had a period of significant recognition. When he gave me a copy, he wrote in the front 'for David, what the actress said to the bishop'.

It is startling to realize, as I write this, that as Tom's literary executor I now own the copyright of that book, will hold it until my own death, when by the effect of my will it will go to his niece.

Twenty-nine

The air was close and hot, the noise of the cicadas so loud it might have been coming from an amplifier. An odd smell, sweetish, tropical, came from the fields, perhaps the smell of human excrement used for fertilizer. Hard to believe, but late in the summer of 1987 I was in China, walking down a road outside the Shanghai airport, wandering off on my own as the group I was travelling with waited for a bus to arrive. A call had come earlier in the summer, from Doris Heffron. I had first known Doris many years before, when she was a Queen's student, had seen her now and then at meetings of the Writers' Union after she had begun to publish young adult novels. It appeared that a writers' trip to China was to take place in late August, and she felt that there were too few serious writers on the list. She was calling around to encourage others to join. We were to pay our own air fare, but expenses in China were picked up by the Chinese Association for Friendship with Foreign Countries. She phoned Tom Marshall and me, and we both committed ourselves to go. Also on board when we left Vancouver were Robert Harlow and Merna Summers. The delegation was led by Gordon Yearsley, a tall, vital, idealistic, old-left-true-believer from Nanaimo, who had, I suspect, organized the trip as a way of getting himself to China, a country he had worshipped from afar, but never visited. Seeing him on some occasion having his picture taken sitting on the back of a camel, Tom aptly likened him to Don Quixote.

We spent close to three weeks in the Middle Kingdom, having meetings with writers in all the cities we visited, being taken to a certain number of tourist sites, and now and then finding ourselves free to wander through the streets. Translators were provided for the meetings, but we were also helped along by the presence of Alison Bailey, English by background, now a doctoral student in Chinese at the University of Toronto. She had previously lived in China, so she had more than language skills to offer. One afternoon in Xi'an, when we had some free time, she guided me through the old city to one of its more exotic locations, the ancient mosque.

Though the meetings with writers were rather stiff and formal, it was possible, through conversation with our guides and the young men in the streets who constantly turned up wanting to practise English, to get a little sense of the current state of things. In Shanghai, one of our guides was a man named Gu Boxi. It was obvious that he felt real excitement about the sense of liberation that was abroad in those days. In late August he already knew that during the October Communist Party conference in the fall of 1987 there would be new faces, younger men elected to the central committee. He was, I suppose, part of the party bureaucracy, and somehow word went out about the direction things were going. There was a certain poignancy to the way he told me, more than once, that I could ask him anything, anything at all. We talked about his spell in the country during the Cultural Revolution. When he was sent away to labour in the countryside with the peasants, he accepted it, at first, believed that it was good for China. Chairman Mao was a hero and to be trusted, and Chairman Mao made a distinction between (failed) Russian socialism, which had really changed nothing in forty years, and a purer socialism that was to be developed in China. (A pure idea, and therefore dangerous, like the very pure socialism of Pol Pot.) The Cultural Revolution – that period of turmoil in the late sixties, with the young people of the Red Guard fomenting a kind of authoritarian anarchy – was the old wound of many of the writers we met. A few talked about it. But that was the past; the present was all the young people who were in school learning English or teaching it to themselves, on hand wherever we travelled to try it out, the sense that under Deng Xiao Ping, a new freedom was possible. Ask me anything, Gu Boxi said, anything at all. He seemed almost eager to tell me about the poverty of the more distant cities, though it's significant that when I asked him about relations with Russia he answered, for the first time, in Mandarin, letting a translator put his words into English. A touchy subject, clearly, and he wanted to be careful about what he said.

While staying in a brand-new hotel in Shanghai we were taken for a day to the ancient city of Suzhou, the train passing fields of an intense, brilliant green, entering a city that was vivid with life and yet carried a weight of ancient history, gardens of rock, water, green leaves, an old house where I saw a blond young man I took to be a German tourist. Weeks later I found out that he was Michael Macklem's oldest son, Tim. We were led, as always (foreign currency to be earned), to a place where you could buy Chinese goods to take home. I didn't buy a lot of gifts and souvenirs in China, but in Suzhou there was a man writing out ancient poems in a quick, cursive calligraphy, on long white sheets of paper. I couldn't resist a poem by Chang Ji.

Moon falls. Crows cry in a sky full of frost.

Maple Bridge; the lights of fishing boats
doze off in the gloom.

Outside the ancient city of Suzhou
lies Hanshan Temple.

At midnight the sound of the bell
reaches the passenger's boat.

Some places remain in memory with a weight of significance, authority, something like holiness: Suzhou is one of those. (Siena is another.) There is a Chinese proverb that says in Heaven there is paradise, on earth Suzhou. In the overwhelming heat, I sat on a huge stone near one of the ancient canals as trains of working barges passed by, the captains howling out instructions over the loudspeakers. Old men with faces from ancient paintings. Men and women passing by carried umbrellas and parasols to keep off the killing sun. Labourers used a piece of bamboo held on the shoulders as a yoke, a load of bricks hanging at each end. The young woman who guided us around a silk factory remarked to our translator that we must be very important people since we had so many guides and attendants; it was addressed to him as an aside, but for some reason he translated it to me. He also told me that the privately owned souvenir stores were dangerous. Deng Xiao Ping had begun to encourage a certain level of free enterprise, but where we travelled most of it was still on the fringes.

Flown from Shanghai to Beijing, we were housed in a large hotel close to the Forbidden City and Tiananmen Square. Across the square stood the memorial hall where Chairman Mao's body was on view, long queues waiting to pass by the waxy corpse. After a ceremonial banquet, a small group of us persuaded our guide, Wang Shuanglin – much against his better judgment – that, guided by Alison Bailey who had lived in the city for some time, we could walk back to the hotel. It was a long trek, down dark streets with occasional patches of brightness, booths selling clothing, hot food. We stopped to rest in Tiananmen Square, and immediately men and women gathered to talk to us, the crowd steadily increasing as strollers stopped to see these North American tourists, to listen to English spoken, or have the chance to speak it. I was to remember that night two years later when demonstrators took over Tiananmen Square and then the army moved in.

China was in a period of transformation. It gave the impression of being a country filled with energetic and determined young people. The regime had promised a new kind of life, and the promise of change always creates excitement, though not everyone was eager for a more liberated economy. Alison Bailey told me of two colleagues from her days in Beijing. They had all worked together on a magazine. Now one was moonlighting all over the place, making lots of money, one of the new men. The other, still a revolutionary idealist, thought this wrong. Along with this, bitterness over a promotion: they were no longer speaking to each other.

On our second day in Beijing I came down with the diarrhea foreigners are warned about – carelessly swallowing water in the shower, I suspect. So I took my pills and stayed close to the toilet in the room Tom and I shared while he and the others went off to the Great Wall, but by the next day I was able to go to a meeting at the Foreign Languages Press. We were introduced to Israel Epstein, a man of late middle age, who had spent his life in China. He had been born there, of Polish parentage. At birth officially a citizen of Tsarist Russia, he was stateless for many years, but he had become part of Mao Zedong's revolutionary movement, and now this was his country. A charming man, at moments resembling Buddha, at others an ancient turtle, he was one of the old China hands, the band of outsiders who'd become part of its modern history. While in Beijing, Gordon Yearsley had gone off to visit the sickbed of Rewi Alley, a New Zealander who had also cast his lot with Mao's China, and this sense of a European presence at the fringes of the country's history was the hint that led to the Chinese section of my later novel, *Just Say the Words*.

While the group was in Beijing, three of us, Doris Heffron, Alison Bailey and I, spent a day in Tianjin, two or three hours away by train. In Toronto, Doris had met the Chinese writer, Feng Jicai. He had returned to China on our flight and had invited her to visit his home. She suggested that I join the trip. Alison got us through the mayhem of the train station,

In Tianjin with Doris Heffron, Feng Jicai and his wife.

and as we rode through the countryside, explained that the little conical hills at the edge of roads, in the farm fields, were graves, situated there according to the principles of *feng shui*.

Feng Jicai met us at the station, a tall, handsome, broadly smiling figure, once a professional basketball player, trained as an artist, now a writer. Doris had lent me his impressive book, *Chrysanthemums and Other Stories*. He spoke no English, so all our conversation, inconsequential enough for the most part, went on through Alison's translation. His apartment was jammed with books, antiquities, stuffed birds. He told Alison, in a gesture that may have been meant as flirtatious, that she would have a complicated life. (From what she told me, she already had.) Then at a certain point he began to speak, at length, with deliberation, about the Cultural Revolution – how his mother was paraded around the streets, mocked and harassed. How after an earthquake he was terrified that manuscripts he had buried near his house would come to light, so he offered to clean up the wreckage of the house where he lived, and of course got ordered to continue with the work, to clean up others. He did find his buried stories, showed us some that he still kept rolled up in a drawer, a way of memorializing the time. After he and his wife, a very pretty woman who said little while we were there, only laughed nervously, first got married, they lived in a single room, the only piece of furniture a bed they'd constructed for themselves. The room was underneath a Red Guard headquarters, and the young Red Guards would come to the window, shine lights into the room and taunt them.

Now he was in the process of creating an oral history of the period. He had placed an advertisement in a newspaper, asking for stories of the Cultural Revolution and got far more than he could use. He was shaping the narratives into a book, repeated to us some of what he'd been told, about a woman doctor who, when her mother and father had been driven to desperation, killed her father at his request, then driven wild by what she had done, leapt out a window hoping to kill herself. It was very clear, as he said all these things, that he was speaking for the record, a man giving his witness, saying what must be said. (Once back in Canada I wrote to Cynthia Good, who was my publisher at Penguin Books, telling her about his oral history, which I thought could be successfully published in North America. She showed no interest. *Voices from the Whirlwind,* an English translation of fourteen narratives from the book, came out in the United States in 1991 from Pantheon Books, working in collaboration with the Foreign Languages Press in Beijing.)

It was on the way from Feng's apartment to a restaurant where we were to have lunch that I fell into a hole in the ground. We were walking down a quiet street in the late summer sunlight, and without a second thought, I stepped onto the round metal cover of a manhole, and as I put my weight down, the circle of heavy steel which covered it tilted in its supporting ring, and I began to plunge into the hole, one leg on each side of the metal lid, a fraction of a second from being injured, quite possibly emasculated. As I fell, I instinctively threw my arms and shoulders backward and my hands hit the pavement and caught my weight so I hung suspended over the abyss. Feng was quick to move round behind me to pull me out, but I allowed him to do it only when I was sure I had shifted my weight safely backward, so the centre of gravity was outside the manhole. And in a moment it was all over; apart from a scrape on my hand I was unharmed. I dusted myself off, and we proceeded to lunch, though I have been wary of metal covers and grills in roadways ever since.

Before we left Tianjin that afternoon, there was a certain amount of picture-taking. Feng, as he'd told us, had been trained as an artist, and with the grace of an urbane and generous host he offered to paint something for us. On my wall is the classic drawing of bamboo I watched him create that afternoon, perfectly articulated strokes of black ink on rice paper, textures of light and dark, the lines leaving space for an inscription which reads (in the translation Alison provided): 'The ancients praise bamboo by saying that it has a hollow heart, with joints. [Flexible but strong is the implication.] A selection of three stalks of spring bamboo. Presented to Mr He Dawei. Drawn and presented by Feng Jicai, August 27, 1987.'

Not only was I offered this astonishing gift, I was given a new name.

Back in Beijing late in the day, we passed through the usual crowds outside the train station, old men with caged birds, one of them to be heard singing out over the clamour of voices and the noise of traffic. On the street outside our hotel passed the constant flow of bicycles, often with one of the precious children in a seat on the back.

A day later we were off by train to Shijiazhuang, the site of Norman Bethune's grave, where we were given a hospital tour, patients stuck with acupuncture needles, a smell of some burning herb that had an odour much like marijuana. The writers we met made speeches about Bethune, in part a gesture of politeness to these visiting Canadians, no doubt, but also homage to a mythological figure from their revolutionary history. There was a painting of him in the hospital reception room, an heroic figure with diabolical arched eyebrows. Four years later, in 1991, Tom published a book called *Ghost Safari*, with a poem from China, and a prose commentary, partly provoked by that hospital visit, in which he analyzed Bethune's difficult, contradictory character, the arrogant womanizer who became a saint, a doctor so careless of his own health when he was working with Mao's army that one might take him to have been suicidal. However you interpret him, a character on a large scale, though I suspect his story may soon be lost in the vaguenesses of our time without history.

Another world: from the trains that carried us across China, I observed all the vivid details of a new landscape, terraced fields, a dry water course, hill towns hanging precipitously on the edge of a gorge, huge construction projects, the exhalation of dragon's breath from the holes in the hills where lime was being burned in huge cave furnaces, men and women living in houses excavated from the dark yellow earth, a wide river foaming with pollutants, all the sudden images that make any train trip like the experience of a poetic film. Other people's hard lives: I recalled the character in Mary McCarthy's novel, *Birds of America*, who says, *'il faut se méfier du pittoresque'*.

In Taiyuan, a large industrial city, parents pointed me out to their children and watched tolerantly as the children stared at this exotic bearded stranger. One afternoon I was walking across the road from a huge park to the hotel with Alison Bailey when a middle-aged man on a bicycle stopped to chat. Alison talked with him while I could only watch and smile. The man was very pleased to discover that he and I were the same age. After he pedalled off Alison told me more of the conversation. At one point he asked if she was overseas Chinese. Now Alison, in appearance, was a perfect English rose, skin pink and white, blue eyes, blonde hair, but for this man, far off in the interior of China, appearance meant little beside the fact that she spoke his language. If she spoke Chinese, she must be Chinese.

It was while in Taiyuan that we were taken to a steel-rolling mill out in the country, an example of the small-scale private enterprise that was now being encouraged. The owner had begun by digging wells, and somehow, with the collaboration of the local party secretary, a man with a face like a toad and crossed eyes, he had created this factory, in which the workers handled molten steel with only minimal safety gear, a few hard hats, light slippers on their feet. The factory gave us a little banquet, at which we were urged to toast repeatedly in the local distilled spirit that Merna Summers called – its prairie name – white lightning.

Wherever we went, when we talked to the local writers, there were memories of the Cultural Revolution, that great storm that shook the country now a distant thunder.

Night train to Xi'an, arrival at 4.30 a.m., no one to meet us.

We huddle on the long
unlit station platform
waiting for morning.

The ancient capital, Chang'an
was built here, buried here.
Rain speaks its memory.

A train arrives, departs.
Purposeful men and women
move in the gloom.

A woman stands on the track
crying out into the night.

Old poet, why does she call your name?

'Wang Wei. Wang Wei.'

Xi'an, like Suzhou, is a city with a long history. The great poets of the Tang period refer to it, and it still has ancient walls, ancient temples, only a few miles away the famous terra cotta army, hundreds of life-size figures discovered in an imperial tomb and restored, under a sheltering roof, a whole landscape of tall clay soldiers, faces detailed and alert, frozen in hardened red clay, watching us in their mystic future. From a bus we saw camels, pomegranates. Old men worshipped in the local mosque.

But the night streets were full of a modern energy, a parked bus turned into a diner, long bright rows of food stalls. All the truly great dynasties, one of our guides said, were open to the world. China, in 1987, felt itself to be increasingly open to the world. Behind each small shop, the glow of a TV set turned on. You can ask me anything, Gu Boxi had said, you can ask me anything. Just watch what will happen, Wang Shuanglin said, at the autumn party congress.

Two years later, it became evident that the new liberation would only be allowed within strict limits. Tiananmen Square, the huge space between the Forbidden City and the memorial hall that contained Mao's preserved body, took on a new mythic meaning. Seventeen years later, China is sending rockets into orbit. The children I saw, so precious, one to a family, riding on the backs of bikes wearing tinsel crowns, are grown up, some of them perhaps at work in the space program. The dissidents are still in prison. When Merna Summers bravely raised the question, our guides were quick to assure her that of course the people she mentioned were in prison; they were criminals.

Thirty

While I was working on the novel that became *A Postcard from Rome* – a novel about opera, aspiring to an operatic form, I decided that I must go to Italy, and if I was to go to Italy, I wanted to be able to speak Italian. I discovered that for only a few dollars I could enrol in a Queen's University introductory Italian course as an auditor. As an auditor you weren't supposed to have your written work marked, but the teacher Antonino Mazza – himself a poet, as it happened – said there was no point having me there if I didn't do the written work. So by the time we set off for Italy in the spring, I had enough of the language to read the newspapers and carry on a simple conversation.

A year or so after coming back from China, and perhaps inspired by the contact with another culture, I enrolled, once again as an auditor, in an introductory course in Russian. Italian, for someone who had some French and some Latin, had been comparatively easy. Russian was another thing altogether, a strange alphabet, an inflected language, a verb system of a different nature from ours. When I walked into class the first day, I saw a familiar face, Zal Yanovsky, once a member of the Lovin' Spoonful, once the husband of my sometime theatrical colleague Jackie Burroughs, now the proprietor of Chez Piggy, the cool place to go then, still, and probably Kingston's most successful restaurant. So Zalman and I took up our seats at the front, worked hard, glanced half-surreptitiously at each other's work to make sure the other wasn't getting ahead, while around us the young people lived their young lives. No fear of being too much of a keener in this class, look at the two old guys up at the front. This went on until early spring when Zal felt compelled to travel south for the Blue Jays' training camp.

You don't learn Russian in one year, so the next year I was back for the higher level course, and halfway through the second year, I also began to attend an evening seminar on translation. We worked through a lot of exercises, and then toward the end of the term, we were told we could choose any piece we liked and turn it from Russian to English. I'd earlier been complaining that it was impossible to find books in Russian, and

Maggie and Kate, who were both living in Toronto, collaborated to buy me a pile of Russian texts on sale second hand, including a three-volume collection of the stories of Anton Chekhov. I knew his plays much better than his stories, and decided that for my project I would tackle one of the stories from the collection. The three volumes were arranged chronologically, so I chose, more or less arbitrarily, the last story that Chekhov wrote.

It wasn't easy work to translate it, but I enjoyed the challenge. I laboured mightily, but even so I found that there were a few lines of dialogue that left me non-plussed. A noun seemed to be in the wrong case, the allusions to the parable of the prodigal son were complex and apparently confused. I took the little passage to Anna Matzov, who had taught me in the first-year course; she had been born and raised in Russia, leaving only in adult life, so surely she could explain. She looked at the lines of dialogue. 'But that's in the wrong case,' she said. Just as I thought. Clearly the speech was ungrammatical, and presumably the muddled references reflected the same sort of confusion in the speaker's mind. So I went back to the lines and worked out an English version that seemed to reflect what I'd found in the Russian.

Once the story was finished I decided to check it against an existing translation – I'd been determined not to use a crib while I was translating. I went to the library, found the Oxford complete Chekhov stories and looked up the last one. To my astonishment I discovered that the respectable academic translator hadn't taken the problem passage I'd been struggling with seriously. He carpentered up a bit of dialogue only vaguely related to the Russian. And when I checked some of the other dialogue I found that he had used a kind of stage cockney that was, to me, wholly unsuitable. I tucked this information away in my mind.

In the meantime I had sent a copy of my translation to Michael Macklem. I had no designs on him at that point, but I thought he'd be interested. He wrote back to say that he'd read the story on his annual trip by car from city to city across western Canada – that was still the way he and Anne sold their books – and if I wanted to do a book of translations he'd publish them – Michael at his best again, always ready for a project that seemed to him worthwhile. My Russian was anything but fluent, but for literary translation, what is essential is a knowledge of the language into which you're translating. There is a long tradition of literary translation: Pasternak had the audacity to translate Shakespeare. So I decided to have a go. I chose the last six stories in the last of my three volumes; that gave me a title, *Last Stories,* and a project of reasonable size. I had never, so far as I knew, read any of the stories in English.

Our house on Montreal Street – at the top of a hill overlooking a few blocks of downtown Kingston and beyond that the Cataraqui River – was four storeys high. The basement was where I had my study. We lived on the next two floors, and the top floor was a guest room, wide open, bright, hidden away at the top of a long staircase. Though I had written a number of books in my downstairs study, for the translations – perhaps to separate them from the rest of my life – I set up a table and chair on the top floor, and for hour after hour I laboured there. I had two large dictionaries, and using these I wrote out a rough literal translation, by hand, leaving space for corrections. I went back and in the interlinear spaces, I wrote a more polished translation. Then I moved to the typewriter. Hour after hour I was immersed in Chekhov's words. Now and then I went to the University library to use their copy of the Dahl dictionary, the Russian equivalent of the O.E.D. It was slow, laborious work, but I loved it, the struggle to catch the tone and meaning, to communicate them in English. My rule of thumb was that when I was in doubt, I should stay close to the literal, to avoid trying to be smarter than Chekhov. I was probably influenced in this attitude by my admiration for George Johnston's saga translations.

Once again I looked at no other translations until my own were completed and polished, then I made some comparisons lest I had perpetrated a clutch of schoolboy howlers. No signs of that, though I did find a line or two I had lost altogether in the long laborious course of the work. (Years later I discovered that in my polishing I had also elided a metaphor that was explicit in the Russian.) On the whole the translations stood up well beside the others I looked at. I didn't make a systematic check of other versions, but in spite of the fashion for mocking Constance Garnett these days, my impression was that hers were the most satisfying of the ones I scanned.

So Michael published the book. A couple of years before he'd used, on the cover of my poetry collection, *The Hundred Old Names,* a wonderful pencil drawing of me done by my daughter Kate, and I asked her to do a drawing of Chekhov for the cover of this book.

Reviews: I've never believed the writers who say they don't read them. Writers are notorious liars, and reviews are reflections of how at least a few readers have responded. In the case of the Chekhov, I wasn't putting my own personality on display, and responses weren't reactions to who I was, so looking back at them I am in a more detached position than usual.

Eve Drobot writing in the *Globe and Mail:* 'There is not one [story] that has not already appeared in a previous anthology or collection. That leads me to wonder why Helwig bothered, except perhaps to display his skills with the Russian language ... I can't quarrel with his vaunted technical prowess, but to be frank, there are some mistakes that don't need to be corrected, for example every version of 'The Lady with the Little Dog' ... has the attractive young woman arrive on the scene with a Pomeranian. Helwig has her with a 'white spitz'.... Does it matter?'

Merna Summers, writing for the *Edmonton Journal:* 'the translation itself – Helwig's version of Chekhov – is quite simply inexpressibly wonderful. I knew all of the stories but one, and knew them pretty well, but I finished reading the Helwig translation with the feeling that I had experienced Chekhov's writing in a new and somehow more accurate way. I am not speaking here about accuracy of the translation of words – I am not in a position to compare either translation with the original Russian – but of something else: the way that writers use language to evoke emotion, and non-writers sometimes do not ... Individual lines could be compared to demonstrate the felicity of Helwig's translation, but it is less in the individual lines than it is in the progress of rhythms that his version demonstrates its superiority. Helwig's rhythms are more graceful, his sentences more muscular, and the result is that our emotions are evoked – we feel – more as Chekhov himself might have chosen to evoke them if he had done his writing in English.'

Of course one prefers positive reviews, but the Summers review is a serious one, an attempt to encounter the book and write accurately about it, while the *Globe* review is representative of the glib, not very attentive reading, the superior tone that has sometimes been the tendency of the book page in Canada's National Newspaper, creating the illusion of having standards without paying the price in care and disinterested attention.

On the other hand the senior editors of the *Globe and Mail* were perfect: after all they hired me. It was sometime in 1990 that I got a call from John Cruickshank, then the managing editor. I had known John some years before when he was a young reporter at the Kingston *Whig-*

Standard. He asked if I was interested in writing regularly for the new Facts and Arguments section on the *Globe*'s back page. I was, and I began to appear there about once a month, essays on a wide variety of topics, everything from eccentricity to the magic of looking in and out of windows. I would phone with an idea, to make sure I wasn't repeating something recently published in the paper, then send them off the essay. Initially I called John Cruickshank with my suggestions, later Philip Jackman, who was editing the Facts and Arguments page. The pay was good, and there was a lot of response to the pieces I wrote: CTV called to ask me to be on a talk-show panel, I got calls from old acquaintances. One day as I was riding my bike along a Kingston street, someone shouted from his front lawn that he'd enjoyed my essay that morning. Around the income tax deadline, I wrote an essay on taxes, about the fact that while I was willing enough to pay my share, but I resented being turned into a bookkeeper in order to do it. Early in the morning I got a phone call: a male voice said he was calling from the federal tax office. Turned out to be a joke: the voice was a retired taxman who now earned his living as a consultant, and he gave me a useful tip. When I wrote about how the Senate might be reformed – my argument being that members should be selected by lot from lists of names provided by the main religious, artistic, scientific, scholarly, business, labour, and native people's councils – I got shifted off the back page and the argument appeared on the commentary page, opposite the editorials. I still think my idea was a good one.

For a little more than two years I wrote for the Facts and Arguments page, and I had a high old time doing it. I wrote lightheartedly about talking back to the television set, seriously about secular values and facing death, discussed all kinds of other things, art forgery, travel. The column that got the most intense responses was one about unlived lives. In my own case that was singing, but I suggested that everyone has an awareness of roads untaken. Not long after the essay I got a call from someone I'd met years before who'd recognized herself in the essay. Later a woman in the choir in Montreal told me she'd found the essay on her partner's bulletin board, read it, then sat down and cried for twenty minutes. I could never have guessed that in that particular essay I was speaking for so many others as well as for myself.

In the years when I was putting together the Chekhov translations and writing those pieces for the *Globe,* I was looking for a publisher for what I believed was the best novel I had ever written. *Just Say the Words* had begun to come to me in the summer of 1987, first characters who connected to a summer place near Kingston we had rented for a couple of weeks, then on the trip to China, the sense of the expatriates who had passed through or stayed. The first Chekhov story I translated found its way in, and a splendidly theatrical performance in drag by a touring actor who played Kingston for a few nights. The book was full of event, but it was held together by characters, not plot, especially by four older characters: Martin and Ruthie were once, long ago in England, married, but in the novel's present, are amicable friends, long divorced, Martin living out his life as a gay man and an actor still struggling to get work; Charles and Vera met up in Shanghai just before Mao's army arrived, but soon separated after their return to England, Charles taking up with Ruthie. The four characters all find themselves in Toronto, Vera and Ruthie sharing a house, Charles married again to a young Vietnamese refugee. Another younger generation of characters is beginning life around them. It's possible that these younger characters are less vividly realized than the quartet of ancient ruins, but the whole is carefully woven together, the first and last sections taking place in Toronto in 1987–8, the second in Shanghai in 1948, the third in London in 1953. By the last section of the novel, Charles and Ruthie are dead, and sweet, rueful Martin is onstage as Prospero in a production of *The Tempest* financed by a bequest in Ruthie's will. (Ruthie is onstage too – her ashes in an attractive pottery container.)

In the early drafts there was a section from the 1930s, written in letters and mainly about Ruthie's father, but I decided it wandered too far, and I extracted it, and it was published as a separate novella, *The Blueberry Cliffs*. The London section was added after my daughter Maggie read a draft and made the oracular pronouncement that though the book was long, it should probably be even longer. There is always a bit of a letdown at the end of writing a novel. In the case of *Just Say the Words,* I found myself terribly lonely for the characters who had been my companions for the previous many months.

Viking Penguin had been my publisher for the previous four novels. The second of them, *A Postcard from Rome,* was a willed book, which came together well enough perhaps, but never quite sprang to life. Then came *Old Wars,* a short but neatly shaped spy story, developed from the radio play written years before. The last of the four, *Of Desire,* was in part a reflection of a slough of despond in which I found myself, and even as I read the final proofs I was tempted to withdraw it, but that meant returning the $7000 advance, not huge, but significant. So I let it be published. It's not a book I care to look back at, and probably I should have withdrawn it, at whatever cost. *The Bishop* had sold best of the four, and I suspect that even before seeing *Just Say the Words*, Penguin had decided to drop me from their list. (They dropped Douglas Glover and Matt Cohen about the same time.) And the version they saw still contained *The Blueberry Cliffs*, which made the book too long and episodic. So they rejected the book, and I found myself, for the first time in more than twenty years, looking for a publisher.

I tried one or two other commercial publishers, one of them McClelland and Stewart. Ellen Seligman, who was their fiction editor, was an acquaintance, and I called her before sending the book. Yes, she said, send it. But she went on to say, quite explicitly, that even if she liked it, she might not be able to do it. That was what happened. I got a call from Ellen, after she read it, expressing a good deal of enthusiasm for the book, and we discussed it in some detail. This was, however, a period of economic recession, and when the book went to the editorial committee, the sales people said no. Ellen, very kindly, sent the book to another publisher with an explanation and recommendation, but it sat there unread for months, and I asked for it back.

I hadn't tried every single large publisher, but the book had been around a bit by now. I was probably going to have to go to someplace smaller. I decided not to mail it all over the country, and I sent it to Michael Macklem at Oberon. Michael had gone on publishing my poetry over the previous ten years while others published the novels, and it had always been his contention that I was a poet led astray, but when he read *Just Say the Words,* he responded with great enthusiasm (an enthusiasm that led to a bit of overstatement on the blurb when the book came out), but it was a relief to have the book in the hands of someone whose belief in it was passionate.

The recession in publishing also affected the CBC, and less work was coming my way. I had the regular *Globe* essays, but after ten good years of freelancing, I began to find that money was tight. I was glad enough to get a writer-in-residence gig at the Pickering Public Library, and pleased when Queen's phoned and asked me to teach a single course for one year – my beloved nineteenth-century fiction seminar. At the last minute they decided I had to teach some Victorian poetry as well. I didn't know it and I didn't like it, I said, but I made a few gestures.

A few months later, I got a letter from Michael Macklem. He had access to some money to pay me if I would acquire and edit some books for them – four a year for three years was what he proposed, not more than one of the four to be poetry. Their small staff was completely preoccupied with the day-to-day running of the business. *Where to Eat in Canada,* always their best seller, took a good chunk of time. No one was free to search out good new things.

I think what he had in mind is that I would draw in existing manuscripts from good writers that I knew. I happily agreed to take on the job, but what I had in mind was something else. I thought I might create a whole new series of books, serious non-fiction, something Oberon hadn't often done, and a kind of book that was likely to get some attention and even sell. I'd recently read William Styron's book *Darkness Visible,* a book-length essay on depression, and I thought the form was an interesting one, the memoir-essay, of a length to be read in a single evening, a kind of conversation between one mind and the world. Oberon was very nervous about all this non-fiction, but I think the books did well for them. I saw six of them into print. The first, *Nothing Sacred,* by Amy Friedman, had its roots in columns Amy had been writing for the *Whig-Standard,* columns in which a tough-minded woman, who had always considered herself a feminist, argued with some of the more rigid assumptions she saw around her in the women's movement. The book got a good deal of attention when it was published. Another of the series began when I read a short story about a nurse leaving the distant native reservation where she had been working. My assumption (correct) was that the story was largely based on reality, and I got in touch with Judy Smith, its author and suggested she write a book about her experiences. It came out as *Native Blood.* The other four were all by men who were members, more or less, of my own generation, who wrote about their lives, and the central idea that informed each of those lives. I'd known David Lewis Stein since university, and I asked him to write about his life in the city of Toronto and his involvement in urban affairs; he'd studied urban planning and had been the *Star*'s city columnist for many years. Peter Harcourt had founded the Queen's department of film studies, and he wrote about his upbringing in an earlier, blunted, puritan Canada, the struggle to escape that and the movement from the study of music to literature and then to film. William Aide was another university friend. I'd heard him play in concert and in private, over the years, and asked him to write about how, a boy from an ordinary, not very musical family, he found himself a concert pianist. Prompted by the group suicide of a cult near Montreal, I suggested to Terry Rigelhof that he consider those events and write about the emotional force of religion, how he set out to become a priest then turned away from it. All of these books were commissioned, and I saw them through from the first discussions to their publication. All of them got significant attention, and Rigelhof's book, *A Blue Boy in a Black Dress* was nominated for the Governor General's Award. The one book that never happened was a book about a musical life to be written by Anton Kuerti. I'd got to know Anton in the early 1980s when he was playing the complete Schubert piano music in a number of Ontario cities, including Kingston, the concerts part of his project of recording the complete Schubert. I wrote to him, we talked about the book, and he agreed to write it. He liked the idea. I met up with him at least once, and we had dinner in a Chinese vegetarian restaurant to discuss the project, but between his commitment to playing, studying new music and composing, the book never quite happened. I think he still plans to get to it someday.

The fiction I edited came to me as completed manuscripts, though I had a hand in the arrangement of the story collections and worked on the structure of a couple of novels – my years at the CBC left me with a sharp eye for plot problems. The grant money that Oberon was paying me ran out after a couple of years, but I was willing to amortize the money over more books, and they were willing to have me. Over four or five years I edited more than twenty books, going on until Nick Macklem and I had a serious disagreement over the editing of a book, and I decided that the occasional problems of working at Oberon – you had to send the same message to two or three different people or it would likely be lost, that kind of thing – were more than I wanted to handle.

One of my favourites among the books I edited, and one that apparently, and regrettably, sold poorly, was a collection of letters called *A Magic Prison*. I had found myself back in touch with Henry Beissel, a poet I'd first met in the 1950s when he was a graduate student at University College. Henry had earlier left Germany and was remaking himself as a poet writing in English, and by the early 1990s, he was the head of the Creative Writing department at Concordia University. He was, it turned out, still in touch with the brilliant and wacky Edward Lacey.

In 1958 I was one of the editors of the University College literary magazine, the *Undergrad*. The college had a fund which provided awards for undergraduate writing, and the winners of this contest were offered to the *Undergrad* for publication. One of the winners was someone named E. A. Lacey, for a group of translations from the eighteenth-century poet André Chénier. These translations are impressive even now, cleverly rhymed, metrical without being forced or laboured. I'm not sure that I knew then just how good they were, though we published them.

I can't place my first meeting with Edward but I do remember that by the next year it fell to me to try to persuade him to give us something new to publish. At first he said no, but finally agreed that we could publish a few things under a pseudonym. The pseudonym he chose was NBC. He suggested that apart from the television network, it might stand for Nellie Blythe Carr. One of the poems was called 'Doctor Death'.

'Incurable,' says Doctor Death
Of this disease of drawing breath;
'I can prescribe an opiate, faith,
A purgative, hate, a palliative, hope,
And my old secret cure-all, rope.'

That epigram was typical in both its wit and polish and its essential despair. One might say that it was the premature and unearned despair of an undergraduate except that it was at the core of Edward's personality, so far as I can see, for the rest of his life. As was the ambivalence about publication. He had the common desire for what he had written to be read but alongside that a desire for privacy or concealment. Henry Beissel has explained how Edward insisted that his reviews in *EDGE* be presented under his own name with a note claiming that this was a pseudonym. Just his kind of joke.

I think it was in 1958 that Edward got thrown out of the University College men's residence. Male undergraduates were expected to show a certain amount of bravado and rebelliousness, but Edward managed to do this, as he did everything, in his own way. The residence had a dining hall attached, with student waiters and a student headwaiter, a man with a certain ponderously serious manner about him. On one occasion Edward, having had one dinner, went back for another. (Or it may have been a second dessert; I have most of this story at second hand.) The headwaiter told him he mustn't take the second helping, and Edward was defiant. This led to some kind of trial before the residence disciplinary committee, known – how very English and how very pretentious – as the Caput.

That august body decided that Edward should be deprived of his food privileges for a period of time – one week or two, I believe. This put Edward on his mettle, and he replied by writing to all his professors – he was at this time a senior student in Modern Languages and an outstandingly brilliant one – to say that since he had been deprived of his food privileges, he would be too weak to attend classes and would have to languish in his room until his period of enforced starvation was over.

Edward had put the cat among the pigeons. The student newspaper became involved, and there were many late night meetings over the issue. It was a perfect example of his inventive malice. A year later he came close to being refused his degree when, though no longer living in the residence, he drunkenly assaulted one of the residence dons, pounding him on the chest and calling him a prick. He explained to me that since everyone called the man a prick behind his back, he thought it was time someone said it to his face.

He was a loony and a troublemaker, but his brilliance and thoughtfulness were undeniable. Though we weren't close friends, he would now and then appear at the door of my room late at night, thin, nervous, voluble, coming in to chat for a while. One of the things we had in common was a liking for minor poets. You could get at them, somehow, weren't held off by walls of historical piety. Edward appeared to remember every line of poetry he'd ever read, and he didn't quote to show off, simply to make a point. Alternatively he would express malicious intentions toward his best friends or tell me stories about his war with a West Indian student who claimed to have a gun and was planning to shoot him.

When my first book of poems came out in 1968, Edward reviewed it in *EDGE*. It was a long review, probing, unforgivingly astute and analytical; by the end I felt as if my brain had been subjected to a kind of spiritual X-ray. He concluded that there were at least a handful of poems he'd keep for an anthology – a not-unfair assessment of the book. I knew that Edward had gone off to South America – his review of my poems had been sent in from Rio de Janeiro – and at some point he had come out of the closet. In certain corners of the world he became something of a hero as Canada's first openly gay poet. After that I had lost track of him, but Henry Beissel explained that he was in fact in a nursing home not far from where Henry lived in the far eastern corner of Ontario. He had been struck by a car in Bangkok, seriously injured and repatriated, having by then spent all the significant amount of money left to him by his parents. When I mentioned that I was editing books, Henry told me he had kept all Edward's letters to him during his years of travel, and the two of us went to the nursing home and broached the idea that they might be published. Edward seemed to regard this as on odd idea; by now, like Tiresias, he wanted only to die, but I got hold of the bundle of largely hand-written text, photocopied it and returned the originals to Henry. Then I sat down with the pale, almost illegible photocopies and started to assemble a book. The text of the letters was remarkably perfect – Edward did not make errors in syntax or spelling, even when he was scribbling in noisy hotel rooms in the third world. The writing was focused and often brilliant, and I did a careful editing job, selecting from the pile of letters enough passages to create a self-portrait, tell the story of his life and travels without a lot of interlinear explanation. When I had selected, marked, arranged the letters, I took the heap of horrible photocopy to my friend Jean Shepherd who had a small business creating and designing texts, and she turned them into legible type. The book's cover was a portrait of Edward as a young man, painted by Barker Fairley, the scholar and artist.

In the course of making arrangements for the book, I visited Edward in a Toronto hospital, where he was part of some rehabilitation program, and then in a boarding house in downtown Toronto. A street near Allen Gardens, large brick houses, old trees. I went in a door at street level, and one or two men were standing around in a common area with a coffee maker and some old chairs, and then I went up a dark staircase, two floors, and there was a long narrow hall with a window at the end, and along the hall, closed doors. I made my way to the third or fourth door on the right and knocked and waited.

It was a boarding house for burnt-out cases, drink, drugs, madness, failure. Edward had earlier signed a letter of agreement with Henry Beissel about the existence of the book, and I now had a contract ready for his signature. I knew that if someone didn't actually deliver it into his hands, it would vanish into the disorder of his life. I knocked and waited and knocked again, assured by the man across the hall that he was in there, and finally I roused him, and after a few minutes talk, he got out of bed and dressed and we walked down to Queen Street and found a Turkish restaurant where Edward told me a little about the Turkish language and bickered amiably with the waiter over the distinction between Turkish and Lebanese food. I got the contract signed.

Two days later, I went back to see him again before leaving Toronto. I knocked and once again woke him and asked, too quickly perhaps, if he wanted to go out somewhere. No, he said, this time. He was sleeping. If he got up, his sleep would be spoiled. So I closed the door and left him there. A few months later, and before the book appeared, he had a fatal heart attack. The book was shown some support by other gay writers, who reviewed it here and there, but even by the standards of a small literary press it sold badly. Few people had heard of Edward. He wasn't part of the accepted story of Canadian literature. Still, *A Magic Prison* strikes me as a fascinating portrait of a complex and intriguing personality, and of a life which was in equal parts self-creation and self-destruction. Perhaps it has no place in an age of piety and cheerfulness, but it is an energetic, elegant and fascinating book. Does it matter whether anyone remembers Edward, reads his words? One feels that it should, but it's hard to say why: we get one life, we do what we can, we go, like thousands every day.

Thirty-one

Nancy and I bought the old house on Wolfe Island in 1988. It is said to be the oldest standing residence on the island, and though I've never been able to date it exactly, I'd guess that it was built around 1840 or perhaps even earlier. I can date a later interior wall from a newspaper pasted on it: 1881. We discovered the place by accident after being sent to look at an altogether different house by Barbara Rubens, the imaginative real estate agent who had sold us the tall stone building on Montreal Street five years before. The building we'd come to Wolfe Island to see was interesting, no more than that, but as we made our way back to the ferry, we saw a long, low frame cottage at the edge of the water, just off the main street and tucked in behind another more modern house. The unpainted clapboard was darkened by years of weather. The house appeared to be empty, and on the front was a sign for an auction sale. We both knew from the first moment that we must have it.

We later learned that the former owner, Tyner (familiar for Antoine) LaRush, who was crippled by polio in childhood and later injured by a serious fall while painting the ferry, had lived all his life in the old family home, and nothing much had been altered in the seventy or eighty years of his time. When he was told he could no longer use the outhouse – which still stood, the hole placed so that everything falling through it would drop on the shore close to the waterline – his nephew got hold of a portable toilet and had it set up in the tiny backyard. When Tyner died, he left the house to that nephew – Des, his name was. With some help from Barbara Rubens, we managed to meet with him and have a look at the interior of the place. Des was one of those innocent souls who believe that if you hang on to an old house, the price will keep going up and eventually you'll be rich (the truth being that eventually the house will fall down and you'll have nothing), but while I looked over the inside of the house, Nancy, who was always quick and clever in negotiation, convinced him to sell it to us.

The wide front door of the house, old pine with solid panels, hung crooked, but it opened and closed. Inside was a substantial room with a low ceiling of tongue-and-groove pine, four small windows, and doors to a back porch and a pantry with walls of wide pine boards. To the left was a doorway to another large room and a small dim back bedroom. A cook-stove sat in front of the chimney, sold in the auction but not yet collected, and hidden behind a board wall was a narrow stairway that led to three more rooms upstairs. Though most of the contents of the house had been sold off, there were still old clothes, a few books, letters, and a lot of cheap Roman Catholic religious art. Behind the house was a low, deteriorated boatshed, and a long rickety wooden dock, at the end of which a neigh-bour tied his small inboard.

The shoreline a few feet beyond the house lies at the entry to Barrett's Bay, an inlet that once led to a canal crossing the island. Looking to the west a few degrees, the city of Kingston is visible, and the causeway that passes over the Cataraqui River. This is the point where Lake Ontario meets the St Lawrence River, and it's always puzzling to know how to describe the body of water close by the back wall – ducks and muskrats swimming past a few feet from the windows. Is it the bay, the lake or the river? All three are joined at this point. Wolfe Island, which lies between the Canadian shore and the American, between the past and the present, and the house, an anomalous survival on a tiny patch of limestone and grass, suggest some borderland world where everything might have a multiplicity of names.

The old frame cottage, its sills resting on bare limestone, had been moved to this location from somewhere else, and as I worked on it over the next several years, I came to suspect – another anomaly – that it had once been two small houses that were later joined together. Each half had possessed a front and back door. During its long history the house had been a school, a grocery store and a bootlegger's, called Flynn's Saloon. An old woman who was raised on the island and still owned a little cabin she visited every summer, told stories about how the back porch once went all the way across the house, and in it there would be dancing with Louis LaRush, Tyner's father, playing the fiddle. More stories about how, when he was drinking and on bad terms with his wife, Louis would move into the boathouse.

The strange old dwelling, wide wooden doors, low ceilings, so close to the water that when you looked out the window you felt as if you might be on a boat, was a magical place. I had sold the house at Ompah, and in the good weather I began to spend my time at the island, doing nearly all the renovation with my own hands – though I was making no attempt to modernize, only to patch and paint and prevent too much deterioration. The windows, when I started, were all unmatched, and I got a local craftsman to build me new sashes, wooden mullions, six panes over six in each sash, and I took all the window frames apart, rebuilt them, and installed the new sashes. Within a year or so, even though they were painted with clear preservative, the wind and weather darkened them, and now, sixteen years later, they look as old as the walls around them. I came upon a farmhouse a few miles away which was on the point of falling down and with the owner's agreement stripped off some of the old clapboard to match what we were missing. I remember a cool spring day when I was prying off the old boards. The house was on the south side of the island, not far from the narrow channel between Wolfe Island and the American shore, and a huge flock of Canada geese was feeding in the nearby fields, the air clamorous with their gabbling. I used that sound in a radio play I was writing, about Confederate spies hiding out on the island during the American Civil War, preparing a plan to assassinate President Lincoln, then learning that someone had beaten them to it. The island, that house, gave me constant inspiration.

Again the green air is filled
with the quick unreelings
of the blackbird's call.

Across the sunstruck pale water
life and death wait.

The cormorant flies close
over its black watery shadow.

In summer the air was full of swallows, in autumn you'd see big flocks of migrating ducks. The second year I turned the dim little back bedroom into a summer porch, breaking through the walls overlooking the water and putting in French doors. When I began to knock holes in the plaster, looking for the studs, I discovered there were no studs. The framing was post and beam construction, with wide spaces between the hand-hewn vertical members. A little nervous about bringing the structure down on my head, I knocked out walls only between the posts;

nothing vertical was cut, but where I removed a small window, I found the framing of an old doorway, so it was safe to break through there. I cut another, narrower opening beside one of the hardwood posts. Jack Chapman, the Kingston woodworker who had made the new sashes, manufactured the French doors, and I set them into the walls. Their only failing, after all these years, is that a north wind will blow rain in at the bottom. I've spent many hours in that room, alone or with company, reading or staring out across the bay, watching the ferry arrive at the dock, half hidden by the Manitoba maple that grows like a weed beside the old outhouse – which now serves as storage for paddles, life jackets, a lawnmower.

While I was opening up the little room to the light, I hired Bob Naismith, a Toronto actor who was working with a troupe rehearsing on the island, to tear down the boathouse. I'd looked at it carefully and decided that it couldn't be saved. The old wood was badly rotted. The theatrical troupe Bob was working with had some horses and a wagon, and they were preparing a performance which they planned to tour to various communities, giving outdoor shows. Obviously the pay for such a venture wasn't much, and I had all the work I could handle in the house itself, so Bob agreed to deal with the boathouse. One day when I was painting in the newly refurbished room, Bob turned up.

'I looked at the boathouse,' he said. 'It's full of wasps.'

I saw that could be a problem.

'I thought I'd better smoke them out.'

I agreed that made sense and went back to my painting, noticing now and then that he was going back and forth making his preparations. He had, mysteriously, a hose from Erricos' restaurant, the *Sportsman's*, a few feet away across the gravel road. Then he had a can of gasoline. Large can. Then he was lighting a piece of newspaper and tossing it into the boathouse, which exploded into flame and a ball of black smoke. Within seconds I had put down my paintbrush and the two of us began to haul buckets of water from the lake to damp down the flames rising from the dry old wood soaked with gasoline. Erricos came out and moved his truck to safety away from the flames. I expected to see the volunteer fire department arriving, but Wolfe Island is an easygoing place, and everyone ignored the conflagration. Nancy appeared from the ferry and did what she could with the little spray of water from the hose. In an hour Bob and I were both black with soot, the fire was out, and the boathouse was gone except for the chunks of tin that had been nailed on the roof. It was a memorable afternoon. I moved that fire from a summer afternoon to a winter night, and from Wolfe Island to Prince Edward Island when I wrote the novella, *Close to the Fire*, a few years later.

In the spring of 1991 my father, who'd had two operations for bowel cancer, was discovered to have lung cancer, inoperable at his age and in his state of health. In the previous months he'd been showing signs of dementia, especially at night. He had six months or a year to live, I was told, and I arranged for my parents to move to a seniors' apartment in Kingston, where I was close by. Wolfe Island was one of the places I took them, where my father might sit in the sun by the water and take whatever pleasure was still possible. It was a hectic and distressing summer, and I didn't do much work on the old house. My father died in October – while I was in the midst of serving, with Ann Copeland and Guy Vanderhaeghe, as a juror for the Governor General's Award for fiction – and at the end of December, Nancy and I looked at the mess I was making of my life and decided to split up for good. She kept the house on Montreal Street, and I kept the one on Wolfe Island, which was still only half renovated. The next summer I spent a good deal of my time there. I remember Tom, who'd had a heart attack in the spring, coming over for dinner, and saying, as I walked him to the ferry in the evening, that he was anticipating his last, best years. He didn't get to have them.

That summer I renovated the main downstairs room, once a kitchen, now a living room, while as much as I had of a kitchen was in the back porch. The plaster in the front room had deteriorated so badly that daylight was visible through it. I packed the walls with Styrofoam and plastered over top. When the back porch had been built, it had covered over four or five inches of an old window, so I decided to move the window a few inches to the right. Sounds simple enough, but one of the oddities of the building was that many of the walls were filled with very old, soft, unmortared brick. I don't know why. My guess was that brick – which in the nineteenth century sometimes came in as ballast for the ships that were to be loaded with timber to be sent to England – was cheap or free, and someone had thought it might provide a bit of insulation. What it meant in this case was that above the window opening, the wall was filled with loose brick. If you took out the framing of the window, the brick would fall on you. I managed somehow, working alone, to keep the brick supported by a mixture of new and old horizontal framing until I could nail in place a crosspiece strong enough to support it. I worked at such things all day, then cleaned myself up a little, made some sort of meal, and lay on a wicker couch with a beer, reading and staring across the water, sometimes fell asleep there.

When everything else in the room was done, I set out to paint the floor. I painted my way out the door, locked up and set out to Montreal to meet up with my old friend Henry Shapiro, who had rented an apartment and was spending a season there, away from his haunts in Saint Louis, where I'd visited him in the spring. A day or so later we were walking down a street in his Montreal neighbourhood. The city was, we both noticed, a wonderful place.

'Have you ever thought of living in a bigger city?' Henry said.

'No,' I said, 'I don't think I ever have.'

On we went, but his question stuck in my mind over the following days, and within a couple of weeks I'd decided to move to Montreal. Simple as that. Time to move on. My life in Kingston was a muddle. Nancy and I had made a final severance, and Judith was lost to me, though she drifted by sometimes. I felt I'd been in Kingston too long; the city was rank with the smell of my life. The only thing I felt pleased about in those days was the volunteer work I'd been doing in the pediatric department of Hotel Dieu hospital: I was good with children, and it felt worthwhile to offer them company, to give their parents a break.

I remember someone asking me how I could stand it, being among those sick and suffering children, some of them dying, but I have never found other people's distress contagious, so I could accept that the situation of each child was as it was and do what little was possible to improve things for a few minutes. The one time I remember being upset was in the case of a young boy with some kind of wasting disease. I never learned the exact diagnosis, but I had spent time with him once or twice, playing a board game or reading. It seemed to me that he was getting weaker and was unlikely to recover, but in the introductory sessions held each day when the volunteers arrived no one had mentioned that possibility. Perhaps I might be misreading, misinterpreting; I was rattled by this. But the day came soon enough when the nurse who went through the list of patients at the beginning of an afternoon session said out loud that the boy wasn't going to get better, and knowing I wasn't exaggerating his situation, I could turn my mind to taking him out for a walk in a wheelchair, a small enough thing, but a break from his hospital room at least.

One memorable afternoon I found myself with a little girl, two or so years old. She was said to be suffering from severe back pains, though the doctors were finding no organic source. I took her off to the playroom while the pediatrician spoke with her mother. She didn't want to go, and I was wary of picking her up lest I hurt her back, but the doctor somehow made clear to me that it was all right to carry her, so I took her away, screaming, to the large bright playroom, closed the half door and sat down on the floor with her. I made a few gestures toward playing with her, but she rejected them angrily. I rolled a big soft ball toward her, she kicked it furiously back. So I rolled it gently toward her again, letting her kick it or throw it and generally be as angry as she wanted. I ignored the rage and noise. At least one of us would be calm and happy. In a few minutes, I asked her if she wanted to read a book. That got a loud 'No!' Fine, I said, but I thought I'd read it to myself. So I began to read aloud, and before long she couldn't resist having a look at the pictures. I remained studiously detached, but within an hour she was happily walking down the hall with me, hand in hand, while we fetched her a Popsicle. Of course I only had to deal with her for two hours, then I could go home and wait for my headache to dissipate.

Once I had decided to leave Kingston, I acted quickly, and by September I had moved to Montreal, to a small apartment on the Plateau Mont-Royal, which my daughter Kate had found for me when I was prepared to take something much less appealing in Little Burgundy. The flat was a *co-propriété indivise,* on avenue de Chateaubriand where it formed a quiet *cul de sac.* The building was three storeys high, the ground floor the office of an architect, which looked as if they had begun to renovate it but never got past the tearing down – bare walls with more or less random areas of plaster and bare brick. The architect owned the whole building, but to get some cash, he sold me the apartment on the second floor and was planning to sell the top floor apartment as well – at the moment his brother was living there. Within a few months the third apartment was sold to a young man who was a waiter at a nearby restaurant. He forced the issue of getting the building legally constituted as three separate condominiums, a complicated bureaucratic process, but it went through – and very fortunately, since the architect went bankrupt a year or so later, and we could have been in a terrible legal mess.

It was a typical Montreal apartment, a steep stairway leading up to the landing, a string running through metal eyes down to the door so you

Maggie visiting in Montreal.

could unlock it without going down. Inside, the classic Montreal *salon double*, the front room with a little alcove where I set up my work table. The hall led back past a narrow bathroom with a window opening onto a light-well, to the kitchen and the doorway of a small bedroom. With high ceilings, front and back windows, the apartment was bright enough to be pleasant, and it was my home for the next three and a half years. I remember the place with affection. It was where I rebuilt my life, learned to accept solitude in a quiet corner of the splendid city that spread its varied neighbourhoods all around the mountain.

For the first month or two of my time there, Henry was still settled in his apartment in lower Westmount. In NDG were my friends the Shepherds. Thirty-five years before, Henry and Harvey and I had lived in the same University College residence; now we were all in the same city again. In October, Henry went back to St Louis, but by then I had begun to sing in Patrick Wedd's choir at the Church of St John the Evangelist, and the music there became the centre of my life. I had acquaintances in Montreal, the writers Ray Smith, Terry Rigelhof, Ted Phillips. Kerry McSweeney, a colleague at Queen's, was now at McGill. Michael Rasminsky, who had written *Katy Cruel* with me a lifetime before, was practising medicine and doing research. Even so I experienced moments of despairing solitude. It was always worst, somehow, in the crowded aisles of Provigo on Mont-Royal, where I went to do my shopping. Nights I explored the neighbourhood on foot. My car was usually parked on a nearby street, but twice a week I had to move it so they could send the street-sweeping machines past. I developed the habit of driving up the mountain and walking for an hour through the woods, then driving back when the parking was legal again. You make a life out of small habits like that.

I began a novel, abandoned it. *I'm afraid I have no people in me,* I wrote in a notebook around that time. I wrote a few pieces for the *Globe* and then got a call saying that all the professional writers who'd been used to start up the commentary column – my old friend from university, Erna Paris, was one of the others – were being dropped, and all the contributions were to come from readers – the equivalent of a radio phone-in show. My impression when I looked at the paper later on was that the writing was much more confessional. You whine about your sorrow and I'll whine about mine, was the way I've sometimes put it – unfairly I'm sure – but it was odd to think that you spend a lifetime learning to work away from your own experience, to create something a little more detached, objective, stylish, only to find that you're replaced by the merely personal. Still, I'd had a good run, and I reused a number of the columns in two later books of essays and memoirs – in fact it was the work for the *Globe* that started me writing essays and led to those books. And by that point I had begun to review books for Bryan Demchinsky at the *Gazette*. While I was still in Kingston the previous book editor, Mark Abley, had commissioned a couple of pieces, a review of a complete collection – Russian with English translations – of the poems of Anna Akhmatova (which prompted me to do some translations of my own), and a centennial tribute to Pasternak, and when I got to Montreal, I had lunch with Mark, and he introduced me to Bryan, his replacement, and also suggested I get in touch with Jane Lewis at the CBC. Bryan and Jane became my most important professional contacts in the city.

So I woke alone in the mornings in the little back bedroom, made breakfast, sat down at the table in the front alcove and worked. Another novel begun and abandoned, a character I liked, but nothing to do with him. Books edited for Oberon. Choir practice one night a week. Another Sunday morning practice and then the service. An occasional weekday service. A couple of months after I moved I got a call telling me that my friend Bill Barnes was in hospital, kept alive by machines, heart failure the last of the complications of diabetes that had afflicted him. I drove to Kingston to visit his inert body, his chest lifting and falling with breath that was not his own. I returned for the funeral after the machines were turned off. I was also making frequent trips to Niagara to see my mother, who was still well at eighty-six, but lonely, and being diabetic, in need of someone to make sure that she remembered her injection, tested her blood sugar. I had arranged to pay a local woman, a decent but disorganized soul, to come in each day and make sure everything got underway safely. She did this, but her own life was botched and messy, and at some point she got evicted and suggested strongly that since she had no place to go, my mother might take her in. Even at eighty-six and weakening a little, my mother wouldn't go for that. I might, I suppose, have given in to what my mother wanted and moved in with her, but I couldn't do it. I came and went. *Sauve qui peut.* My eldest cousin Margaret, my father's niece, had settled in Niagara with her second husband, and she and Ross were always attentive in my parents' later days. By Christmas of that year, my mother had began to fall asleep in her chair, something she had never done in her life: to sleep in the daytime was a confession of unconscionable weakness. After Christmas I went to Niagara more often, struggled to find someone reliable who would come in daily. Her blood sugar began to go out of whack, and she spent days in hospital. One of her feet became infected and had to be soaked in Epsom salts.

It was late in April while I was staying at my mother's that I got a call to tell me that Tom Marshall had been found dead in his little house on Victoria Street in Kingston. 'A dear, stumbling, large-souled, mystic man' was what I said of him when the *Whig-Standard* asked for a comment, and I can live with those words as an epitaph for my old friend. I drove to Kingston for his memorial service, which was held at the Public Library, with a boozy wake afterward at Chez Piggy, one of his favourite haunts.

Back in Niagara, I was sitting with my mother at breakfast one day and her eyes closed, as if in sleep. When she didn't wake, I carried her into the front room and set her on the couch. It didn't take me long to decide that she wasn't asleep, that she'd probably had a stroke, and I called her doctor. He came to the house, confirmed the obvious, and admitted her to the small local hospital. She came back to consciousness, but she was unable to speak, and partly paralyzed, she lingered for two or three weeks and then died – almost by choice, she refused to eat – just after her eighty-seventh birthday.

So within ten months I had moved to a new city, experienced the deaths of two of my closest friends and my mother. Now I had to clear out her house, sell or move the furniture, put the house on the market, settle the rest of her estate. I stared at the objects that were part of my parents' life. My mother's purse still lay where she'd last set it down on a delicate upholstered bench with curved legs in front of the bedroom window. She had disposed of some of my father's things – I had begun wearing his watch, still do – but there were drawers and closets and files and more drawers. These things were important to someone once. I filled garbage bags, took clothes to the Salvation Army, arranged for a local man who handled estates to sell off some of the furniture from the house. The rest of the furniture, a lot of it fine work saved from the antique business, I packed in a truck, leaving some at Wolfe Island, some in Ottawa for Kate, taking a few things on to Montreal. I told myself that when this was all done I was going to take a trip to England or France, just to get away, an escape, but that didn't happen for a year.

Most of the summer I was at Wolfe Island. In my driven and

obsessive state I drew on the walls with coloured pencils, pasted paper frames around the drawings. When I rose from bed in the morning I would walk into the little room beside the bedroom and stand naked by the French doors, looking out across the water, studying the play of light, the changing colours, luminous pearl under a morning mist, or pale blue with little orgasmic shivers where the breeze struck, the metallic green chop on a windy day. Sometimes I would see a tall, ominous great blue heron standing on its long legs on the remains of the old dock. There was no running water in the house so I bathed in cold lake water in a round enamel tub. I was Tom's literary executor, and his brother, who was overall executor of the estate, agreed that I could take back to the island a couple of photographs of Tom – one I'd taken twenty years before – and they watched over me, still do, one more occult presence in that timeworn house.

That summer I spent a lot of time at Tom's, sorting out his papers. There was a barren intimacy to those hours. Everything in the house was familiar. Notes that Tom had written to himself on scraps of paper or restaurant napkins, lay on chairs and tables. Plans for future books. At first all the pictures and furniture were in place, but gradually things were sorted, hauled away. His brother, his sister-in-law and I were taking apart his life. The snapshots were put in boxes, the papers tidied, the arrangement of wise sayings from Chinese fortune cookies disposed of.

The house had a damp smell, and the front rooms were a bit dim. I knew the exact place where Tom had fallen and died. When I heard sounds, I would remember how in his first weeks in the house Tom heard its noises and imagined its ghosts. As I worked through his papers in a small crowded room which I shared with a large ugly chair, a table, shelves and filing cabinets, I had a strong sense of Tom's presence, an articulate spirit, a little irritable at having to endure the intrusion of an outsider messing with his work. The papers went to the National Library. While sorting them I found enough unpublished poems to make a posthumous book.

What was I writing that summer? I'm not sure. Not much perhaps: *Just Say the Words* hadn't yet appeared in print. At the island I worked on an upstairs bedroom – a room with only one west window, a little dim so I painted everything white or off-white, including the floor: it's a wonderful place to sit now, at the hour when the evening light is reflected from every surface. I decided to put a skylight in the dark windowless room at the top of the staircase. I pedalled my bicycle around the back roads of the Island, speeding along the gravel roads as if I might catch up with something. Judith turned up now and then. (I remember staring out the back window of the big downstairs room, watching her as she stood a few feet out in the water in her bathing suit, bare legs, the crease at the top of the thigh, and suddenly, as if my craziness had summoned it, the air was vibrating with a deep ominous hum, the sound possessing the ear and the stunned brain as swarming bees flew everywhere around the house, thousands of them, tiny dark forms moving so fast and randomly against the light, their penetrating dire unison enclosing me.) I wrote letters, writing more frequently to Judy, my most impassioned of old friends and lovers. I knew that she felt isolated in her life, though she had three daughters and was busy with that and teaching school. She had been Tom's friend in her Kingston years, and he had visited her when he gave a poetry reading on PEI. I told her about his death.

By the autumn I was settled back in Montreal, which began to feel like home. I remember arriving for a weekend in late August, setting off in the darkening evening through the busy streets. I followed a gathering crowd until I found myself on the Jacques-Cartier bridge, which was closed so that hundreds of people could gather there to watch a huge fireworks display. Another evening I came upon a black gospel choir performing in Parc Lafontaine. In the fall I got a call from Richard Handler, who was producing *The Arts Tonight* at the CBC. It was then on the air just after suppertime. He wanted some writers to comment on the election that was about to take place and asked me to be one of them. I wrote the piece and recorded it at CBC Montreal with Jane Lewis. Richard liked it, and asked me to do a series of occasional pieces for them – much what I'd been doing for the *Globe,* but a little shorter and to be read on the air. So every month or so, Jane – tall and slim and red-headed like her sister the model – led me through the maze of the CBC building to a studio to record the little talks and afterward we might have coffee, and she would tell me about her grandmother's huge garden at Port Neuf, which she was now reviving, or we'd discuss photography or Quebec politics.

I was building a new life. My French was good enough for day-to-day life, though there were always mysteries. The pleasant woman in the laundromat began chatting to me one day. Her French was slangy and colloquial, but I usually managed to understand; however on this morning I was mystified – numbers, she was mentioning numbers, *six, quarante-*

neuf, what was this about? It was a long time before I figured out that she was discussing the next 6/49 draw, about which I knew nothing in any language. As always I was singing twice a week or more often, and now I invited people to my apartment for lunch or dinner, and often on weekends I'd get a call from the Shepherds late in the afternoon asking if I wanted to join them for a meal. I had my regular stops in the neighbourhood, a small bakery, the second-hand stores which sometimes offered odd or interesting items – a print now hung at Wolfe Island or a handmade pine picture frame. Sometimes I walked up to Fairmount for bagels. The metro station was close by to take me down to the art gallery or over to NDG. In the evening I might drop in at Champigny, the excellent French bookstore on St Denis, which was open until ten – now and then I bought art books there. Some days I had breakfast at Aux Deux Maries, a *brûlerie* and café that had recently opened and where I bought my coffee and dark chocolate, which came in a wonderful gold foil that could be put to all kinds of uses. Kate was married, living in Ottawa and working at the Canadian Conservation Institute, and she and her husband, Claude Royer, would drive to Montreal to visit me. Maggie was settled in England with her friend, Ken Simons, like her a political activist, and one of the editorial pillars of *Peace News.* My parents, though they had never had much money, were careful with what they had, and they died without debts, so when their house was sold there was a small estate for me to invest, which I did, with some care and some luck.

In the spring of the next year I travelled to England, to visit Maggie in London, to seek out my mother's mysterious birthplace in Somerset. I explored the financial district of the City, previously unknown to me, another day walked the towpath from Richmond to Kew, the woods full of bluebells and primroses. I journeyed by train through the West Country, a region I'd never seen before, stopped at Corfe Castle to see Maurice and Nancy Strike, my parents' friends from Niagara-on-the-Lake. Maurice, who had spent years as a theatrical designer and worked at the Shaw festival, was now the Anglican rector of the small Dorset town. I climbed one of the enormous hills just behind the town, where the ruins of the castle overlooked steep slopes covered with golden gorse, which, I was told, hides poisonous adders. I began writing poems, including one about Hardy which was set down in a small hotel in Dorchester after I had walked along the river Frome – one of those narrow English streams, often no wider than a creek, but deep and fast in the running – through the fields and woods to see his family house at Bockhampton.

These low sloped cottage ceilings
    and steep stairs
from small room to small room, with a boy's feelings
    and the old cares
of country life are the first inspiration:
    the neighbourhood wears
his words for its daily ways, and the reelings
    of stars across night stir imagination
    and he dares, dares.

From Dorchester to Bockhampton is an hour's
    walk in the fresh green
of spring, river babbling; a thousand flowers
    bloom between
the leafing trees in the neighbouring wood,
    yet these things mean
only what time, space would, what chance could,
    what no kind powers
    gave them to mean.

A tour bus is parked at the top of the lane
    and the touring crowd
solicit the images of his delicate brain
    as shadows of cloud
race over the green fields, chasing the sun.
    Spoken aloud
with love or pondered in silence, his words contain
    all that's been suffered and done
    and done again.

On through Exeter, and I settled for a while in Penzance, and each day got on a local bus and rode to St Ives or St Just or Cape Cornwall. From the narrow country roads I got a glimpse of the great standing stones that have endured from some pre-Christian past. Sitting in a teashop in Marazion, tired and hungry after walking out to Mount St Michael, I became aware of a handsome blonde woman in her forties sitting with a young man who was probably her son.

'I'm trying not to cry,' she said, her hand to her mouth, controlling sobs, and her son was holding her hand. Her husband had just died, I supposed.

'I try to think about the good times.'

No, not died, abandoned her.

'If...,' and she murmured something, 'it wouldn't have happened.'

All the pain of a stranger's life: I paid up and left as quickly as I could, not to overhear any more of her sorrow.

The next day, at Land's End, I stared west from the top of the steep cliffs, thinking that there was nothing but ocean between me and Canada. Not yet knowing that when I returned, my life would change yet again.

The early death of a friend shakes everything; it makes you rethink the world. Tom's death had stirred Judy to recall her earlier life in Kingston, old friends she hadn't seen for years, so she came to Kingston that summer, and suddenly we found ourselves in each other's arms. Two years later we were living together.

One evening Judy and her friend Janet Troughton were at the island for dinner, hamburgers cooked on my crude barbecue, charcoal burning in a circle of stones on a limestone outcropping. Somehow Janet, who hailed from Picton, a few miles west along the lake, got talking about the rum-runners in the neighbourhood, and how her mother, as a young girl, had been pals with some of them. I had recently agreed to do a reading when I went back to Montreal – a part of the Urban Wanderers series in a bar on St Laurent at Duluth. For this occasion I was to read something that I'd written in the previous twenty-four hours; I'd agreed to do this even though I wasn't writing anything but the occasional poem. Janet's story about the young girl and the smugglers stuck in my mind, and I began to do some research into that period of local history. The east end of Lake Ontario, from Wolfe Island down to the Bay of Quinte, had been one of the great centres of action during American prohibition. Though there was prohibition of a sort in Canada as well, the distilleries were open, and it was perfectly legal to buy a boatload of booze to be shipped to Cuba. No one fussed too much if you were to load more whisky for Cuba the next day.

All this began to form itself into a story, but it was only very partially worked out when, back in Montreal, the day came for my reading. So I sat down in the morning and wrote a passage about a young girl's involvement with one of the bootleggers, and how he was killed. It's a gripping episode, the girl rowing out into the lake to find him after she hears gunfire in the darkness, and it worked well when I read it aloud that night, but it launched me into the writing of a book before I'd figured out where I was going, so that the novel, *The Time of Her Life,*, was a slow and difficult struggle over the next year or so, a number of intersecting stories at first, until I came to see that the life of the book was in the chronicle of the life of one woman. I found that what I was creating had a certain quick, elliptical movement, and remembering *Party Girl,* the radio play from almost twenty years before, I decided to tell the story with a similar gapped, hurtling rhythm, avoiding many of the conventional climaxes and transitions, the usual dramatic turns. Fiction is, after all, a traditional but not necessarily true way of imitating the shapes of human experience. Life has no shape until we impose one, the story the family told us, or what we have learned from television, film, books, gossip. Beyond that our being is arbitrary, random, impenetrable. Bad dreams. At the core of us, perhaps, something inert. *The Time of Her Life* tried to evoke that layer of existence, while at the same time being a chronicle of an adventurous life. It got some very strange comments from reviewers: Jean, the main character, was said to lack a brain or a soul or a heart or morality. So do we all; so much of our lives is an imitation of what we've been told living should be.

> The gods are neither
> good nor bad
> nor bad nor good
> but violent, lordly and final.

The next summer Judy came back to Ontario, and in a rented car – by now I had given up owning a car, I didn't need one in Montreal – we drove around Prince Edward County, south of Picton, and looked for locations for the story of the girl and the rum-runners, which I was now writing, day by day. The idea had come to me on Wolfe Island, and the house I owned there became Jean's childhood home, her bed in the dim room at the top of the stairs, but I shifted its situation many miles along the lakeshore. In the spring of the year, the choir of St John the Evangelist travelled to New York, to sing a concert at a church on Long Island and a service at another near Times Square. I used my spare time on that trip to refresh my sense of the geography of parts of the city. A beach on Long Island and sections of Greenwich Village entered the book.

In September I travelled to France, a few days in Paris then south to Marseilles where musical friends from Kingston, Russell and Pamela Davidson, lived for part of the year. I was sniffing out background for the period of her life that Jean spent in France during the second war as the wife of a French count who is an adherent of one of the right-wing royalist parties.

I had a couple of wonderful moments of discovery while staying in Marseilles. I took a local train and visited, for the first time, that golden city, Aix-en-Provence. All the *hôtels* from the seventeenth and eighteenth century had walls of a rich ochre, like gold leaf. The cathedral baptistery goes back to the fifth century, when the south of France was an important religious centre of the early church. Another day I spent wandering on the white stone hills of Les Îles de Frioul overlooking the Mediterranean. A ferry from the Vieux Port at Marseilles carried me out to a small port on one of the islands, once separate chunks of rock, now joined to each other by a causeway. The water around them was as clear and brilliant as amethyst or emerald, perfect green and perfect blue. White cliffs rose from the edge, marked here and there with the dark shapes of small plants. I walked along a deserted road, down to a little beach of round stones. On both sides the rock walls of the *calanque* rose steeply. White light – as if it radiated from the white rock itself. The hills were rounded; centuries of time had scrubbed away the sharp edges. The larger rocks cast pale shadows on the ground.

Photographs I took, which lack human figures to give them scale, don't make clear the immense height of the white hills above the *calanque,* but I can remember seeing minuscule figures at the top, tiny as ants. On the rock, dwarfish green plants, which appeared to be growing almost without soil as if they could sink roots in the rock itself, bore little yellow or pink flowers. At the top of a cliff, looking down, I tossed over a stone, and it took several long, slow seconds to reach the water. At the edge of the islands were abandoned gun emplacements and concrete pillboxes left from the Second War, built during the German occupation, I assumed, to repel a possible invasion. Staring out across the dark sea, I knew that the closest land mass was North Africa. In the old section of the city I had seen Arab faces in the narrow streets, immigrants from the Maghreb.

Visiting in Paris just then – by coincidence – were both my daughters, and I met Kate, looking stylish and elegant, in the courtyard of the Louvre, where she had been giving a lecture to the staff. Talk of parental pride. Then we joined up with Maggie and Ken, who were busy walking at high speed all over Paris – Maggie, by now the author of several books of poetry and prose, six months pregnant with my first grandchild.

Autumn days on Wolfe Island, the lake whipped into whitecaps, little flocks of ducks beating across the sky of driven clouds as I imagined Jean on a short trip back to her roots, and thought about my own future. It was a near certainty, by now, that Judy would leave her husband and the two of us would live together. We both existed largely in our daily correspondence. At night I built up the fire in the little Franklin stove, covered myself with blankets to sleep, waking to the splash of waves on the shore only a few feet away. Back in Montreal I finished a draft of the novel and begin to write poems about my neighbourhood, the pretty redhead on the *terrasse* across the way, the sight of the mountain at the end of a long narrow street, the sound of the winter wind booming through the metal balcony, as if it was a giant set of wind-chimes, the beggars, the café where I sometimes had breakfast.

At the winter solstice, Nancy, who had gone to England for the arrival of our first grandchild, called to tell me that Maggie's daughter Simone had been born, though what was intended to be a home birth was protracted and finally took place in hospital. I'd been trying to call, getting no answer, growing panicky, and now after all the years of worrying about Maggie, frightened at times that she would not survive the storms of her intense, idealistic nature, the good news was almost too much. I cried, I phoned friends all over the continent, I drank until I fell down.

Thirty-two

An evening in late April, the third and final night of singing for a disc that the choir of St John the Evangelist was recording, a liturgical year in music. We finished late, and some of us went to Ben's delicatessen for food and beer. My apartment was empty, the furniture on its way to Prince Edward Island, and the next afternoon I would get on the train. In a day I would be there too.

In January I had flown to the Island and bought a house, a large frame construction built late in the nineteenth century, not in the best of shape, but livable. Upstairs it had four bedrooms and a little room for my study, so there was space for all Judy's daughters to stay. Mary, the oldest, was on the West Coast, attending Pearson College, but the other two were at home. The house was on a bus route to the high school Caitlin was attending, though just outside the school district for Christina's elementary school, which meant that for the next three years I drove her back and forth during the times – every second week was the arrangement – that she was with us.

Spring on Prince Edward Island is late and cold, and the old house had no heat in any of the upstairs rooms. If I stood on the red earth floor of the basement and looked around me, I could see daylight through holes in the foundation. In the room that became Judy's study, a bay window had plaster falling from the ceiling. An airtight Franklin stove came with the house, but it was set on loose brick which was full of bits of wood and bark, an obvious fire hazard. The old building, once the doctor's house, with a former medical clinic on a piece of severed land beside it, stood on a corner in the village of Eldon on the Trans-Canada highway a few miles from the Nova Scotia ferry, Cooper's general store across the road in one direction, the post office in the other. Behind the grassy yard, a patch of woodland and a smaller frame house standing empty. The aged woman who owned it lived somewhere in the United States, and only got to the Island to see her childhood home for a few hours in the summertime. It was close to derelict.

Past a tumbledown shed was a bed of strawberries, and a row of red currant bushes. Beyond them apple trees ran wild at the edge of the woods. Up the road stood one of the oldest frame churches on the Island, built by one of Judy's ancestors. Just down the hill below it lay a millpond and John Macpherson's sawmill, still driven by waterpower. I began to do the necessary repairs on our house, one job after another, one room after another, working alone in the chilled air. One day, waiting for Judy on a street in Charlottetown in the cheap car I'd bought a few weeks before, I heard a voice, couldn't make out the words and was unable to see anyone who might have spoken to me. Unexplained voices, the cold spring, empty houses: all those things came together in a short story, 'Missing Notes', the first short story I'd written in twenty years, a product of the stress and revelation of a new life, the cold and rain, the spookiness of the vacant house next door. As I wrote the story, and began some poems about our life on the Island, I plastered and painted and rebuilt, and I had finished Judy's study, the kitchen, and a guest room ready when Kate and Claude visited that summer. The four of us visited the beach at Panmure island.

Berries like sudden blood,
and the salt-and-protein
of edible flesh
comes to light
out of the sea
in the incipient downpour.

You walk in the colour of rain
in the old way
of slow hunting,
seeking with your skin
through the falling mist,
wet clothes, a long line
of ocean inlets under clouds.

The birds have gone mad.
Soft shells break.
Run to the sheltering car.
Sky lets loose all its water.

Judy in our house in Eldon, PEI.

In August Judy and I made our first trek from PEI to Wolfe Island, what became an annual trip, a little strange always to leave one Island paradise for another, but it meant that I could visit family and friends, spend a little time in big cities. Judy too had old friends in Kingston, and by now Maggie and Ken had moved to Toronto, with Simone.

September of that year, I think it was, that Judy and I were wandering about a second-hand bookstore in Charlottetown and saw the Edgar Johnson biography of Dickens, two volumes on sale at a good price. So we took it home with us; we were both Dickens fans. A lifetime before, Judy had planned to write a graduate thesis on his novels, though that never happened, but as we both read the books, we got to discussing Dickens' unfinished novel, *The Mystery of Edwin Drood*. It's possible that Judy tried to convince me that I should write a completion – there had been a couple of attempts at a conclusion, which she'd read, unsatisfied. I speculated about doing some such thing, began a little unfocused research, reread the dark autumnal novel. By now it was fall, each evening a wood fire burning in the Franklin stove safely set on its new tile base. I stared into the flames, imagining things. Late one Sunday afternoon after a long walk in the woods beyond John Macpherson's mill, I heard a voice in my head.

I spake unto the Dutchess, and she said, 'You wouldn't dare.'

I wrote that down, and a couple of lines following it, and I was on my way into the novella I at first called The Man Who Finished Edwin Drood, though it was published as *Close to the Fire*, a wonderful little book to write, and to read, I hope, about fire and darkness, love and death, all wound around the mystery of the uncompleted Dickens story. Although it has a death at the centre of it, somebody called it a truly happy book, and that's the way I feel about it. I was absolutely astonished (still am) that Michael Macklem, when I sent it to him, turned it down. Many years before he'd rejected *A Sound Like Laughter*, and I could understand that – the comedy was too harsh for many people – but in the novella, though there was a certain amount of graveyard laughter, the comedy was a good deal warmer and more genial. Wicked Uncle, as the narrator calls himself, is 'convinced that he's got away with something and hopes to go on getting away with it'. That's how my friend, the Quebec writer Judith Cowan put it, very astutely I thought. When Wicked Uncle's devious, somewhat theatrical, but much-loved wife decides to bring Orland, her former husband into their house to die, Wicked Uncle grumbles and orates, but somehow he accepts it, and he is the one who is with Orland in his last moments.

In the spring we were in Fredericton for a choir workshop, and I noticed the sign on the front of Goose Lane Editions, and I decided to send them the book. They were very quick to decide they wanted it, though there was some delay while we worked out whether they would also be offered *The Time of Her Life*. In the event, they published both books.

Close to the Fire was the first of three novellas I wrote over the next four years. All of them are about characters, of middle age or older, who, whatever the difficulties and pain of their earlier lives, have outlasted them. In each of the books the comparative brevity allows for a lightness of tone that might have been impossible in a more protracted work. *Duet* was the second to be written, in 1997, but because other books pushed their way in – poetry, essay collections – it was the last to be published, in 2004. It is a tale of two very prickly characters, not in the best of health, who have a kind of irascible, wintry romance. *The Stand-In,* written in 1998 and published in 2002, is the most eccentric in form – three lectures delivered by a retired professor brought in at the last minute to replace a suddenly dead colleague. It hints at a number of dark stories, including a possible murder, but the speaker, whose future beyond those three lectures we'll never know, is having a high old time giving his talks. When I think of those novellas, I'm reminded of the D. H. Lawrence title, 'Look! We Have Come Through!'

Living on the Island I was a long way from the centres of journalism and radio. I continued to write reviews for the *Gazette,* did magazine pieces about the Island for *Canadian Geographic* and *Imperial Oil Review,* but gradually I found that my connections were disappearing. Illness felled Richard Handler at the CBC, Bryan Demchinsky left the book page at the *Gazette,* my last regular radio drama producer, Bill Lane, with whom I'd worked for something over ten years, moved on to new things. I'm sometimes reminded of Peter Harcourt's wisecrack, that he's ending his career as it began, writing about movies no one will ever see for magazines no one will ever read.

In the summer of 1999, just after *Close to the Fire* was published, I was asked to teach for a week at the Maritime Writers' Workshop in Fredericton. I had done such things over the years – in North Bay, twice in Fort Qu'Appelle, twice in Kingston. A week had always been my limit (two weeks in Saskatchewan once, but that wasn't a workshop: I was there as an editorial consultant). There are, I know, all sorts of writers, some of them famous, who have taught creative writing – Clark Blaise, Alastair MacLeod. By now every university has a department, but I am a relic of an earlier world, and I could never be comfortable doing it. At least if you are teaching Jane Austen or Charles Dickens you get to read aloud the words of those great writers. No doubt young writers learn, must learn, but what each has to discover is unique, has to do with a singular history and talent. How is it possible to teach a young person to be anything but what the teacher recognizes and values? Doesn't that mute originality, the rebellious will that makes writers what they are? It sometimes seems to me that there are more people learning to write than learning to read. It was better for me to peddle my skill from door to door as a freelance.

As for workshops a week long, they have, for some of the participants, the aura of a summer camp – a week away from the regular pattern of life, a chance to do nothing but write and think about writing, a refreshing change, usually among new people. I can understand why they value the experience, and some of them find their way through to a lifetime commitment to putting words on paper. At a short workshop, the teacher's business is to stimulate, and for a few days I can do that, take the deck of cards in my hand, throw them into the air and say, Catch what you can. Many beginning writers are trapped in limited assumptions, commonplace habits, easy ways out. Over the years I invented a few exercises, small, mechanical, the equivalent of a musician playing scales or studies, but they have the possible benefit of not allowing automatic responses. Though there are many things in my life that I've done for money but would have done without being paid a cent, teaching writing in not one of those. Still, you get to travel a bit, and to meet people. In North Bay I got to spend time with the wonderful fabric artist Micheline Beauchemin. On the prairies I met a lot of interesting people, including Bonnie Burnard, who was in both the workshops I gave there, and later appeared in both *Coming Attractions* and *Best Stories,* and Peter Stockland, a journalist whose stories I published, and who later became editor of the Montreal *Gazette.* (After a political argument in a Saskatchewan bar, Peter accused me of 'guerrilla rhetoric'. I thought that very flattering.) One summer while I was doing a workshop in Kingston, Carol Shields, who was also teaching there, and her husband, Don, took me to lunch at the Faculty club, where he, as a teacher from another university, had an honorary membership. Over that lunch – as Carol later reminded me during a party at Don Bailey's in Winnipeg – I proposed that she write an essay on the treatment of sex by Canadian women writers. Whatever prompted that idea? And why did she remember it? When she mentioned it in Winnipeg, she seemed to suggest she thought it was something worth doing, though she couldn't do it. She had been reading the recent biography of Margaret Laurence and was much preoccupied by Margaret's difficult childhood and the even worse childhood of Mavis Gallant, but I don't think there was any connection.

The summer I taught in Fredericton I had a high old time with the other writers who were teaching there, Paul Kropp, Carol Gibson Langille and Pamela Donoghue. One of the requirements of the Fredericton workshop was that each of those teaching give a talk, and I took that as a reason to compose, at long last, an essay that I'd had it in mind to write for many years. I called it 'A Short Walk Round Hugh MacLennan'.

And then I went home to my little unheated room upstairs at the back of the house, and every morning, I sat there to arrange and rearrange words, to tell lies. By now Judy and I had developed our ways of shaping the week. She taught for five days while I wrote and did renovations, and on Saturday we had lunch at the Charlottetown Farmer's market. I got recruited to sing in a church choir, and that filled Sunday morning. At the March break we travelled, if there was money available, and in summer we worked in the garden, Judy creating new rock gardens and flowerbeds while I tried to keep insects and our greedy and omnivorous dog out of my vegetables. In good weather we walked on the beach just a few miles down the road, often having the whole length of it to ourselves, staring across the long reach of water to the hills of Nova Scotia.

The quotidian, the habits of daily life: in 1979, being interviewed by David Prosser for the Kingston *Whig-Standard*, I said I wanted to do another book of poetry – to keep a day book, throw some out, what was left to represent the cycle of the year. I was astonished when I came on that clipping recently since it described what I did twenty-two years later.

It began in that odd week between Christmas and the beginning of the new year. That interlude has twice led me to find a new direction in poetry. In 1982, it was *Catchpenny Poems*. In the year 2000 I had spent the days before Christmas, as I usually do, visiting my children and grandchildren in Ontario and Quebec, arriving back in PEI just in time for the holiday. On my return there was a pile of letters, including one from Colum McCann, a young Irish writer now living in New York, who had been reading my collection *This Human Day* in the weeks since the two of us had met at the Harbourfront International Festival. He remarked that it was now on his shelf next to the American poet, Wendell Berry. I hadn't read Berry, so I went off to the library and came home with one of his books, *A Timbered Choir: The Sabbath Poems,* and began to find my way through it. Berry created the book out of his habit of spending time on Sundays walking, thinking, and each week writing a poem. Something like the pattern that I mentioned in the interview so many years before.

Also in that mail was a review of *This Human Day,* not the first to refer to my occasional habit of aphorism. In the previous months I'd been writing rhyming poems, some of them in very close forms, a great pleasure, but it leaves you wanting to take deeper, slower breaths. The lines I now began to write were longer than usual, mostly between eleven and thirteen syllables, with only a few variations from that. From the first day I had a long, relaxed line, a sense of how it might move, the impulse to include the details of everyday life. The days after Christmas are the anniversary of the death of my friend Claudette Hoover, and that entered the poem, along with the sense that all my friends, living and dead, might be listening.

It was a winter of storms and heavy snow, so the background of the seasons forced its way in. If the poem was to be what I called in the opening lines 'a landscape of thought', it would have to contemplate many different kinds of things. I'm not sure exactly when I decided that it would continue through the year. The beginning of the New Year, the argument that this was the true first year of the millenium, the feeling that it was time to take on something big while I still had it in me, these were all part of the commitment. I thought of other poems that had followed the year, looked at Spenser's *Shepherd's Calendar,* but it left me cold. I read in an anthology some chunks of James Thomson's *The Seasons,* which I'd once owned in an edition decorated with charming woodcuts as endpieces, and that had more resonance. I quoted a line of it as a kind of homage. Later on I discovered another eighteenth-century poem, William Cowper's *The Task,* which also had something in common with what I was attempting.

I wrote every day, or at least every weekday, with some work on weekends, revisions anytime. The pages typed out on my laptop continued to accumulate. The poem, which was the most demanding thing I have ever written, needed the shape given by the recurrence of its themes, daily life, weather, history, birds, the garden, poetry itself, music, the incursions of the public world, but if it wasn't to be laborious, I needed always to find new tones, new angles of vision. What was merely dutiful would be cut.

At the end of the first month, it was clear that I was in this for the long haul, but worried about sameness, I wrote the February section in shorter, more abrupt lines, then returned to the longer lines in March. May and October were also written in the shorter lines, little scherzos between the meditations. There could be no breaks in the writing if the poem was to give an account of the year, to follow its rhythm. If I was on a train, I wrote on the train. I wrote in stations and airports and whatever room I slept in. It was satisfying, a little overwhelming, but that is what you do, imagine what might be and make it happen. Revisions on the book were more or less finished by the spring of 2002. Rewriting, I didn't allow myself to be wise after the event, could only polish the surface, not alter the content. The book appeared in the spring of 2004 in a beautiful edition from Gaspereau Press in Kentville, Nova Scotia. One of the pleasures of publishing with them was the chance to work with people much younger than I am. Many of my contemporaries in the arts are retired or exhausted or dead, and it was good to have the energy of the young carrying me along. *The Year One* is both an evocation of the lyric detail of our life in a village on Prince Edward Island and a glance backward. In his review the poet George Elliott Clarke called it 'significant, magnificent, and beneficent'. I hope he was right.

Thirty-three

Cold days of early spring, a north wind blew along the grey streets of Toronto, chilling me. I had flown to Ontario for public readings from *The Year One,*, which had been in my hands for only a week. One of the performances was to be at Toronto's Harbourfront. The other, the evening after I arrived by plane from Charlottetown, was in a crowded bar above a restaurant in Hamilton, Ontario. My earliest memory is of standing on a Hamilton street corner with my father and in the darkness watching snowflakes fall. That was mentioned in the long poem among the lyric moments out of the past that sang their counterpoint to the day-by-day progress of the year. The GO bus that brought me to Hamilton stopped to let off passengers in front of the Fred Astaire Dance Studio. I didn't know such things existed any more. A handsome boy from my high school went on to be a dance instructor. Where was he now? As the reading began, my old friend George Loewen appeared in the doorway, a little pale, transparent – he'd recently been through the kind of serious foot infection diabetics are prone to. He had driven down from St Catharines to meet me.

The audience for the reading was large and enthusiastic, six poets performing, the others all in their twenties or early thirties. A pretty girl in skintight pants read Buddhist poems – how to live perfectly in the moment. (The beauty, the sheer extravagant youngness of the young, and me growing older.) A man who had edited an anthology of new poets rang bells and read to the accompaniment of a tape of chanting monks. Soon, he announced, he was going to India to immerse himself in life there, to seek enlightenment. Last before me, Shannon Bramer, a dark-haired young woman who had sat near me at dinner, the light catching the bits of glitter in her makeup. (Remember the young Gwendolyn MacEwen reading forty years before, the big eyes outlined in kohl.) Bramer's poems were intense, inward, a hint of the surreal in the imagery. After the publication of a couple of books and a chapbook with reputable presses she was clearly on her way, wherever it is poets are on their way to. She announced that she was four months pregnant and dedicated the last poem to her unborn child. A whole evening of young voices, new lives finding words.

After the reading, George drove me to the bus terminal, and the GO bus carried me through the glittering night landscape of the industrial suburbs to Toronto, to stay at Maggie's house. I heard streetcars passing in the night, the siren of an ambulance. As I lay in bed in the morning, my granddaughter Simone came into the room and sat on my chest for a while before going downstairs for breakfast. Out in the cold, men and women lined up at the door of Honest Ed's. I can remember at seven or eight years old, in the days when there were still horses pulling the milk and bread wagons through the streets of Toronto, reading in the *Star* the large advertisements for Ed's earlier store – on Bay near Dundas, I think it was. We passed it on the streetcar on the way downtown. Who was writing in Toronto in those days – Morley Callaghan, Raymond Souster, Margaret Avison, Hugh Garner, Robert Finch? Walking along Bloor street from my bank, I reflected that the European restaurants and cafes like the one I used in *The Streets of Summer* had been succeeded by Korean shops and sushi bars, new immigrant communities replacing the old. Late in the afternoon, I passed a lineup of homeless men at Trinity–St Paul's, waiting to go inside for the free dinner.

In spite of the cold, flowers were blooming in the front lawn of Maggie and Ken's house, blue scilla, miniature daffodils. I was born in this city, lived here at three periods of my life, I knew my way around, yet I couldn't get a grip on it all. I could call up memories – spring nights in my first year of university when, a little crazed by the intensity of the examination period, I would roam the dark streets with one or two friends, committing benign delinquencies like moving porch furniture from one house to another – arriving on the early morning train and making my way to the CBC to read a poem on the morning show back when Bruno Gerussi was the host – sitting in Nicholson's restaurant with an impetuous Margaret Atwood who was all but jumping out of her seat raising hypothetical contractual difficulties as we discussed a possible script for *The Great Detective* – an accidental meeting on the subway with Marian Engel, weakened by the cancer that would soon kill her, and we sat down on a bench where she could rest before getting on her train – coming across Alice Munro at the crowded launch of Michael Ondaatje's *Running in the Family,* Alice remarking in a slightly scandalized way that she had a drink *every day* now – meeting Don Bailey in the upstairs bar of the Winchester Hotel and being shown the ancient murals of Canadian landscapes painted on the walls – reading at Harbourfront in 1977, the launching of Morris Wolfe's book of Toronto stories, and half way through the reading of a long story beginning to feel I was going to faint (I found a chair, sat down and the feeling passed) – trying to manoeuvre a rented truck into a narrow driveway in Kensington market while moving Maggie into a basement room she'd rented – visiting, in childhood, my mother's best friend, Cathy Stewart, whose husband, a little older than she was, had an artificial leg and missing fingers, wounds received in the First World War – eating lunch in Brian Walker's backyard near Vaughan and St Clair one summer day, staying too long so that I was nearly late for Nicholas Macklem's wedding at Trinity College Chapel, running along the Danforth looking for a cab that wouldn't turn up, dressed in a suit, hot and sweating and furious with myself – Toronto came back to me in such bits and pieces, neither an exotic place nor my home, though I was born here. Perhaps I experienced the world in moody fragments still, as when I was a young man trying to learn to write about it. I met up with Bill Aide near the university, where he was to attend a five o'clock recital, and at a tiny table in Starbucks we discussed health problems, and he gave me a CD of a Chopin recital he performed in 1979.

In my bag ready to take home with me was my copy of Maggie's new novel, *Between Mountains*. Maggie started out as a poet, then began to publish some highly original essays – one on anorexia has been republished all over North America – and in 2001 brought out her first novel, a beautifully rendered and heartbreaking story that grew out of the political troubles in East Timor, with which she, as a human rights and anti-war activist, had been deeply involved. Her new novel, which dealt with war crimes in Bosnia and the ensuing trials at The Hague, was a more detached, intellectual book, a love story that provoked questions about the nature of justice and language. Once she was known as David Helwig's daughter. Now, I suspect, many people think of me as Maggie Helwig's father. One generation succeeds another.

Four of us were reading at Harbourfront, David Yezzi, an American poet from New York City, Dennis Lee and I, and Souvankham Thammavongsa, still in her twenties, born in Thailand, raised in Toronto, her first book just out. She was sitting across from me at dinner, tiny and silent, and finally said to me in a quiet voice, 'Are you nervous?' Well, no, I wasn't, even though I once came within seconds of fainting during a reading here, but she was, obviously, and the rest of us, all male, larger, older, did our unsubtle best to reassure her, and she performed bravely,

Kate and Émile

her delicate but steely poems catching and holding attention. One of them was about coming from a background that wasn't literary and finding out that words were your calling. Not unfamiliar, that situation, something that happened in every generation, though in my case it was not the experience – so common in Canada now – of being separated from my family by language.

Dennis Lee and I are about the same age. We first ran into each other, I believe, in 1970, at an early meeting of the League of Canadian Poets. We were both nationalists in the age of nationalism, and his poem *Civil Elegies* caught a particular moment of the Canadian experience. It was the word for its time. When I was doing posters for *Quarry* I produced a poster version of Dennis's poem, '1838', a wonderful rhyming ballad about William Lyon Mackenzie which ends, 'But who will speak for Canada?/Mackenzie come again.' Now, at pensionable age, Dennis and I are on the same bill at Harbourfront, reading poems that have turned in perfectly opposite directions. His new book, *Un*, is a collection of short pieces, as intricate as a cryptic crossword, full of delighted games, puns, shatterings, whereas *The Year One* is deliberately long in its developments, including everything, aspiring to a different kind of music. Back home, reading through Dennis's book, I will become aware that the vision lurking in his shards and bobbins is still the one I'm familiar with from his earlier poetry, a grave vision with its roots in Martin Heidegger and George Grant. I expect an objective reader could say something similar about *The Year One*, that it's a new embodiment of a vision woven through a dozen previous volumes of poetry. You can't escape your own soul. We stir ourselves to keep the brain alive, to avoid what is merely habitual, set out for renewal, count ourselves the kings of infinite space, but we are bounded by the limits of our being.

While I was wandering about Toronto in those spring days, reading from my account of one year of my life, my daughter Kate, eight months pregnant with her second child, was at a conference in Whitehorse, delivering a paper on her analysis of some native artefacts revealed by the melting of a glacier, bits of a long vanished culture, human tools hidden and preserved in ice for thousands of years. Within her, as she explicated that ancient history, my grandchild, one small biological consequence of my years on earth, floated in amniotic fluid, the tiny unborn heart beating, waiting for the world.

May, 2003 – April, 2004

Acknowledgements

Lines quoted from David Helwig poems earlier published by Oberon Press are reprinted here by permission of Oberon Press. Lines by A.J.M. Smith reprinted with the permission of William Toye, literary executor for the estate of A.J.M. Smith. Lines by Michael Ondaatje reprinted by permission of Michael Ondaatje.

A few sections of this book previously appeared in *The Child of Someone,* published by Oberon Press in 1997. A short section of the book also appeared in the *New Quarterly.* The manuscript was read, in whole or in part, by my friends Peter Harcourt, Henry Shapiro and the late Joseph Sherman, who made useful corrections and suggestions. I am grateful for their help.

David Helwig was born in Toronto in 1938. He suffered his teenage years in Niagara-on-the-Lake. After studying at the University of Toronto and the University of Liverpool he taught for some time at Queen's University. He was involved, along with other young poets including Michael Ondaatje and Tom Marshall, in the publication of *Quarry* magazine, and he created three series of Quarry posters. While in England in 1969–70 he founded the annual Oberon story anthology, which continues to thrive. During the late sixties he taught in Collins Bay Penitentiary and put together a book with one of the inmates there (*A Book about Billie*, 1972). In 1974 John Hirsch hired him to be literary manager of CBC TV Drama, and he worked at the CBC until 1976. In 1980 he left his teaching position at Queen's and from then on earned his living as a freelance writer, writing for television, radio, magazines and newspapers, as well as doing a good deal of editing. He is the author of more than thirty books, mostly fiction and poetry. *Catchpenny Poems* won the CBC poetry award in 1983, and in 2004, his long poem, *The Year One*, won the Atlantic Poetry Award.

He lives in Belfast, Prince Edward Island. His website address is at www.davidhelwig.com.